D1580992

WEST HAM

WEST HAM
IRONS IN THE SOUL

Pete May

MAINSTREAM
PUBLISHING

EDINBURGH AND LONDON

Copyright © Pete May, 2002
All rights reserved
The moral right of the author has been asserted

First published in Great Britain in 2002 by
MAINSTREAM PUBLISHING COMPANY (EDINBURGH) LTD
7 Albany Street
Edinburgh EH1 3UG

ISBN 1 84018 618 6

A catalogue record for this book is available from the British Library

Typeset in Berkeley and Blur
Printed and bound in Great Britain by
Mackays of Chatham

For Nicola, Lola and Nell

ACKNOWLEDGEMENTS

Special thanks go to Nicola Baird for being a West Ham widow all season and tolerating my endless excuses that it really was work. Also Denis Campbell for his assistance in quaffing jellied eels and researching numerous West Ham details, and top photographer Dave Kampfner (you can see more of his work on www.kampfner.com) for his share of the footie photos. Others worthy of a Di Canio-esque clutching of the club badge are Mainstream's Bill Campbell for commissioning this book, match day announcer Jeremy Nicholas, Steve Rapport, Phill Jupitus, Peter Stewart in the West Ham press office, and editors such as Bill Williamson, Peter Freedman, Andrew Shields, North Bank Norman and Shane Barber for publishing my West Ham obsessed prose over the years. Above all, thanks to fellow fans Matt George, Gavin Hadland, Dan Humphreys, Fraser Massey, Nigel Morris, Mike Pattenden and Joe Norris for their many witty comments and expletives on match days. Hopefully, this book will convey something of the tortured psyche of the genuine West Ham fan. Also worthy of praise are Fleur and Richard for pre-match hospitality before the match at Newcastle, Reno Marioni for providing an American take on English obsessions, Michael Magenis for sneaking me into the Fulham end, and, of course, Carol and her able staff at Ken's Café for pre-match sports nutrition. Come on you Irons!

Pete May
June 2002

CONTENTS

1. HURRY UP HARRY

Harry Redknapp has been sacked. My initial response, gazing at the stark capital letters on page 302 of Ceefax, is one of incredulity. It's 9 May 2001, and season 2000–01 is meandering to a close, with West Ham having secured survival in their penultimate game of the season by beating Southampton 3–0 at Upton Park. It's been a disappointing season for the club. A run to the quarter-finals of the FA Cup included great victories away to Manchester United and Sunderland, before losing at home to Spurs in the quarter-finals. But in the league, form has slumped since a 5–0 Boxing Day thrashing of Charlton, and the club has won just three out of seventeen league matches since then.

The talismanic Paolo Di Canio has struggled with sinus and Achilles tendon problems for two months, playing while taking antibiotics and unable to train properly, and Redknapp has struggled to accommodate the flair of both Di Canio and Joe Cole in the same side. There's also been a hangover from the sale of Rio Ferdinand. Redknapp did brilliantly in talking up his price. He turned down an offer of £15 million from Leeds, resulting in the Elland Road club returning with a bid of £18 million – a world record for a defender. With the transfer system possibly close to collapse and a new stand to finance, the board felt the price was too good to turn down. Protests from the fans were muted as, although Ferdinand had huge potential, errors in concentration still resulted in him giving goals away.

Harry would have been upset at losing a home-grown player whom he described as 'a Rolls-Royce' of a defender, but as befits a legendary 'wheeler dealer', he immediately set about spending nearly eight million of the Rio cash on six signings. Indeed, so many players from around the globe arrived on loan deals or as new signings that it was tempting to think Redknapp had opened a backpackers' hostel at Chadwell Heath and was preparing to flog all the different nationalities a set of discounted Lonely Planet guides to London he'd picked up from a stall by the South Bank (the arts centre that is, not the old West Ham South Bank).

Rigobert Song, Titi Camara, Christian Dailly, Ragnvald Soma, Svetoslav

11

Todorov and Hayden Foxe all arrived as new signings, but none of these players had proved an instant success. Strangely, the two loan signings who had looked most at home in the Premiership, French wing-back Sebastien Schemmel and Finnish international defender Hanu Tihinen, were not kept on by Redknapp.

But, despite the poor second half to the season, Redknapp leaving West Ham is a huge shock to the football world. The announcement makes the national news that evening and Redknapp's face is on the front page of the next day's *Guardian*. The board has announced that Redknapp has left 'by mutual consent' after a meeting with chairman Terence Brown, but most commentators realise this is football jargon for being given the sack. Redknapp, who has two years left to run on his contract, says that it was an argument over funds for new players that had 'gotten out of hand'. He emphasises: 'Leaving the club was the last thing on my mind when I went over this morning. I never dreamed it would happen. After meeting the chairman it all changed and I found myself out of work. Life in the Premiership will be even tougher next season and I wanted three players to get us up to scratch.'

Harry Redknapp had been at West Ham for nine seasons, two as assistant manager to Billy Bonds and seven as boss, and in many ways he was the club. True, when up against the likes of George Graham he was sometimes out-thought tactically, as in the FA Cup defeat last season but a club with limited funds was never going to get anyone better at manipulating the transfer market. Astonishingly, he took the club into fifth place and the UEFA Cup, via winning the Intertoto Cup, while still making a profit on transfers.

My partner Nicola finds my sadness and disbelief difficult to fathom as I stare at the Ceefax page with the expression of a man who has just placed a year's salary on Titi Camara topping the Premiership scoring charts. For amid all the continental coaches, 'Arry Boy was a proper old-style English gaffer – constantly stressed, with a battered face and bags under his eyes, but always ready with a quip for the press. Redknapp and his assistant, Frank Lampard, were always more Regan and Carter than Eriksson and Grip. On 'Arry's manor the cast read like a plot from *EastEnders*: 'Arry's assistant Frank was his bruvver-in-law. 'Arry's boy Jamie had legged it to Liverpool but Frank's boy, Frank Junior, was still at the family firm.

Harry called his wife 'the missus', once admitted to a fanzine that he'd never eaten a curry and said, 'The last film I went to see was *Doctor Zhivago,'* which was released in 1965. When I interviewed him after the launch of his autobiography, he claimed not to recognise Leicester Square, saying he only went out in the East End or in Bournemouth. When he saw a tramp begging on the streets he quipped: 'That's the ex-West Ham manager, that is!' He then compared himself to his son Jamie and his pop star wife Louise. Harry met his own wife Sandra at the Two Puddings pub in Stratford. 'There was a dance upstairs. It was dark and I had a result really. I think she liked my mate better, but got lumbered with me.'

HURRY UP HARRY

After assembling his Foreign Legion in 1996, Redknapp declared: 'I'm just an uneducated East End boy. How can I be expected to speak all their languages?' And you can't imagine Wenger or Eriksson throwing sandwiches at players who don't track back. Harry once confessed: 'I did hit Don Hutchison on the head with a plate of sandwiches at Southampton. He had the lot, egg and tomato, right across the nut . . . he wouldn't accept what I was saying and it all got a bit naughty.'

On hearing that Florin Raducioiu had decided to visit Harvey Nichols rather than be involved with West Ham in a Coca-Cola Cup tie at Stockport, Harry's first reaction was probably: 'Who is this Harvey Nichols and can I sign him on a loan deal for Saturday?'

There will be no more announcements that Harry's seemingly permanently skeletal squad is 'down to the bare bones'. And no more of his famous 'rickets' in the transfer market (can you imagine Arsene Wenger announcing 'I 'ave made ze ricket with Boa Morte'?), such as when he signed 'those dodgy foreigners' Raducioiu, Boogers and Dumitrescu. Like Barry Fry, he fitted revolving doors on his dressing-rooms and, for the first time in my West Ham-supporting life, the club made a profit on many transfer deals. The likes of Bilic, Berkovic, Hartson, Hughes, Unsworth, Lazaridis and Foe were all sold on for big profits while he managed to gain class players such as Paolo Di Canio and Trevor Sinclair at ridiculously cheap prices.

It shouldn't have ended in this manner and it's typical of the lack of glasnost at West Ham that the board has not revealed the reasons for Redknapp's departure. The main reason would seem to be that the board had lost faith in his ability in the transfer market following the disappointing post-Rio sale signings. Redknapp too had perhaps grown tired of competing with the top six with such a limited budget, knowing that at least £6 million of the Rio money would probably go towards the new Dr Martens Stand. Another contributing factor might have been the sheer turnover of players during Redknapp's reign. There were 134 deals buying and selling players, with each deal involving massive signing-on fees and ever-increasing wages. Redknapp later suggested that the chairman, Terry Brown, had taken offence over comments he made in an interview to the fanzine *Over Land and Sea*, in which he said the chairman couldn't add up because he had only spent £9 million of the Rio money and not the alleged figure of £14 million. Whatever the truth, Terry Brown and the board at least owe the fans – the main shareholders in the company – some sort of statement.

You suspect that there is much more to tell and the real reasons will one day emerge. As at all football clubs, there is no shortage of rumour. Redknapp has been airbrushed from Hammers' history. The summer edition of *Upton Park News*, mailed to season ticket holders, has no mention of Redknapp bar a glib admission from managing director Paul Aldridge that the appointment of Redknapp's successor 'caused great controversy in the press and among some supporters'. The first programme of the new season is destined to have a mere reference to 'managerial alterations' and not even a thank you to Redknapp for his nine years of service.

Harry has gone and West Ham fans can only hope that the board has not dropped a ricket.

2. DEATH BY CEEFAX

The day after Harry Redknapp is sacked, *The Guardian* runs a list of contenders for the post of West Ham United team manager. These include Charlton boss Alan Curbishley, ex-England managers Terry Venables and Kevin Keegan, former Arsenal and Spurs boss George Graham and current player Stuart Pearce. Perhaps it is all part of a Baldrick-like cunning plan and the board has decided that the club has gone as far as it can with Redknapp and is now going to appoint a top boss to have us challenging for those European Champions League places. Then again, maybe not.

Curbishley, who has done superbly to establish Charlton as a Premiership side, seems the obvious choice. Still only 43, he used to play for the Hammers and clearly still has affection for the club. But Charlton issues an instant hands-off warning and over the next few weeks Curbishley rules himself out of contention and, damningly, even implies that Charlton might have more potential than West Ham. Kevin Keegan is soon signed up by Manchester City; Terry Venables makes it clear that after saving Middlesbrough he plans to spend more time with his autocue on ITV's *The Premiership*; George Graham is presumably judged to have too much of a defensive reputation to suit the West Ham Academy's tradition of attacking football; while Stuart Pearce is ruled out for not having sufficient managerial experience and joins Keegan for one final season playing at Manchester City.

While no one wants to manage West Ham, England midfielder Frank Lampard makes it very clear that he doesn't want to play for the club again. A little like Private Pike in *Dad's Army*, young Frank is upset because the club has been beastly to his dad and uncle (sacked assistant manager Frank Lampard Senior and Uncle Harry Redknapp). Obviously he's upset at the sacking of two members of his family, but you wonder how he would have responded had he been at, say, Manchester United. Would he just have muttered something about being a paid professional and opted to see who the new manager was?

Meanwhile the search goes on. Last season, when Rio Ferdinand returned with Leeds to play at Upton Park, it was a bit like a successful student

15

returning home to meet a slightly embarrassing blonde ex-girlfriend from Essex. By mid-June it's the club itself that seems desperate for any kind of partner. It's a bizarre feeling not having a manager. During my 31 years of watching the Hammers the club has only had five managers and, whenever there has been a change, an appointment has followed swiftly. But not this time. It's clear the board have sacked Redknapp without having any replacement in mind. Anyone new to the country in the last month would have read the tabloids and assumed that 'Managerless West Ham' was the club's full name. Every day there's the same despairing scan of Ceefax desperately searching for news of West Ham appointing a top manager. But instead all there is to find is Frank Lampard's agent inviting bids and news of reserves almost being loaned to Peterborough. Sartre was wrong. Hell is not other people but waiting for a Ceefax story that never comes.

In *The Soccer Tribe*, Desmond Morris wrote that football fans view their manager in much the same way as some tribal societies see witch-doctors. The witch-doctor is attributed with powers that might result in rain, while the football manager knows similar spells and incantations which might result in a title reign. But now our tribe had lost its medicine man. When Nietzsche wrote that 'God is dead' it was probably while his team was without a gaffer.

And who will defend West Ham's interests among the Darwinian world of the Premiership? Alan Curbishley at Charlton is able to sign youngsters such as Luke Young from Tottenham and Jason Euell from Wimbledon, while all we do is fail to see off the predators. My sense of unease is compounded by the sale of Frank Lampard to Chelsea for £11 million. It's pretty good money and Lampard has less potential than Carrick or Cole. But even so, had we had a top manager like Curbishley, Venables or Keegan installed they might have persuaded him to stay. Now both Ferdinand and Lampard have gone, the board have sent out the message that we are a selling club. Carrick, Cole, Di Canio and Sinclair will surely be next.

Once the early candidates are ruled out it's Steve McLaren, the Manchester United number two, who appears to be about to take the job. He would be an imaginative choice, and is recommended by Sir Alex Ferguson. Only news of his talks with the board leaks out, Middlesbrough move in with a counter offer, and McLaren clearly prefers their brochure to ours. Hibernian's Alex McCleish mutters that it would take 'a very good offer' to entice him from Edinburgh. There are rumours of a move for ex-Holland boss Frank Rijkaard and then silence.

Peter Gabriel keeps telling me 'Don't give up' but then you remember that line about 'so many men no one needs' and imagine them all ending up at West Ham to replace our sold-off stars. It's beginning to look as if William Hague might be retiring a little too early. We may just be needing his leadership skills next season.

You wonder what West Ham must be putting in their job advert. It probably reads something like: 'A vacancy has arisen at West Ham United for the post of Team Manager. This prestigious position offers: a transfer budget of 50 pence; bonus of £25 for avoiding relegation, erm, we mean winning the Premiership; a hugely talented team of injured players; your choice of company car from Dagenham Motors; a couple of rejected Fila tracksuits; the chance to sell a used Lampard to Chelsea or Leeds; company outings to Southend once a year; gratis luncheons in Ken's Café. Ambitious self-starters please apply in writing to Mr Terence Brown.'

Around this time there are rumours that Glenn Roeder might be a candidate. He took over the side for the final game of last season at Middlesbrough, but was told not to bother applying for the post. He has been a coach for a couple of years at the club, but was below Redknapp and Lampard in seniority and had only an average managerial record at Watford and Gillingham.

The club then announce that anyone renewing their season ticket who does not approve of the new manager could have a refund. Maybe the catch is that West Ham will never get a manager. Who could us fans blame if there was no one in the dugout? Ourselves?

By mid-June most fans are praying that West Ham appoint just about anyone to give the illusion that someone is in control of our footballing destiny. Like Michael Stipe, I risk losing my religion if this continues. My club is adrift, rudderless on a sea of Premiership money, no stars to guide this wandering bark, heading towards the murky bottom of the Nationwide.

Finally, on 14 June, after 37 days of footballing purgatory, comes the underwhelming news that Glenn Roeder, yes, Glenn Roeder, has been appointed the ninth manager in the club's history. Cheap option is nearly every fans' verdict. Someone who won't complain while the club is asset-stripped. Maybe all that waiting around wasn't so bad after all.

For his photo call, Roeder stands in a hard hat before the rubble that is the former West Stand, looking like a man who has just failed the audition for *Auf Wiedersehen Pet*. Roeder himself admits that he was not the club's first choice and says that he feels like a 100–1 outsider winning the Grand National: 'The horses fell one at a time and I was the last one standing.'

True, he might prove to be a great manager and has coached England alongside Glenn Hoddle. Like John Lyall, he might be a very nice man. But surely appointing someone with no Premiership experience is a huge risk.

With typical loyalty, less than 100 fans ask for their season ticket money back. But more pressure is placed on Roeder when, at home in Italy, captain Paolo Di Canio publicly questions the appointment of such a low-profile manager and hints that he himself might be driven out of the club. 'I told them what I thought and they did the exact opposite. They listened to some of the young players at the club instead. Naturally I'm not too happy about this and, judging by the reaction of the fans, neither are they,' he declares. 'At the end of last season Paul Aldridge asked me what I thought of Glenn. I said he was a great coach and he should definitely stay on as assistant. But I also said I thought we needed an experienced figure. I still believe that.'

PDC adds that although Roeder was not his personal choice as manager, 'This is Glenn's big chance and I will be fighting tooth and nail alongside him. Who knows, maybe he will lead us to the Premiership and prove himself in battle . . . Still, this does not change the fact that many fans feel betrayed and I feel that my views and those of others were not taken into account. When I return to London we're going to have a serious talk. I would hate to think that someone at the club is trying to push me out. If this is the case they're not going to succeed. I will not be pushed around.'

Most bookies have him odds on for an early dismissal and one even has West Ham down with Bolton as 3–1 to be relegated. Presumably we have to give the man a season to see if he can do the job, although uncomfortable comparisons with Chris Hutching's short reign at Bradford City last season come to mind.

Poor Joe Cole is wheeled out to give quotes on Ceefax about Roeder being one of the top coaches he has played under, although at Joe's age you wonder how many coaches he's had beyond his school games master.

Encouragingly, Roeder starts in a businesslike manner, appointing ex-Hammer Paul 'Sarge' Goddard as his assistant, Ludek Miklosko as goalkeeping coach and, in an overdue move, bringing in John McCarthy, a sports scientist, before arranging some rushed pre-season friendlies. He also insists that Fredi Kanouté, who is rumoured to favour being reunited with his former boss at Lyon, Jean Tigana, now at Fulham, must honour his contract.

Roeder's initial foray into the transfer market is a good one. He buys a familiar figure, French full-back Sebastien Schemmel, who was on loan at the club last season but was inexplicably not signed from Metz by Harry Redknapp. He played in the epic victory at Manchester United in the Cup and from his first game at Charlton looked a very useful, pacy wing-back, even if his crossing was somewhat erratic. Even in the dire second half of the season Schemmel never stopped running in a woefully underperforming team. What's more, his value seems to have reduced from £4 million to a mere £465,000, so it's a relatively risk-free signing for Roeder.

His next move suggests that the new boss might be more than a yes man. No one seems to have known that the Aston Villa goalkeeper David James was for sale. But Roeder manages to sign the England international goalkeeper for £3.5 million. James played for Roeder as a youngster at Watford, so clearly must have some respect for the man. The new boss is bullish about the signing: 'By getting David and other potential signings, people will see that the club and I mean business. When was the last time West Ham signed a current England player with his best years ahead of him?'

The signing of James shows an encouraging ruthlessness, for although Shaka Hislop is a fine keeper, when he returned after injury last season his confidence seemed to dip and he looked suspect on crosses. Only then the unthinkable happens. West Ham's Australian defender Hayden Foxe has already been sidelined after a freak training ground accident where he caught his finger in a bib. Now David James is selected to play for England in a friendly against Holland at White Hart Lane on the Wednesday before the season kicks off. In a collision with Martin Keown he injures the posterior cruciate ligament in his knee and is likely to miss most of the season. Four days before the new season, West Ham's one big signing is crocked. Glenn Roeder describes it as 'a massive blow' and adds 'it makes you wonder if these internationals should be played'. Roeder is not only untried, he's unlucky too. It's the sort of injury that can turn a season and West Ham fans start to wonder if, with a rookie boss, the club will be able to survive in the Premiership for a ninth successive season.

TOP TEN HAMMERS' INJURIES

DAVID JAMES'S KNEE LIGAMENTS: Crocked by an Arsenal centre-back on his own side while playing for England before he had even played a competitive game for the Hammers.

DEVONSHIRE FLU: Alan Devonshire returned after injury for a couple of games, caught flu, and then disappeared for 18 months before re-emerging to help the Hammers finish third in 1985–86.

PHIL PARKES'S SEPTIC ELBOW AND ARTHRITIC KNEES: Has any other goalkeeper ever managed to have both a septic elbow and arthritic knees and still look better than Allen McKnight?

STEWART ROBSON'S CYCLING SHORTS: Nobody knew exactly what Stewart Robson's injury was, but the suspicion was that his entire body was held together by his Lycra cycling shorts.

TREVOR MORLEY'S KNIFE WOUND: Missed the second half of the 1990–91 season after being stabbed following a 'domestic incident' at which his wife Monica was present.

HAYDEN FOXE'S FINGER: Missed the start of the 2001–02 season after catching his finger in a training ground bib in a 'freak accident'. The injury was so bad that another knock might have meant him losing his finger.

WEST HAM

BILLY BONDS'S TOE: The Hammers' skipper once managed to trip over his slippers, fall downstairs and injure his toe.

JIMMY GREAVES'S ALCOHOLISM: Signed for West Ham and, perhaps understandably, hit the bottle.

ALVIN MARTIN AND STEVE WHITTON'S CAR CRASH: Whitton remembers that 'Alvin had this bloody Toyota Supra, a flying machine, and he just put his foot down'. Going round a bend in Stratford the car went through a couple of trees and a lamp-post. Alvin broke six ribs and Whitton broke two ribs and dislocated a shoulder.

SIMON WEBSTER'S LEG: After joining the Hammers he went for a 50–50 ball with Julian Dicks in training – and was never seen again. Now one of the club's physiotherapists.

3. GLENN'S GLORIOUS GLADIATORS

Liverpool 2 West Ham 1 - 18 August 2001
West Ham 0 Leeds 0 - 25 August 2001
Derby 0 West Ham 0 - 8 September 2001

Green Street is my boulevard of broken dreams. Since 1970 I've walked from Upton Park tube station to the Boleyn Ground past shops that defy all attempts at gentrification.

By the station doors stands the West Ham programme stall, which has fallen victim to the greengrocer's apostrophe, offering match day 'programme's'. Stepping over the odd pile of police horse manure, we reach Green Street. On the right is the Queen's fish and chip shop, where on match days legions of fans in replica shirts queue for chips and saveloys. Beyond this is the market, fronted by a stall which appears to sell nothing but outsize bras for Dawn French. Behind the market are what used to be referred to as 'the Beirut flats', a once dismal council monolith full of burnt-out windows, which has at least been slightly improved by some cladding and paint. After the market is the perpetually packed Queen's pub, and beyond this the Belly Busters burger store and the tools and ironmongery shop of Derrick A Cross, the sort of establishment that looks like it's been there since the war and will remain there forever selling useful selections of kitchen utensils, brushes, buckets and mops.

On the left-hand side of Green Street stand halal butchers, kebab shops and proof that feminism never reached the East End. Ever since I've been coming to West Ham – my first match was in 1970 against Blackpool – a sign has stood above a dry-cleaning shop reading 'Don't kill your wife – let us do it!' That sign has travelled from sexist outrage to post-lad mag irony, just through never changing. Maybe it will be listed soon.

By Tudor Road are the front gardens where scarves and old programmes are sold and where from 1989 to 1992 I helped sell the fanzine I contributed to, *Fortune's Always Hiding*. Later, Shane Barber, the editor of *On A Mission*, took over the selling spot and published my column Mayday until he left the country for Germany. Outside Upton Park Domestic Appliances stand numerous old fridges and cookers (Harry Redknapp probably learnt all he knew about salesmanship there), while next door stands Ken's Café, a proper greasy-spoon in which it would be no surprise to see Kaff Beale berating her customers. The food is marvellous value compared to the catering inside the ground – with egg, chips and beans costing only £2 – and it's here that victories are anticipated and defeats digested.

The shops and markets mirror the other London clubs' views of West Ham. Chelsea Village it ain't. Arsenal, Spurs and Chelsea fans all view life at Upton Park as distinctly downmarket. Even the club's nickname of 'The Irons' betrays its working-class roots; West Ham started life as Thames Ironworks in 1895, a works side for the shipbuilding company of the same name. Yet amid the dodgy tower blocks and chip shops, class and romance have mingled with poverty. East London might be where London's unsightly and dangerous industries have traditionally been dumped, but its football fans have always expected a little fantasy, perhaps as a buffer against reality. This has, after all, been the home of Moore, Hurst, Peters, Brooking, Devonshire, Di Canio and Cole, players who with one moment of skill can enliven a week's toil at the typeface.

It's a street of many memories: in the early '70s Geoff Hurst puffing out his cheeks to score the winner against Liverpool in a League Cup tie after a great run by 'Arry Redknapp on the wing; policemen confiscating DM boots from skinheads outside the North Bank; the barracked Bobby Gould diving to score with a header after a Frank Lampard cross in a thrilling 6–2 victory against Leicester; a splendidly sideburned Trevor Brooking firing home a sumptuous goal against Derby; Devonshire and Brooking exchanging countless one-twos on the left; Trev whippin' in crosses with either foot; Frank McAvennie poaching two late goals to beat Everton 2–1 in the season we nearly won the league but because of a strike nothing was televised; Ray Stewart scoring that late penalty against Ipswich; Paolo's volley against Wimbledon and his attempted walk-off against Bradford . . .

Today it's a stultifying, sweaty August afternoon in East London in 2001 as West Ham kick off their first home fixture under the Roeder regime. It's so hot that even East Enders have declined to overdose on saturated fats. Ken's Café is deserted, bar about five people. There's plenty of space to observe the team photos from the '60s, a Hammers mirror and yellowing posters of the likes of Julian Dicks. 'That's how I like it,' declares proprietress Carol, apparently oblivious to the loss in income. Over the years Ken's has been the scene of fanzine meetings, post-match inquests and endless shouted requests for customers to collect 'number 37 egg, chips and beans! I'm not telling you again or it goes in the bin!' It's also where my own football academy meets to discuss the finer nuances of the game.

GLENN'S GLORIOUS GLADIATORS

There's Big Joe, who has been around since the days in the 1980s when we both worked on the award-winning fanzine *Fortune's Always Hiding* and, perhaps rather aptly for a Hammers fan, now works in the comedy industry. Gavin and Nigel are both journalists and closet Uriah Heep fans. Perhaps because of their anti-social activities as both heavy metal and West Ham fans, they have remained friends since their days together at Brentwood School, the alma mater of Frank Lampard Junior. Nigel is Steve Potts's number one fan and Gav is brilliant at finding real ale pubs in the vicinity of any ground in the country.

The rest of our squad includes Dan, who works in the press office at a TV company and has probably wasted more wagers on unlikely West Ham scores than any man alive; Matt, who is a political correspondent with an anorak's knowledge of football, the sort of man who can tell you the combined age of Oldham's midfield; and Fraser, who somehow manages to combine being show-business correspondent for a glossy celebrity magazine and attending glittering film premieres up west with living in Ilford and supporting the Irons.

A midweek visitor is Dirty Den, another ex-*Fortune's Always Hiding* man and *On A Mission* fanzine writer, whose job on a national Sunday newspaper prevents him from attending Saturday games. Despite being from Northern Ireland he's developed an unhealthy love for West Ham and Celtic, and is our own resident expert on the sexploits of Frank McAvennie and the crazed genius of Paolo Di Canio.

West Ham have started the season with a predictable defeat at Anfield. But instead of the anticipated thrashing we've been decidedly unlucky. After Owen's early goal the Hammers came back to win a penalty when Svetoslav Todorov, in for the injured Kanouté and having thankfully ditched the Alice band for a decent haircut, was bundled over by Hyypia. With typical nonchalance, Paolo Di Canio, starting the season with a shaved head, chipped the ball over Liverpool keeper Arphexad into the exact spot where he was standing a second earlier. Paolo then ran to hug his new boss and a slightly embarrassed Glenn Roeder nearly dropped his notebook and pen in surprise.

West Ham played tightly and Song and Dailly did well at the back, alongside the new signing Schemmel and veteran Nigel Winterburn. It's only a moment of brilliance from Michael Owen that won the game 13 minutes from the end. Allowed just a fraction too much time by Dailly, he arrowed a shot into the far corner from a seemingly impossible position wide on the right.

So perhaps Glenn Roeder's reign will not be the disaster everyone expects, even if the Hammers are one of the bookies' favourites for the drop and Roeder is still ranked as a good bet for an early-season sacking.

The Leeds game was in some doubt. Only at West Ham would the ground itself have to take a fitness test. It was only confirmed yesterday that the

23

ground had received its safety certificate, but with Upton Park having recovered from Devonshire Flu the game can now go ahead. The old West Stand was demolished at the end of last season and builders in yellow hard hats now watch the game from the emerging and impressive Doctor Martens Stand. Seeing the structure, the visiting Leeds fans chant 'Is that the Rio stand?', which it probably is, having been partially funded by the sale last season of Rio Ferdinand to Leeds for £18 million.

Interestingly, and typical of the club's lack of openness, is the fact that the programme makes no reference to Harry Redknapp, although former player turned pundit Tony Gale is critical of the side's 'tactical naïveté' last season, perhaps indicating the board's thinking.

But at least match day announcer Jeremy Nicholas is upbeat. 'Let's give a huge Upton Park welcome to Glenn's Glorious Gladiators!' he exclaims, sounding very much like a man who has just discovered the concept of alliteration.

Perhaps sensing the unfairness of his early-season vilification the home fans seem willing to give the unheralded Roeder a chance. A minute's silence for the late Les Sealey, the former Hammers' keeper and coach, ends with a collective roar of hope for the new season.

As the match kicks off our eyes are on the new boss. After nine years of Harry it's a shock not to see an agitated used car dealer on the line; instead we have an implausibly tall and angular man in a dark suit who looks almost like a Dickensian creation. He stands in front of an impressive new transparent dugout. 'He must have insisted on the flash continental style dugout before he took the job,' muses Dan. Only Roeder never actually gets in it, he just stands by the touchline, arms folded, with the demeanour of an East End undertaker trying to prevent 22 players trampling over the floral tributes.

Gavin, who is to football timekeeping what Frank McAvennie is to chastity, then makes his first late arrival of the season, greeted by a cry of 'Legend!' from Nigel. It's immediately apparent that the Hammers have a better shape than last season, when numerous players seemed to play 'off the cuff', as Harry would say. Roeder has said that he hates the words 'free spirit' and has assigned Joe Cole to a left-sided role in midfield as he sticks to a 4-4-2 formation as opposed to Harry's five at the back. The other big shock is Rigobert Song's facial hair; sporting a grey goatee beneath dreadlocks he now resembles Titan from Stingray. It's almost as embarrassing as Julian Dicks's one-time Forrest Gump cut.

A sumptuous 60-yard ball from Di Canio sees Sinclair volley over early on, but it's a welcome sign that Paolo has recovered his sense of magic after his poor form at the end of last season. At one point he beats Leeds's aggressive right-back Danny Mills three times. Viduka heads over for Leeds and it's a tightly contested workmanlike game. Rio Ferdinand has received predictable applause from the home fans as he returns to Upton Park. When he first came back with Leeds last April he scored in an easy 2–0 win. At least it looks like West Ham will give them a tougher game this time.

Even Dailly and Song are playing well again in central defence and honest artisan John Moncur is working hard to compensate for the absence of the sold Lampard in midfield. Young Michael Carrick is taking more responsibility too and goes close with an audacious lob over Martyn from 40 yards out. The thought occurs that this is a working-class club and at least the side are putting in an honest day's labour for once. Too many games at the end of last season just drifted away.

In the relentless heat the game is more perspiration than inspiration, but two minutes after the break Joey Cole has the ball in the net, only for the goal to be disallowed on the dubious grounds that Todorov has impeded Nigel Martyn. Toddy, as Harry liked to call him, still looks too lightweight for the Premiership, but creates a good chance for himself before curling the ball wide. Young prodigy Jermain Defoe replaces him for the last 20 minutes and immediately has a confident strike at goal.

It's Rio Ferdinand who denies the Irons a win. In one sublime movement Di Canio cushions Sinclair's cross, drags it back and sends Mills 20 yards off in the direction of the A13, only for his shot to be blocked by Rio's instinctive, saving challenge.

The game ends in a goalless draw. The side appears to have a shape, and having played well at Anfield and taken a point from Leeds it hasn't been that bad a start to the season.

As we walk towards Upton Park tube Dan and myself are impressed with the new boss's demeanour. 'I think Roeder's been taking lessons on how to stand,' says Dan. At least we now have a boss who poses with the authority of the Wenger-like technician, tie neatly in place and arms folded.

After the match Roeder announces himself 'very satisfied' with the two performances so far and says: 'We've set our benchmark . . . I thought Paolo had scored and so did he. It was just a nuisance Rio came back to haunt us.'

With the Frank Lampard money still to be spent, Roeder's aim is to improve the squad with high-quality players. Later that week he spends a club record £5 million on signing Don Hutchison from Sunderland. Hutch scored 11 goals in 35 games for the Hammers during his first spell at the club and also earned a reputation for drinking and high-jinks. But he has apparently matured while at Everton and Sunderland and was last season's player of the year for the Black Cats.

Hutchison clearly has a good scoring record, and has hopefully given up the habit of hiding his wedding tackle behind Budweiser labels, as he did so infamously in a holiday snap that found its way into the *News of the World* while he was at Liverpool. He uses that very same organ (no, the paper, not that one) to reveal that he has changed lifestyle since his last spell at Upton Park.

'I regret a few of the things that happened last time I was down here but most of all I regret letting the fans down,' admits Hutch. 'I used to think I could go out when I wanted, drink as much as I wanted, then still get up and play football. I was a lot younger back then. I thought I was invincible.'

Opinion is divided among Hammers fans. Joe feels that £5 million for a 29-year-old who he thinks is moving for more money is too much.

'What, we're buying him back because he drinks less?' exclaims Joe in disbelief, after we discuss the *NOTW* interview.

'Yeah, he's down to five pints a night now!' declares one of the more cynical members of our party.

On the other hand, the value of one older Hutch is just under half a Lampard, so it might be about right in an inflated market. Dan comments via e-mail: 'It's good to see we've found a Biro that works and signed someone at last. Pound for pound, he's probably worth the dough. We really need a bit of bite right in the centre and, as we found out last year, he's not afraid to shoot. Just as long as they're not tequila shots, we'll be laughing.'

Hutch makes his début in another goalless draw at Derby, notable for the return of Fredi Kanouté for 53 minutes before the inevitable hamstring injury flares up again. West Ham have defended well, but played three games without scoring a goal in open play. Thankfully the next match is an away tie at Reading in the Worthington Cup. Surely even Svetoslav Todorov must score against second division opposition.

4. DEATH IN THE AFTERNOON

Reading 0 West Ham 0
(Reading won on penalties) – 11 September 2001

11 September 2001 will forever be remembered as the day West Ham were knocked out of the Worthington Cup by Reading.

It's scheduled to be my first away game of the season. Dirty Den is up for the trip and, in that sad manner peculiar to football groundhoppers, we're both rather excited at seeing a new ground. Train times have been checked and we've arranged to meet at Paddington station for our trip to the Madjeski Stadium. Only suddenly grim, deathly reality intervenes to render football irrelevant.

In the early afternoon I turn on the TV to check the West Ham team news on Ceefax, only to find apocalyptic images on the screen. There's the logo 'Attack On America' in red letters in the corner of the screen and black smoke billowing from the World Trade Centre. That morning terrorists have hijacked two planes and flown them deliberately into the towers. A third plane has crashed into the Pentagon and a fourth has exploded in a field, perhaps on course for Camp David.

All work plans are abandoned as the defining image of the new century unveils on live TV. There are slow motion replays of the second plane striking with lumbering, obscene accuracy. Desperate faces are leaning out of windows waving handkerchiefs, an inferno behind them, pleading for some kind of rescue. And you think, they're not going to get out. I remember the time I stood on top of the Empire State Building and couldn't stand by the parapet wall because of my vertigo. Now people are jumping. It must be the worst decision of their lives. Burn or jump. Death by furnace or death by plummeting onto unforgiving streets far far below. There's a horrible, almost pornographic, voyeuristic quality to the nightmare being played out on the TV screen.

And then the unthinkable happens. The tower blocks collapse, falling floor by floor, imploding from the top downwards as a huge cloud of grey volcanic smoke and debris shoots down the side streets with people diving for safety into shops and under cars. This is not a film. No one knows how many people are in those buildings. It could be 10,000. If the attacks were at midday it would have been 50,000.

I phone Denis and ask him if he's heard what has happened, which is a pretty silly question really, as he works for a national newspaper. He's still up for the game though. This attack on America is the sort of thing the IRA were doing to London for years, only on a massive scale. My rational mind tells me that we shouldn't let terrorists win, we shouldn't stop our normal day-to-day activities. Why should psychopathic, suicidal terrorists in America affect my behaviour?

At four o'clock Nicola returns home. She's heard the news while playing with our daughters in the park, and is so upset that she's left Lola's shoes in the sandpit. 'Don't you see, it's the end of everything!' she declares.

I'm not saying that Nicola is a bad traveller, but she panics in the back seat of other people's cars, she doesn't like lifts and is terrified of flying. Now the thought of four planes being hijacked and used as human bombs bringing death to unsuspecting office workers as they arrive at work has left her with all the optimism of Sylvia Plath with a hangover.

She unveils a complex timetable of apocalyptic inevitability involving the collapse of the world financial markets and the insurance industry, the subsidence in her flat never getting fixed, the collapse of the property market, George Bush going mental and dropping nuclear bombs on everyone who isn't American, the Middle East erupting in full-scale war and the end of life on the planet in general. Blimey. And West Ham will probably get relegated as well.

Like most men, emotional intelligence is not one of my strong points, but even I sense that Nicola is in need of emotional support and perhaps football should come second. Part of me still wants to go to Reading; it goes against every instinct of the football supporter to have tickets for the game and voluntarily not go to it. But this is an exceptional, terrible day; Nicola feels we may only have a few days left together, and I agree not to go to the match. We phone Denis. Nicola explains her reasons for not wanting me to go to the game and Denis says he'll try to sell my ticket at the match.

Nicola phones her mother, and with that exemplary practicality peculiar to certain upper middle-class Home Counties women, she announces that of course she's heard about the World Trade Centre but she's going to carry on painting her windows regardless. This emphasis on normality is somehow reassuring.

That evening we sit down with large glasses of chardonnay and watch the rolling coverage on CNN, Sky News and the BBC. Someone called Osama Bin Laden and an Islamic fundamentalist terrorist group called Al-Qaida are being named as the likely suspects. The New York skyline is rent by a void filled with a satanic plume of smoke while people stand gazing on bridges, stunned, cheering rescue workers. I'm no fan of American foreign policy but no one deserves this. As the evening progresses it's becoming clear that the hijackers were acting out of a religious fascism rather than any sense of social justice.

There's an announcement that Tony Blair has closed the airspace over London. There are still planes flying overhead though and every sound of a jet engine now sounds ominously close. There are serious predictions that there will also be strikes on London, talk of poisoning of the water supply and crop-spraying machines spreading lethal chemicals over western cities. I've made the right decision, football tonight would have seemed too surreal.

Details of the heroic, loving last phone calls made by those on planes and in the towers start to emerge. I hope there were no children on board those hijacked planes and think of my own daughters. Will our children be safe from chemical or biological attack? Nell is just seven months old and her life has hardly begun. We have already explained to three-year-old Lola that an aeroplane has hit a tower block. How will I explain to Lola that all her dreams, aspirations, love and hopes might now amount to nothing, that we might be obliterated by the action of a suicidal fanatic who believes that God will reward his martyrdom?

But even as I think this, I know that I'm an incurable addict too, as something inside me can't stop my remote finger flicking to page 390 of Ceefax. Ah, West Ham are drawing 0–0 at Reading and Defoe and Todorov are playing up front and new signing Don Hutchison is continuing in midfield.

Newsnight has yet more theories and explanations: the hijackers were armed with just Stanley knives, they almost certainly took control of the planes from the pilots for the final minutes, security on American internal flights is lax because Americans regard it as their right to board a flight with minimum delay, the passengers might have fought back on the plane that crashed in Pennsylvania.

At 10.40 p.m. I turn back to Ceefax. West Ham have drawn 0–0 with Reading and then lost on penalties, with Defoe missing the vital spot kick. Poor Denis has gone to the game alone, endured a goalless draw, extra time and a penalty defeat, and won't get home till 1.30 a.m., all this on top of witnessing a global catastrophe. Normally I'd be upset at another loss to a lower division side and the likelihood of another trophyless season. But tonight it doesn't matter.

No one even knows if the football season will be completed. Or if someone will crash a plane on Upton Park while 26,000 people are at a match. Normal life can no longer be guaranteed. We have just seen the most horrific, unforgettable images of the new millennium and you wonder if, like the First World War, one act will set in place the most monstrous conflict of the twenty-first century. The world is a newly dangerous place. Maybe five thousand people are dead, Americans will never feel invulnerable in their own country again and some geezer called Osama Bin Laden has attacked the rights of all western groundhopppers by depriving me of a visit to ground number 49. Now that really is a declaration of war.

5. TAKING GOALS TO NEWCASTLE

Middlesbrough 2 West Ham 0 – 15 September 2001
West Ham 3 Newcastle 0 – 23 September 2001

After the terrible events of 11 September West Ham do their best to help return our lives to normality. Even global terror can't prevent such enduring traditions as the Hammers failing to score and then giving away two daft goals at Middlesbrough.

Four days after the terror attacks on America the Hammers arrive at the Cellnet Stadium with new £5 million centre-half Tomas Repka in the side. Following the summer departures of Stimac and Stuart Pearce, another centre-back was an immediate priority for Glenn Roeder. Repka appears to be a good signing; he is a Czech international and has completed more than 100 games for Fiorentina in Serie A. Roeder first spotted him while looking at his teammate Alessandro Pierini and speaks of him as being a tough, committed English-style defender. At least the new gaffer has proved himself able to attract relatively big names. He has now spent all the Frank Lampard money and what remains of the Rio cash on three internationals: the injured David James, Don Hutchison and Repka.

But it all goes awry at the Riverside. Middlesbrough have lost four in a row, but it's an immutable law of supporting West Ham that any losing team will immediately end its poor run against the Hammers. After half an hour Paul Ince's right-wing cross is misjudged by Shaka Hislop to present Brian Deane with an easy goal. And ten minutes later Song's error lets in Johnston for the second. With Fredi Kanouté having only played 53 minutes of football all season (at Derby), West Ham have started off by playing midfielder Hutchison as a lone striker and inevitably struggle to create chances. To increase the Hammers' misery, Repka ends his début by being sent off 12 minutes from time for a second bookable offence.

After four games West Ham have yet to score a goal in open play and have slumped to the bottom of the Premiership. It hardly sounds encouraging

31

when Roeder adopts the standard line of managers in trouble when he tells the press: 'Overall, when everybody is fit, there is enough quality in the squad to get out of trouble.'

With the early season home fixture against Chelsea having been postponed until work on the stand is completed, West Ham only have two home games out of the first seven matches. So victory against Newcastle is vital in the Sunday afternoon game live on Sky.

The first home game since 11 September has me thinking that a packed ground is a prime target for terrorist attack. Mind you, you'd have to be a brave member of Al-Qaida to take on Carol in Ken's Café or risk being felled by a heavyweight burger from the Belly Busters stall in Green Street.

Glenn Roeder appears to be one of the Premiership's more philosophical managers. In the programme against Leeds he commented that the death of former Hammers keeper Les Sealey proved that 'all our lives hang by the thinnest of threads', while in today's programme he refers to 11 September by writing: 'The scenes we witnessed on TV will haunt us forever. I find it unbelievable what mankind can do to each other. It puts everything into proper perspective.'

Roeder must be thankful that Frank Lampard Junior is no longer at the club. 'It's nice to see a sensitive response to global terrorism from footballers,' I suggest to the lads in Ken's Café before the game. In that morning's Sunday papers it's emerged that Lampard, along with John Terry, Jody Morris and Eidur Gudjohnsen, went on a drinking binge 24 hours after the World Trade Centre attack and the Chelsea Four shocked grieving Americans with their boozy high-jinks in a hotel bar at Heathrow.

Newcastle arrive for the match in excellent form, unbeaten after four games and boosted by a thrilling 4–3 victory over Manchester United. But from the kick-off it's apparent that even with just the upper half of the Doctor Martens Stand open, the intensity of the Upton Park experience can still intimidate the opposition. It's the sort of ground where fans are close enough to the action to feel eminently capable of knocking over a cross to the far post, which would probably be missed by West Ham's current strikers.

The day has begun with another 'Di Canio To Quit West Ham' story in the tabloids, but the newly bald maestro again looks back to his best form, contributing tirelessly to both attack and defence. Crucially, Fredi Kanouté has returned. The big West Ham striker is what might politely be called an enigma. He could be a great great player if he could add more aggression and belief to his game. As at Leeds last season, he can terrorise defences on his own, but at other times he misses chances and seems to stroll through the game. We have a theory in the Upper East Stand that he plays wearing a Walkman, strolling around listening to ambient French jazz fusion, then occasionally doing something dynamic in the gaps between tracks.

After just three minutes Robbie Elliott is brought down by Dailly and it looks like a clear penalty for Newcastle, but the ref waves play on. Shearer and Bellamy look dangerous early on, but West Ham almost score after 11 minutes when Di Canio crosses and Carrick just misses getting a telling touch. Then, on 17 minutes, comes the moment we've been waiting for all season. Paolo plays a short corner to French signing Laurent Courtois, who whips in a cross to the far post and Don Hutchison – taunted as a 'greedy Mackem bastard' by the Newcastle fans – dives to head home. There's huge relief all around the stadium. We've scored a goal, we've scored a goal, we've scored one, West Ham's scored a goal . . . And from a corner too.

New signing 'Super' Tomas Repka is instantly reassuring at the back, attacking headers with relish, clattering into tackles and generally getting stuck in. He looks the sort of defensive leader West Ham have lacked since Stuart Pearce departed for Manchester City. Hutchison's experience complements Michael Carrick's promise in midfield and the pair dominate Lee and Acuna. In fact, Hutch looks the sort of goalscoring midfielder we need to replace Frank Lampard. Sinclair has a shot cleared off the line and Hislop makes a fine save from Bellamy's lob to leave it 1–0 at half-time.

On 52 minutes the game is effectively over. Christian Dailly, the man maligned last season as an inadequate replacement for Rio Ferdinand, suddenly looks like Franz Beckenbauer as he plays a sweeping long ball out of defence for Di Canio to run on to on the left. He's faced by Warren Barton and it's a mismatch that should really be covered by the Geneva Convention.

Paolo dips his shoulder to send the journeyman full-back halfway down the Barking Road before firing a perfect shot across Given and in off the far post. He celebrates with his usual equanimity, leaping into the Bobby Moore Stand and being engulfed by back-slapping fans. Prominently attached to his captain's armband is a rolled-up Stars and Stripes flag, which he brandishes to the crowd. This is Paolo's tribute to the American dead.

Shortly after the goal comes a staff announcement on the PA. 'Mr Moon has left the stadium,' we learn to ironic cheers. This has been going on for years and everyone knows that it is some form of coded security announcement, probably meaning: 'There's five tonnes of explosive under the main stand, don't panic, Mr Roeder, don't panic!' I imagine shady Al-Qaida operatives crouched in bunkers declaring: 'OK, we wait until the Infidel Mr Moon has left the stadium before we strike.'

West Ham are now dominating the game and Fredi is looking for his comeback goal. Given makes a fine save from a long-range drive before he settles the game ten minutes from time. Di Canio back-heels, Hutchison dummies and the big Frenchman fires under Given. Fredi turns down the avant-garde jazz fusion on his Walkman for a few seconds and does his trademark shrug, grinning like a man who has just been pleasantly surprised by the arrival of the number 73 bus.

Then comes John Moncur, on as sub for Laurent Courtois. 'He's there, he's every fucking where! John Moncur!' sing the crowd, and such ubiquity is usually accompanied by nefarious activities. Moncs was a skilful midfielder and at 35 has been a loyal servant to the club. But in recent seasons his principal function has been to come on as a substitute and get booked or sent off as quickly as possible, which is certainly great entertainment for the fans.

'He's still got four minutes to get booked in,' suggests Matt.

'I'll give him three minutes, any increase on that?' says Dan.

'Make it two,' adds Joe.

'I'll go for two bookable offences and a straight red,' I suggest.

Moncur then exceeds all expectations by clattering into a late tackle and being booked after just 30 seconds. Huge cheers reverberate around Upton Park and all around us in the stand fans are guffawing.

'Well, he said he'd worked on his temperament,' I remark. 'And there's still time for him to be sent off.'

The whistle blows and it's been a vibrant home performance from the Hammers; the best home performance since the Boxing Day demolition of Charlton in 2000.

Match day announcer Jeremy Nicholas has never knowingly underplayed a victory. He must love the early days of the season when one victory can send a team soaring at least 75 places in the league. 'We're off the bottom!' he hollers. 'We go above Southampton! We go above Leicester! We go above Derby! We go above Ipswich! We go above Charlton! We're 15th!'

After the game Newcastle boss Bobby Robson complains about being denied an early penalty but concedes: 'From the moment West Ham scored to the end of the game they were the better team.'

Meanwhile, Paolo Di Canio continues to act as a one-man global ambassador in the new world order. When asked about the behaviour of his former teammate Frank Lampard he responds with some eloquence: 'If you go out drinking all night after what happened you don't understand the enormity of the events. It's right to fine them two weeks' wages but they should have been left out for a month after doing that. It was terrible.'

As for the Stars and Stripes on his armband, 'I didn't wear the armband because I had any friends in America, I just feel like all the American people are friends and family to us. It's so sad what happened and I just want to live in a peaceful world – but we must not give in to the terrorists.'

When I return home Nicola can tell by the sound of my footsteps walking through the sitting-room that we've won. Which just proves that West Ham fans are a bunch of walkers; jaunty gait equals victory, morose plod equals defeat. Football still doesn't seem to matter as much as it once did, but after such a vibrant attacking performance against an on-form side, West Ham's season surely starts here. Repka and Hutchison look fine buys and Sinclair and Carrick are back to their best in the middle. And an away win at Everton next week will see us challenging in the top half of the table.

6. FOUR THOUSAND HOLES
IN BLACKBURN, LANCASHIRE

Everton 5 West Ham 0 - 29 September 2001
Blackburn 7 West Ham 1 - 14 October 2001

Even more nauseating than watching your team lose on Ceefax is watching them lose on the Sky results service. This morning we were convinced that West Ham's season had turned. After the way Glenn's Glorious Gladiators had played against Newcastle, the lads would surely get a result at Goodison, even if I did see us get stuffed 6–0 there two seasons ago. Every West Ham fan should have known better.

Arriving back from a family outing to Lauderdale Park in Highgate, it's time to tap in 46 on my digital box, desperately hoping that I don't discover match summariser Iain Dowie in huge earphones looking uncannily like a cyberman from *Doctor Who*.

Fuckety fuck, as Hugh Grant once said. Incredibly, West Ham are 3–0 down. The Sky printer reels off lots of useless and annoying information. Gazza has gone off injured after five minutes (and still we couldn't win?). Doubly annoying is that the really painful bits are in capital letters at the bottom of the screen:

'HUTCHISON SCORES OWN GOAL AGAINST FORMER CLUB.' Plonker.

'GRAVESEN SCORES FIRST GOAL IN A YEAR.' Oh great.

Then we are 4–0 down.

'WATSON SCORES FIRST GOAL OF SEASON.'

Ah, yet another first. That well-known striker Steve Watson.

'West Ham are 4–0 down now,' I tell Nicola, and, frustratingly, she doesn't seem at all surprised.

'RADZINSKI SCORES FIRST GOAL FOR CLUB.' How many more firsts is this sodding game going to produce?

'West Ham are now 5–0 down!' I declare in disbelief, expecting at least some sympathy from Nicola.

35

'Well, what do you expect?' she snaps cruelly, as if rank ineptitude were normal when West Ham travel to Merseyside, which, of course, it normally is. It gets worse:

'PETE MAY FOLLOWS PATH OF FORMER WEST HAM MANAGER SYD KING AND TOPS HIMSELF. FIRST SUICIDE BY WEST HAM FAN SINCE FRED SMEGGINS LEAPT INTO THE RIVER LEA AFTER A 12–0 DRUBBING BY ACCRINGTON STANLEY IN 1912.'

Actually that's a joke. The only consolation is that Spurs have lost 5–3 at home to Man United after being 3–0 up at half-time. At least we don't lose 3–0 leads. Oh, actually we do; against Wimbledon, who were hardly Man United in 1998.

At least Joe retains some humour on the phone that evening: 'At least it's an improvement on when we went up there two seasons ago and lost 6–0. We've gotta sort out the defence and get rid of Dailly . . .'

It doesn't get any better watching it on *The Premiership*. There is one good chance early on when Schemmel crosses and Di Canio puts the ball wide when he should have scored. At the back West Ham badly miss the suspended Repka. Campbell outjumps both Dailly and Song for the first goal. The second sees Hislop and Don Hutchison go for a free-kick after the exposed and ageing Winterburn has hacked down Alexandersson. Exhibiting all the communication skills of Ian Paisley on a visit to the Vatican, Shaky Shaka fumbles, Hutchison lashes at the ball and it bobbles into the net for the ugliest and most comical of goals, all without an Everton player in sight. Cue Danny Baker punching the air and anticipating another bumper video sale for Hammers Own Goals and Gaffes next Christmas.

For the third goal Thomas Gravesen runs from the halfway line as Dailly, admittedly left unprotected by his midfield, retreats like a man on the return leg of a bungee jump. Gravesen's fine low shot from the edge of the net finds the corner. Glenn Roeder maintains his human pencil pose on the touchline, arms folded, looking like the son of Blakey from *On the Buses*, about to shout 'I hate you, Dailly!'

The fourth is the sort my five-a-side team concede when we've been playing for an hour and a half and our hungover jelly legs no longer respond to instructions. Watson has enough time to read Proust's *Remembrance Of Things Past* before crossing, Shaka cuts it out with one hand, an Everton boot flicks it back, and Steve Watson pokes an embarrassingly feeble shot under Hislop's body. The fifth is a triumph of collective ineptitude. The ball skews off Song's ankle into the air, Dailly should hoof the ball away first time, but instead allows it to pinball off him and Radzinski scores from an acute angle as the hapless Dailly flounders on the line.

As Glenn Roeder leaves the pitch he gives a quick contemptuous glare at his players, then disappears down the tunnel with the expression of a man who has just discovered the entire squad performing deviant sexual practices with the Dagenham Girl Pipers on the eve of an FA Cup semi-final.

The Times's Martin Woods is particularly perceptive in his Monday morning comment that 'the elongated figure of Glenn Roeder resembled a fastidious choirmaster listening to his boys singing at a school prize-giving as if they had feasted on helium gas. "Just you wait, Carrick!" you could almost hear him whisper.'

'We have let our fans down and I want to apologise for that,' says a stunned Roeder after the match, mentioning 'diabolical defending' and the last four goals being 'absolute shockers'. 'We've had a long talk about things and what was said will remain behind closed doors,' he continues. 'We need to stay tight as a team.' Which is the only time that West Ham have been tight all afternoon. The next day's *News of the World* concludes: 'West Ham's defending will result in only one thing – relegation.'

West Ham don't play the following week because of yet another break for internationals, so at least we avoid defeat. Meanwhile Paolo Di Canio defends allegations that he misses or doesn't perform in away games. 'I've played for AC Milan, Lazio and Celtic – some of the biggest clubs in the world. Would these clubs have signed me if I didn't perform in away games . . . I do play hard in away games. I scored at Liverpool on the opening day of the season – a "big balls" goal. Another player might have felt pressure in that situation, but I didn't.'

Unfortunately, the side's performance at Everton might also be described as a big balls performance, but Di Canio apologises for this. 'I went over to the West Ham fans to say sorry – not because I hadn't tried, but because they are such great supporters who spend so much time and money following us.'

At the end of the first week in October comes another jolt from the world of Ceefax. 'SINCLAIR ASKS FOR TRANSFER' read the stark capital letters. What was it Harry said about no longer being a selling club? Rio went, then Lampard, now Sinclair. Then Fredi, Di Canio, Carrick and Cole will surely follow.

Sinclair's statement reads like a poorly written CV, where you try to detail the reason why you left your last job and have to make it sound vaguely professional rather than telling the truth that you told the boss to shove it.

'Given the club's current state of transition, at this stage of my career my ambitions are more likely to be fulfilled elsewhere,' says Tricky Trev. For 'state of transition' read selling off our best players, although he's being unfair on Roeder who has made three decent-ish buys in James, Repka and Hutchison.

'I've enjoyed my time here immensely and have a great relationship with the fans, but a fresh challenge will help my performance levels,' continues Sinclair. Is all that stuff about performance levels just a coded way of saying he's not trying?

Roeder is clearly annoyed. On the next day's Ceefax he declares that:

'Players come under incredible pressure from outside their club to become "restless".' On Teletext West Ham fanzine *Over Land and Sea* declares: 'The timing of this is pants. It's all me me me, but what about us, Trevor? The punters who have given you the best support any set of fans could. Where's your loyalty to the club?'

A week later it's time to discover further cruel and unusual ways of watching West Ham lose. At least the televised game at Blackburn can't be any worse than watching us get stuffed 5–0 on Sky's results service. We are now in the second week of October and West Ham have hardly played a game at home – in fact five of West Ham's first seven games are away and, with the game on the box, I'm again being a Part-time Percy and going to a local pub rather than wasting my money on an expensive rail fare up north.

'Are you West Ham?' asks the barman in the Famous Cock Tavern at Highbury Corner, having presumably spotted my expression of hopelessness and fear. The pub is half empty for the Sunday game which kicks off at 2.00 p.m. A few groups of drinkers and perhaps half-a-dozen exiled north London Hammers fans stare hopefully at the numerous TV monitors, presuming it can't get any worse than the 5–0 defeat last week.

I admit to the barman that I am indeed a Hammers fan. 'I used to go to school with Joe Cole,' he says. 'We played for the same boys' team.' In Highbury there must be at least 50,000 people who claim to have gone to school with Joe Cole.

'You should never have sold Ferdinand,' continues the barman, repeating the mantra that every sodding know-all fan has been telling me since Rio went to Leeds last November. Following the Rio sale every other football fan now sees West Ham as a selling club once more. Although the problem wasn't really the Rio sale as much as Harry Redknapp blowing half the money on the aptly named Titi Camara, Song, Dailly, Soma and Todorov (and, of course, letting loan star Tihinen leave) rather than buying one or two class players.

'Well, I don't think many clubs could have afforded to turn down £18 million,' I say.

'You'll be in trouble this season, now Redknapp and Lampard have gone,' continues the fatalistic barman, even though the game has started and I'm trying to watch the monitor.

'Well, we've got to hang on to Carrick and Cole,' I admit.

'He'll be off to Man United.'

'Or Arsenal, he is a local lad.'

'I don't know if we'd want him, he's always injured.'

Yes, yes, thank you, thank you so much. I settle down to watch the match, alone with a pint of lager, a packet of peanuts and a copy of *The Observer*. At least it's 0–0 after five minutes, which is a result on recent form. Repka has replaced the hapless Song, Moncur is in midfield and Soma – wasn't that the drug they used in *Brave New World* to induce a false state of tranquillity in the masses? – has replaced the injured Winterburn at left-back. A Hutchison cross even whizzes across the face of the Blackburn goal. It doesn't seem too bad for 30 minutes.

Then Grabbi is allowed to float inside and turn on the edge of the box and jinks a lofted ball over the Hammers defence. Christian Dailly strolls back with the air of a contented goatherd sedately counting his flock at dusk as Flitcroft speeds past him and gently heads the ball over Hislop.

It gets worse. There appears to be an EU set-aside policy around Dunn, who is allowed several hectares of room outside the area by our non-tackling midfield and cracks a superb shot over the flailing Shaka. 'Are you Burnley in disguise?' chant the home fans. The answer is no, we're not that good. Di Canio misses a good headed chance from close in. Two minutes later a cross from Tugay on the right is headed on by Grabbi and again the Irons' defence is late to the second ball, feebly claiming for offside as a splendidly isolated Johnson pokes the ball over the line from a yard or two out to make it 3–0.

Then, maddeningly, those bastards in claret and blue start playing. Carrick cuts inside on the left and scores with a fine low drive. At 3–1 we might just stage a comeback as we look more urgent in every area.

At least Roeder takes decisive action at half-time. Dailly and Moncur are taken off to be replaced by Foxe and McCann. Di Canio swings over a free-kick and Trevor Sinclair, completely unmarked in front of a yawning goal, scuffs his header down into the ground and wide. This is the same Sinclair who has just asked for a transfer in the manner of a mid-ranking Mondeo executive – all talk of 'periods of transition' and 'career prospects' in a coded message which might be more satisfyingly precised as 'West Ham . . . you're shit . . . aaarrgh!' He wants to enhance his chances of playing for England on the left by signing for a new club, even though he's just made the England squad with West Ham, but has, satisfyingly, probably just caused Sven-Goran Eriksson to wince in disbelief at his error. 'They only started playing when they were 3–0 down!' Joe Cole's mate behind the bar is telling a latecomer who has asked the score.

Kanouté puts another header straight at the keeper and I'm fantasising about a 3–3 draw. Until Repka brings down Grabbi and is sent off for his second bookable offence. The second booking looks a little unlucky, but there was little excuse for the earlier agricultural lunge and he is red carded for the second time in three games. Another dismissal and he may get to take the referee home. Still, at this rate he'll only be sent off another twenty times before the end of the season.

An innocuous cross is curled into the Hammers box which should be easily volleyed away. Comically, Grant McCann, who looks like a 12-year-old with severe acne, slices the ball into his own net. He actually goes to kick with his right foot, misses completely and the ball cannons off his left shin into the net past a hapless Shaka, who is starting to wear the bemused expression of a man in yellow pyjamas who has run out on to the street at 3 a.m. because his house is on fire. Glenn Roeder purses his cheeks and gives a passable impression of a man sucking a wasp. There's a close-up of McCann – whose pockmarked face looks as if he's been refuelling on burgers from Belly Busters – looking distraught. Acne? We have a sports scientist at Upton Park now. What chance do we have if we can't even cure acne?

My mind is rewinding, and to quote Peter Gabriel, 'digging in the dirt, to open up the places I got hurt'. Through a lunchtime lager haze I can see Steve 'Wally' Walford on a sunny winter afternoon at home to Southampton in 1984 and some 30 yards from his own goal without a Saints player in sight. He turns and instantaneously unleashes a vintage lob over keeper Tom McAllister. Tragically for Walford his attempted mother of all own goals strikes the angle of post and crossbar; but the floundering McAllister has clearly decided that Walford's effort is worthy of a goal as the ball strikes his backside and gently bobbles over his line. Those in the Chicken Run that day stand in stunned silence, not quite knowing if they have witnessed an act of genius or folly. Grant McCann, you have just entered Hammers history.

More beer is needed. Typically, with West Ham down to ten men, Tugay, given too much space again, fires home Blackburn's goal of the season with a sublime shot from 25 yards. It doesn't stop either. As W.B. Yeats (whoever he played for) might have put it: 'Things fall apart; the centre cannot hold.' The defensive pairing of Foxe and McCann display about as much cohesion as the various warring tribal factions of Afghanistan. Dunn ambles through West Ham's midfield and shoots, Shaka parries and Jansen shoots home the rebound. Sky's summariser mentions Hutchison's 'pitiful tackle' (what, has he seen those Budweiser pictures too?) and helpfully mentions that 'but for several wonderful saves by Shaka Hislop this could have been West Ham's record defeat'. Our record defeat, an 8–2 mauling, also at Blackburn, on Boxing Day in 1963, is nearly equalled when Blackburn's forwards are given a huge amount of space on the left, a shot is going wide but sub Craig Hignett, disgracefully unmarked, fires in from an impossible angle to make it 7–1. There is no spirit, no pride, our overpaid, overrated stars are just not playing for Roeder.

Of course, there have been other thrashings. Driving back in the rain from a 6–0 semi-final defeat in the Littlewood's Cup after standing on a soaking open terrace at Oldham ('Never mind, lads, there's always the second leg'). That 6–0 thumping at Everton two years ago, a 6–0 débâcle at Liverpool when Dalglish and Hansen were awesome and all we had was Steve Whitton at centre-forward and Phil Parkes's arthritic knees and septic elbow in goal.

I've seen Dowie and Newell up front. I've seen Steve 'Nellie the Elephant' Whitton charging down the wing like a tranquillised rhino. I've seen Paul Hilton playing up front and Alan Devonshire develop two-year flu. I've seen fire and I've seen rain. But I never thought I'd see West Ham be so crap again.

There's still time for 38-year-old Mark Hughes to open up the Hammers defence with a sublime pass which Hignett, who should have scored, pokes wide. The final whistle blows and Paolo Di Canio tears off his captain's armband, looking disgusted with his teammates.

I sit in the pub unable to move. 'Their defence was non-existent!' a barmaid is telling another Hammers fan who has said: 'I need a beer after that.' I even find myself thinking that TV pundit George Graham, currently berating the Hammers' defence with Richard Keys, might do a better job for the Hammers. What's the use entertaining when you let in seven sodding goals? I mean, seven bloody one.

Poor Glenn Roeder does his best in front of the cameras. He looks likes a man making a police appeal after his entire family, pet dog and budgerigar have just been viciously slaughtered by a serial killer, and mumbles comments about 'now's not the time . . . individual errors . . . embarrassing defeat for the whole club'.

I stumble out of the pub into the unforgiving light and shuffle home dispiritedly across Highbury Fields. The worst thing is that those tossers created enough chances when they decided to play for the odd 20 minutes. 7–1. Dailly has been given enough chances, Soma looks lost, Kanouté's Walkman batteries appeared to have run out, Carrick underachieved, Sinclair's thinking of Sunderland and so might be Hutchison, McCann and Foxe are raw, Di Canio looks like he's totally dispirited.

My body aches after the morning's five-a-side. There's a *Sunday Times* left on someone's doorstep with the headline announcing that Osama Bin Laden has advised English Muslims to steer clear of aeroplanes and high buildings. Maybe the so-called alliance against terrorism could undermine his morale by beaming satellite coverage of West Ham games into his cave. Apart from the prospect of aircraft plummeting out of the skies and the possibility of an envelope full of anthrax arriving in the post (the latest act of terrorism to hit the US) there's not much to worry about at all.

Monday's papers make grim reading. Even *The Guardian* is speculating on Roeder being the next Premiership manager to be axed, which is unfair on a man undermined by his own board from the day of his appointment, through their admission that he was not even first or second choice.

In his post-match comments, Roeder points out that the club has been struggling for some time. He's right that the problems started last season. Showing a lack of professionalism in allowing themselves to become distracted by an FA Cup run, from Boxing Day to the end of last season the players won only three out of eighteen league matches. 'We had players out there who can do better and players who did their best but just can't do better,' admits Roeder. He talks of a rebuilding job and being four or five players short. Despite the result I'm not in favour of his sacking. As the board placed so much faith in his talents in the summer, it would be pointless not to give him a whole season.

Worryingly, Glenn then goes on to reveal his choice of in-house movie: 'In times like this I always think of the *Rocky* films. You can either lie down and be carried out of the ring or get up and start swinging.' Does the giraffe-like Glenn Roeder really fantasise about being Rocky? But if it means he's fighting, then good. Roeder's four big signings, James, Schemmel, Repka and Hutchison are all good players. But if he's 'lost the dressing-room', as they say, then he'll have to sign more. And even the man who likened himself to a 100–1 Grand National winner is now contemplating becoming an unseated rider: 'It hurts. I hope I get more time but whether it's me or someone else, who knows?' he wonders out loud.

Later that week Nigel e-mails to tell me: 'I'll be going to Roeder's penultimate game.' Big Joe and myself do what West Ham supporters do best – despair. Joe has several complaints: 'That was a cracking result, we scored an away goal, haven't done that since Liverpool . . . Hutchison is never a £5 million player . . . never mind Newton who was only good enough to play for the Under-21s, we'll have McCann, that's one for the future . . . what other club has received £29 million for Ferdinand and Lampard and got nothing to show for it . . . at least George Graham won't get us relegated, he'd have too much professional pride for that.'

By midweek it's like *EastEnders* minus the sexual abuse. The directors – who hate controversy and seemed happiest with a nice but underachieving manager like John Lyall, whose most controversial move was to carry on painting his house after being sacked – must be appalled at such family infighting.

Paolo Di Canio has entered into his 'I must speak my mind for a man not true to himself is not a man, you think I am not a man, you insult me, you insult my family, I score you the big balls goal, if not I kill you' mode and, hilariously, has become the first ever Premiership player to call his own side 'shit'. Admittedly 26,000 fans do so nearly every week, but you don't expect such candour from a player. Imagine Trevor Brooking in the '80s announcing: 'Well, in all fairness we played like a right team of faaacking caaants today, John.'

Di Canio is certainly an antidote to all those 'looking to the next game to put it right' clichés, although you do wonder what effect such public vilifying will have on his teammates. He's aware of this himself: 'Maybe some people will say I have to shut my mouth and work harder, but even if I had scored three goals we would still have lost.'

Di Canio says, quite rightly, that 11 fans could have performed better than the West Ham side at Blackburn and adds that he is 'very, very angry'. And as he's not exactly the most placid of individuals, that must mean that he's now resembling Jack Nicholson in *The Shining* and at any moment the irate Italian is about to strike an axe through the door of the dressing-room at Chadwell Heath. 'I don't want to blame my teammates,' he claims, before blaming his teammates.

'You have to look at your face in the mirror and ask if you are a true professional, a true footballer or the opposite,' declares Paolo in his customary lyrical fashion. 'There are players who didn't show their quality and commitment. This is not possible in the Premiership, especially at a glorious club like West Ham. The manager is intelligent and I think he will now be tougher with the players.

'I have played for 16 years at the top level and I run for 90 minutes. Some players who haven't shown their quality yet play for 20 or 30 minutes. Either they are not ready for the Premiership or they don't have strong characters. In both cases we have to change. Only if we realise how shit we are can we improve.'

His English usage is certainly coming on. Di Canio speaks for the fans though, and, as a man who stood on the terraces with the Lazio ultras as a teenager, he knows something of the passion of supporting a side like West Ham through thin and thinner.

I wonder if we should make Paolo manager. In his autobiography he admitted: 'Because I am right-wing I am fascinated by Benito Mussolini . . . I own dozens of Mussolini biographies, I think he was a deeply misunderstood individual' – so at least Paolo would make the training run on time. And possibly change the kit to fetching black shirts. That line about 'a glorious club like West Ham' is telling. You could imagine him restoring some Roman pomp to Chadwell Heath with triumphal arches all along the Eastern Avenue and then announcing that Abyssinia is really a part of Essex.

After Di Canio's outburst former gaffer Harry Redknapp decides to wash his boxer shorts on the Mile End Road and tells the *Mirror* that he's 'disgusted' with Roeder's comments. In an extraordinary attack on the man he himself appointed to the staff, Redknapp rages: 'It's absolute rubbish to suggest that the rot set in when I was there. Glenn Roeder should stop making excuses and get on with it. He's got Cole, Carrick, Sinclair and Kanouté – all absolutely top-class players. But he's blaming everyone but himself. Everywhere I look he is blaming this or that. The fact is there's no excuse for getting beat 7–1. Accept it.'

Then, rather disingenuously ignoring the fact that Roeder received £11 million for Frank Lampard, Harry adds: 'He's saying that he wants more money for players but the board have backed him. He has spent £14 million on players already this season.'

It's undignified and unfair after just seven games and frankly Harry should be above making this kind of personal attack. Beneath the Redknapp quotes in the *Mirror* is a piece with the headline 'Cole is crocked again'. 'Cole's finished, isn't he?' says Nicola after I've made her read Harry's comments. 'Of course not,' I counter, mentally believing she might be right.

Even new director Trevor Brooking, more used to sitting on defence than lambasting West Ham's, has, gulp, said something controversial. He's told the press that the club has 'around the seventh highest wage bill in the Premiership, but I can't get near to seeing that sort of quality' – which in Trev terms is the equivalent of the Queen Mother suddenly declaring a liking for revolutionary communism.

Ron Atkinson is commenting on the situation in *The Guardian* and perhaps offering himself up as a Red Adair at Upton Park. He voices what most West Ham fans felt in June. 'I think several experienced guys didn't take too kindly to the appointment of a fledgling manager. Sometimes that type of player responds more to an experienced manager than to someone who is cutting his teeth.' Pertinently, Big Ron adds that coaching is very different to making the tough decisions required of a manager and that, 'If I was running a multi-million pound enterprise I don't think I'd want inexperienced people at the helm.'

Roeder refuses to respond to Harry Redknapp's attacks and maintains his dignity during a torrid week, but suddenly next Saturday's game at home to Southampton has become a game West Ham and Roeder dare not lose. After just seven games West Ham are in crisis, just one place off the bottom of the Premiership and apparently on the Roeder nowhere.

TOP TEN RIGHT HAMMERINGS

BLACKBURN 7 WEST HAM 1: A disastrous own goal, a sending off, and taunts of 'Are you Burnley in disguise?' – all shown on live TV. Afterwards the West Ham captain Paolo Di Canio called his own players 'shit'. The most embarrassing West Ham defeat ever.

OLDHAM 6 WEST HAM 0: Disaster on a plastic pitch for the Hammers in the first leg of a Littlewoods Cup tie in 1990. Plus an open terrace, heavy rain and ubiquitous mud. Presumably gaffer Lou Macari announced on the coach back home, 'Don't worry lads, a quick seven goals in the second leg and we'll be through to Wembley.'

NOTTINGHAM FOREST 4 WEST HAM 0: A 1991 FA Cup semi-final on live TV was not the best place to get thrashed. Throw in the iniquitous sending-off of Tony Gale and Parris, Allen and Quinn labouring against Brian Clough's fine side of dedicated young men and you have a wasted trip to Villa Park, only partially redeemed by the fans' marvellous 30-minute mantra of 'Billy Bonds' Claret and Blue Army!'

MANCHESTER UNITED 7 WEST HAM 1: Paolo Wanchope made the mistake of scoring an early goal in 2000. Then Beckham, Scholes, Keane and Cole took over and walloped the Hammers with ease. At least it was an improvement for keeper Craig Forrest, who let in nine when he last visited Old Trafford with Ipswich.

LIVERPOOL 6 WEST HAM 0: In 1984 Dalglish mesmerised the Hammers defence and Souness and Hansen were imperious in midfield and defence. Phil Parkes was so busy that his legendary blow-dried hairstyle was almost put out of place. 'Brucie, Brucie what's the score?' chanted the Kop at the sedentary Bruce Grobbelaar, who then held up six fingers. West Ham were denied even a late consolation when Steve Whitton sliced the ball horribly wide in front of an open goal.

EVERTON 6 WEST HAM 0: At the back end of the 1998–99 season the lads were chasing fifth place. So Ruddock and co. proceeded to make Don Hutchison, Kevin Campbell and Scott Gemmill look like svelte-footed players of genius as they capitulated to a mediocre Everton side. Strangely enough, we still finished fifth.

LIVERPOOL 5 WEST HAM 0: Even the presence of *On A Mission* editor Shane, trouser-dropping John and lobster-quaffing Steve and Jenny for the *On A Mission* end-of-season bash at the Adelphi Hotel in 1998 couldn't raise the Hammers, who were 4–0 down at half-time. The case of Michael Owen versus David Unsworth has since been referred to the League Against Cruel Sports.

ARSENAL 6 WEST HAM 1: Some might have thought that the lads were taking it a tad too easy before the 1975 FA Cup final. As ever, the Irons concentrated on the Cup and played like men dispossessed in the league.

LIVERPOOL 5 WEST HAM 1: All West Ham needed to do to avoid relegation was win at Anfield, home of the Champions, in 1989. It started well when Leroy Rosenior made it 1–1, but once Ince was crocked by McMahon the lads slumped to a 5–1 defeat and into the second division.

WEST HAM 3 WIMBLEDON 4: Not strictly a hammering, but special marks for clasping defeat from victory. At the start of the 1998–99 season the Hammers romped into a three-goal lead in the first half. Wimbledon responded by playing four giants up front, new signing Javier Margas wished he was back at home in Chile, and the Dons went from 3–0 down to 4–3 up.

7. HAMMER HORRORS

We might have just lost 7–1 to Blackburn, but things have been worse. Since Harry Redknapp joined the club as assistant manager in 1993, fortune had not been hiding quite so much. The club is at least an established force in the Premiership, and before finishing 15th last season West Ham had finished three successive seasons in the top half of the table, something even the side containing World Cup winners Moore, Hurst and Peters never achieved.

You only have to go back 14 years to realise how far the club has come. There was one particularly horrifying match against Sheffield Wednesday in 1987, just after the side that finished third in 1986 had rapidly imploded and spent several seasons seeking relegation. This was back in the days of standing in the Chicken Run; I can still remember it with all the lucidity of a mishit Kevin Keen cross.

'You're stupid! Why did you join us?' hollers an irate fan at new signing Gary Strodder. And that's just the warm-up. After two minutes comes a cry of 'Come on Hammers, why aren't we losing?' The lads duly oblige by conceding the softest of goals. The Chicken Run fans chant mockingly, 'Here we go, here we go . . .'

Someone verbally admonishes the 'claret and blue dustbins' as they toil listlessly in an attempt to score, presumably not realising that striker Frank McAvennie, so brilliant the previous season, has a cocaine habit. 'Lyall out! Lyall out!' come the chants. Hammers full-back George Parris thumps the ball hopelessly into touch. 'Ball out! Ball out!' comes the modified chant.

'What have you got in that bag Parkes, a respirator?' greets the West Ham custodian when he takes his place in goal for the second half. The Irons continue to suggest that they are the real cause of Arthur Fowler's nervous breakdown in *EastEnders*. A bald bloke in a black leather jacket, who sounds like Ade Edmondson in *The Young Ones*, is possibly the angriest Hammers fan in the world. Later I discover that this is Steve Rapport, aka North Bank Norman, editor of the fanzine *Fortune's Always Hiding*. He shouts 'Brilliant, absolutely brilliant!' and 'Dangerous!' as West Ham's lame movements fizzle out. Then he turns his ire towards West Ham's diminutive forward line,

47

shouting: 'Don't worry, Cottee, Snow White and the other six will be coming soon!'

All the West Ham players come in for similar haranguings. 'Who can we blame now?' asks one fan. 'We've blamed the entire team, we'll have to start shouting at ourselves!'

Then comes a classic example of a footballing breakdown. As the ball ricochets inside West Ham's area our defenders are as statuesque and immobile as table footballers. Ade Edmondson hollers, 'Don't clear it, West Ham, it's only in the box! Don't clear it!' Wednesday's Shutt gently rolls the ball over the West Ham line. 'Aaaaaaaagh!' exclaims Ade in a primeval wail, beating his head with his hands.

'Condoms! Condoms! You're playing like a team of condoms!' shouts another fan, at least proving that West Ham fans have taken in the safe sex message of the government's AIDS ads. Things become even worse as McAvennie is sent off. At least he'll be in Stringfellows early, but for Ade Edmondson it's too much. 'Remember goals, West Ham, they were big in the '70s!'

The police move towards the touchline as the end nears. 'Officer, arrest that lot on the pitch for loitering without intent!' demands an irate supporter.

As the fans leave the ground one supporter is consoled by his girlfriend. 'They were terrible last week too,' she says.

'No, that was just bad, this was absolutely dismal,' he mutters.

The next season it got worse. McAvennie had left for Celtic, Alan Devonshire had contracted 18-month flu, and West Ham had tried and failed to buy Kerry Dixon, Mick Harford, John Fashanu, Kevin Drinkell, Colin Clarke, Peter Davenport, Nico Clausen, Lee Chapman and quite possibly Eddie 'The Eagle' Edwards. For five months John Lyall had played frail midfielder Alan Dickens up front in the least effective conversion of footballing history. Ken Bates refused to let Chelsea's Kerry Dixon rejoin Arsenal for fear he might rediscover his goalscoring touch, but had no such worries about him joining West Ham, immediately agreeing terms, only for the player himself to reject the deal and Lyall to claim: 'You have to be patient when you are pursuing quality.' One paper then labelled West Ham 'the lepers of football'.

During a dire draw at home to Portsmouth there was a cry of 'Bring on the *Neighbours* video!' from the Chicken Run. This was followed by 'Stewart! It's that green thing with lines around it!' as the full-back pumped another ball towards Stratford. During a game against Oxford a frustrated fan ran on to the pitch and curled a beautiful shot around Hammers' keeper McAlister. He was embraced by a steward before being ejected by police who assumed that witnessing a goal at Upton Park might lead to scenes of public disorder.

Finally, West Ham signed striker Leroy Rosenior from Fulham, and amazingly he seemed to want to play for us. He made his début against Watford and I took my old school friend Alison O'Brien, just back from Spain, to her first game in a decade. Upon taking her place in the Chicken Run she remarked: 'It's just like walking into a room full of really bad-tempered men.' As a returning expatriate, she had many questions: 'Are West Ham still having all the game and failing to score? Is Billy Bonds still playing? Is John Lyall still saying he's waiting for the right player at the right price?' I had to answer yes on all counts.

'Do something Lyall! Resign! Anything!' raged one fan as a petition for a change of manager went round the Chicken Run. Only as the game moved towards another terrible goalless draw the impossible occurred. Rosenior raced through the Watford defence to plant a firm shot into the net. There was a stunned silence before the ground erupted. 'We've scored, we've scored, we've scored!' screamed a fan beside me, starting to resemble Basil Fawlty in a fire alarm. 'It's only one . . .' muttered the man with the petition. True enough, West Ham survived that year, but achieved the inevitable relegation in 1989.

It was the best of times, it was the worst of times. West Ham might be looking at impending relegation in the autumn of 2001, but at least we've been there before.

8. FORTRESS UPTON PARK

West Ham 2 Southampton 0 – 20 October 2001

As if the Americans haven't suffered enough with the World Trade Centre – some of them have started going to West Ham. My pal Reno moved to London from San Francisco in the summer and has announced that he wants to sample this Limey sport that isn't called soccer. So here he is at West Ham versus Southampton.

Big Joe was delighted to shift his ticket: 'Great! I can lose 30-odd quid to the bookies now instead of watching that lot!' he enthused. 'Don't worry about your mate, if he's American then he'll be shell-shocked anyway . . .' We agree that watching West Ham lose to Southampton will be the ultimate authentic West Ham experience.

At least the game should match the global mood of tension and apprehension. Will the US invade Afghanistan? Will Glenn Roeder ever smile again? Southampton's new young manager Stuart Gray is also under pressure following a poor start to the season. Yes, it's ridiculous but true; eight games into the season the press hype up the game to claim that whichever manager loses will be sacked. In my view, having given Roeder the job we must give him at least a season to prove himself.

Roeder reveals some of the inner pain he's felt since the Blackburn thrashing. 'Watching those last 20 minutes at Blackburn was the lowest I have ever felt in football. I looked at my watch and prayed for the time to pass quickly . . .' confesses the Hammers boss. 'Last Sunday was the most excruciating, horrible, painful, hurtful time of my life. Please, God, don't let it happen again.'

The experience has also taught him who his friends are in football, and it seems fair to think that he won't now be sharing a cup of tea and a toasted cheese sarnie with Harry Redknapp in Ken's Café.

'What I found amazing was that so many other managers and coaches phoned to commiserate. These were the people I always hoped were my friends and they phoned to prove it. They know the pain. They actually know how I felt. They offered a shoulder and I'm grateful,' says Roeder.

In fact the beleaguered boss is sounding like he's recently been sitting in a plastic chair in a group therapy session of Managers Anonymous: 'Hi, I'm Glenn and I've been abused at Blackburn. My captain's called my side "shit". My ex-boss has told me my excuses disgust him. Last Sunday was the most excruciating, horrible, painful, hurtful time of my life. I need help and guidance . . .'

The experienced Nigel Winterburn, returning today after injury in place of the unimpressive Soma, offers his beleaguered manager support: 'He was good enough when appointed seven weeks ago and he still is. Glenn has been let down. Too many players have gone missing during the last two defeats.'

Has Roeder lost the players? He at least seems to be maintaining faith in his ability: 'I think first of all you need genuine belief that even in adversity you can get through it.' After the 'eerie silence' in the dressing-room following Sunday's defeat, the players had a 'good honest 45 minutes' after their Monday training session, according to Roeder. As Winterburn says, 'It's better this has happened earlier in the season rather than later – if we had only lost 1–0 we probably wouldn't have said anything.'

Poor Reno doesn't realise that he might be about to see 25,842 people have a collective breakdown. Still, seeing this tribal ritual – the West Ham relegation six-pointer – through an outsider's eyes is instructive. Reno regards Ken's Café as the best thing he's seen since *EastEnders*. Inside we meet Dan, Martin from Scotland, Nigel and Gavin. Reno particularly enjoys the ambience of unreal coffee and chips that aren't ever known as fries and then being playfully shouted at by an authentic Cockney proprietress for only having a £10 note. 'Hey, that was great . . .' He then asks for tomatoes pronounced the American way, before hastily correcting himself. If Ken's could ever get itself on-line then it would surely be packed with American tourists . . .

We enter the East Stand and Reno insistes on a pint of watery lager from the Lower East Stand bar. He then stares in disbelief at something he's just seen. 'Gee, what's that stuff they're selling?' Reno's spotted men with white coats selling seafood. In the age of global cuisine it seems that the club's latest innovative marketing tactic is the assumption that all East Enders really do eat jellied eels.

After I explain the basics to Reno – West Ham have just been walloped 5–0 and 7–1 and have a rookie manager who stands on the touchline in a dark suit with his arms folded rather like an East End undertaker – we take our seats.

The atmosphere is strangely muted, the crowd are still shocked by the horrible capitulations at Goodison and Ewood Park. DJ Jeremy Nicholas, rather like those brave jocks in Vietnam who had to convince their troops that they were really winning the war, proceeds to announce the West Ham team as if they are Real Madrid.

'In goal Shaka Hislop! Number 30 Sebastien Schemmel! Number 3 Nigel Winterburn!! Number 7 Christian DAAAAIIILLY!!!' (Smattering of tepid applause punctuated by serial groans.) The crowd do find sufficient energy to boo Trevor Sinclair's name, though. 'What, you boo your own players?' asks Reno, initially shocked by the revelation that English fans jeer some of their own men. If only he'd heard Lino, the noisiest fan in London, hollering at Kevin Keen from the Chicken Run back in the 1980s.

The first half is a mess. Southampton look as bad as West Ham and both teams lack confidence. Schemmel and Sinclair, apparently revitalised by the boos, bravely attempt to break down the Saints defence on the right flank. Glenn Roeder keeps his arms folded on the touchline. At one point he does make some weird motions with his hands which must surely be indecipherable to the players. 'Maybe that's why he keeps his arms folded, perhaps he's like Dr Strangelove, his arms go all over the place if he doesn't hold on to them,' suggests Dan.

At half-time Reno nearly chokes on a meat pie – 'Jeez, you pay for these things?' The second half kicks off and I'm thinking that maybe Di Canio can't play in a struggling team. His body language portrays a man who is seriously frustrated. And maybe he's feeling his 33 years. However, he is still involved in most of West Ham's best movements.

Repka has been solid at the back – and remained on the pitch – while Dailly looks a different player at home. West Ham are much livelier than Southampton after the break and at last the goal comes. Di Canio finds the indefatigable Nigel Winterburn, 37 years old, racing down the left, and his excellent cross is headed in by Fredi Kanouté who, oh wondrous joy, has scored a predator's goal rather than a masterpiece. It's a good moment for Winterburn, the only former Arsenal player not to be permanently injured or to treat Upton Park as a retirement home (see Suker, Robson, Radford etc.). The second comes after good work by Sinclair on the right, Di Canio hits the bar and Kanouté heads home the rebound for another simple goal.

Southampton look spineless, but who cares, the result is everything. The ball spins towards Glenn Roeder on the touchline and he traps the ball, earning an affectionate cheer from the crowd. He has maintained a dignified stance, speaking honestly and sensibly during the last fortnight and surprisingly few fans have attacked him. They realise that he is basically a decent man who has perhaps been put in a position he shouldn't have by a bungling board. The Bobby Moore Stand belatedly break into song with 'Stick your blue flag up your arse!' 'Why are they singing "up your bum!"?' asks Reno. I explain that this is a traditional East End folk song directed towards Chelsea, whom we play on Wednesday.

Jeremy Nicholas greets the result with his usual tongue-in-cheek jubilation. 'We go above Southampton! We go above Derby! We go above Ipswich! We go above Fulham! Ladies and gentlemen, we're 15th!!! We're unbeaten at

Fortress Upton Park!!! Crisis, what crisis?' he hollers. In fact we've yet to concede a goal at Fortress Upton Park, despite those twelve in two games at Everton and Blackburn.

We head towards the tube. Three points, a clean sheet. It's an improvement on wondering if we will ever win again. Reno is then left utterly bemused by nearly 26,000 people meekly joining a queue. 'Hey, what is it about you Brits and queues? In the States everyone would just pile on!'

After the game Glenn Roeder explains that he simply asked the players to 'show some good old-fashioned East End bottle'. All except Tomas Repka, he explained, who had to have it translated into Czech. This must have made for an interesting exchange.

'Boss, you want us to play with ze bottle and glass?'

'No, no, Tomas, bottle and glass means arse.'

'You vant us to play on our arses?'

'No, without bottle your arse goes.'

'You vant me to go to Arsenal?'

'No, just show some bottle . . . oh, never mind, just don't get sent off!'

Now we just need enough bottle for the Blues on Wednesday night . . .

9. STICK YOUR BLUE FLAGS UP YOUR . . .

West Ham 2 Chelsea 1 – 24 October 2001
Ipswich 2 West Ham 3 – 28 October 2001

'Up your arse, up your arse! Stick your blue flag up your arse! From Stamford Bridge to Upton Park, stick your blue flag up your arse!'

It might not be eloquent, but it does scan nicely, and whenever West Ham play Chelsea it lodges itself inside my cranium with all the catchiness of 'Agado' by Black Lace. Four days have passed since that vital win against Southampton and sadly, as the press had predicted, Saints manager Stuart Gray was sacked eight games into the season after defeat at Upton Park.

It's a drizzly, late October night as I arrive at the Islington office of Big Joe. His Millwall-supporting colleague asks us if we're going to win and Joe answers with the habitual pessimism of the long-term Hammers fan, 'Of course not!' I mutter that we might get a 1–1 draw.

Then it's into Joe's BMW for another stressful drive across London in the rush hour. In between taking calls on his hands-free mobile concerning peripatetic comedians, and cursing bus drivers and cyclists, Joe is in confessional mood, admitting that he plans to go to fewer games this season. 'It's all right for you, you've got your family. I'm investing all this time in something I have no control over,' he muses.

We discuss team news and then the conversation turns towards West Ham's forgotten signings. 'Gary Charles! If I blew a million quid I'd be sacked!' exclaims Joe in disbelief. 'Gary Charles, he'll never play for us again, Scott Minto, he'll never play for us again . . . Camara, he'll never play for us again . . . as for Hutchison, I tell you he's never a five million pound player . . .'

Discussing our defensive frailties, Joe suggests that Hayden Foxe had better be good as Redknapp made such a fuss about waiting for his permit. In the end Foxey married his French girlfriend and after a Godot-like wait gained EU residency.

'Who was that Bosnian geezer we tried to sign . . . Jarni, we never got him

55

either.' Joe has been involved in getting work permits for comedians recently and knows something of the technicalities involved in enticing temperamental overseas performers to comedy venues in Green Street.

'Can you imagine a West Ham work permit application?' he muses. 'Reasons for rejection of application: candidate failed to drink ten pints a night . . .'

'Candidate refused to get plonker out in a bar, refused to date a page three model and refused to ask for a transfer and blame the fans at the first sign of difficulty . . . If we were still doing *Fortune*'s we could have had some fun with this,' I add.

'Candidate refused to drive while drunk, took training seriously and was too good – would have shown up the rest of the squad,' chuckles Joe.

We arrive at the ground in good time for once, enjoy a cup of tea in Ken's Café and take our place in the East Stand. Unlike the moribund affair on Saturday, the crowd are up for this one, with huge chants of 'Bubbles' and a rousing 'Stick Your Lampard Up Your Arse!'. Maybe it's a little unfair on Lampard, who chose to leave after his father and uncle had been sacked. His early career was dogged by accusations of nepotism – not helped by the fact that whenever he did play he was deemed unsubbable. 'Lamps', as he was imaginatively nicknamed, matured into a good player who scored a lot of goals, probably at his best when playing just behind the front two and maximising his long-range shooting ability. Mind you, as we'd often point out in the stands, he tended to fade out of the game when confronted by Keane or Viera and, at £11 million, my own view was that he was slightly overpriced. Carrick and Cole are surely better longer-term prospects.

We'll do well to get a point against Chelsea's expensively assembled team tonight, but following Saturday's win you sense that the fans are starting to warm to Roeder. There have been yet more unhelpful comments from Harry Redknapp about the new West Ham boss in this morning's *Independent*. When really he should be keeping silent, Harry asserts that no team in any league should get beaten 5–0 and 7–1, and then says of Roeder: 'He's ended up with a great job that he never in his wildest dreams saw coming. I gave him a job two years ago. I met him at a dinner one night and felt sorry for him. He was out of work, a nice fella, with a family, so I said: "Come in a couple of days a week." He helped me out with the reserves, did a lot of scouting for me. From being where he was to being manager . . . a dream.'

Upton Park becomes a different stadium under the lights – even with the bottom half of the Dr Martens Stand still a building site. Surely we can't beat a side with Hasselbaink and Zola up front, a club that can spend £7 million on squad players? We start well, very well. After five minutes a quick-fire interchange between Di Canio and Sinclair sees the ball ping to Michael Carrick who fires a precise shot into the corner from 19 yards out. YES!!!

'Only another 85 minutes of defending left . . .' I mutter. After 12 minutes, incredibly, we're 2–0 up. Trevor Sinclair, who's hardly playing like a man who wants a transfer, launches into a lunging tackle and the ball squirts to Kanouté who, in his deceptively powerful but languorous style, thumps the ball home. What are you doing West Ham? Kanouté is looking inspired after his third goal in two games, holding the ball up superbly and beating players for skill despite being 6 ft 2 in. tall. It's as if he's changed the tape on his mental Walkman from cool French jazz to The Buzzcocks. Hmm. Maybe he wants a move to Stamford Bridge, we muse with typical cynicism.

Hammers fans never feel completely confident though, and sure enough on 22 minutes Zola plays a fine through ball to Hasselbaink who, despite the attentions of Dailly and Winterburn, scores with a fine angled shot that fizzes past Shaka Hislop. Lampard is still being booed and relatively subdued, is just before half-time he emerges in the penalty area to prod a cross towards goal which Shaka somehow saves with his feet.

At half-time we all descend into the bowels of the East Stand and discuss our chances. The conversation moves on to how we signed Repka from Fiorentina because the club was going bankrupt. Apparently we might be moving in again for his defensive partner Pieroni. Courtois, who is having a good game on the left, signed for us because his club were in financial trouble too, says Joe. 'We also do house clearances. There's a piano we picked up over there,' adds Dan, pointing towards the Sir Geoff Hurst Suite.

The injured Courtois is taken off by Roeder and replaced by Defoe, who within minutes of the restart slices the ball wide. Di Canio also goes close after a typically mazy dribble on the left, but then Chelsea really come at us. Repka is having an outstanding game at the back and Dailly, of all people, looks a much better player alongside an old-fashioned centre-half who enjoys whacking the ball into the stand and leaping for headers with his neck muscles bulging. Super Tomas looks like the man we have needed to dominate our own penalty area.

But Chelsea's side is full of expensive, world-class stars, and inevitably chances are created as they now dominate midfield. Hasselbaink hits the post and Shaka Hislop produces an incredible stop to deny the striker. All this from the keeper who was on his way out after the signing of David James. Shaka has just carried on with the job, and tonight he's superb. Then it gets even better. Lampard is substituted ten minutes from the end. So much for £11 million. There's the usual tense period of injury time lasting several aeons and then blissful relief. Upton Park rises. Roeder rewards himself with a clenched fist salute.

Ken Bates aka Father Christmas! David Mellor! Tony Banks! John Major! Frankie Lampard! Can you hear me Frankie Lampard? Your boys took one hell of a beating!

We've beaten bloody Chelsea – their first league defeat of the season – and what a great result for Glenn Roeder, a week ago out of his depth and on his way to the sack. The government has just relaxed the law on cannabis, but this is, according to the evidence of most of my senses, reality.

DJ Jeremy Nicholas, boosted by write-ups of his comments after the Southampton game, repeats his post-victory mantra: 'We go above Charlton! We go above Fulham! We're 14th!!! We're unbeaten at Fortress Upton Park! Crisis, what crisis?'

After the match the normally undemonstrative Roeder hugs his coaches and players and tells his critics: 'The snipers should know better. I was a West Ham fan as a kid and I wouldn't do anything to harm this club.'

Elated by the win, Nigel, Gavin, Fraser and myself, plus two Chelsea fans who are friends of Nigel's, make for the Prince of Wales behind Upton Park Station. There's a familiar, happy victory hubbub among the four-deep queues for the bar.

'I think Redknapp's been really childish,' says Gavin as we discuss our ex-manager's outbursts against Roeder. One of the Chelsea fans is asking Nigel: 'You'd seriously rather West Ham won the league than England won the World Cup?'

'I'd rather West Ham won the Worthington Cup than England won the World Cup,' observes Nigel, quite correctly. Sod national pride. It's 21 years since West Ham last won a trophy and it's 20 years since we reached a major cup final. What kind of a trophy-ridden world do these Chelsea fans live in where they could trade the odd pot for a World Cup win? We'd see England lose 10–0 to Germany in exchange for West Ham winning a trophy. We are desperate men. This is our jihad. The decadent consumerists from the West will never understand.

Nigel's Chelsea mates seem nice enough guys, with newborn children and media-type jobs. But football and tribalism are never easily separated. There's still a part of me that's mentally chanting: 'Up your arse! Up your arse! From Stamford Bridge to Upton Park! STICK YOUR BLUE FLAG UP YOUR ARSE!!!' And, boy, that's what we did tonight.

The following Sunday West Ham play away to Ipswich in yet another match that's televised live. Only how do you get sodding pay-per-view to work? Curiously, Ipswich versus West Ham is listed under special events and not sports, but after much fiddling with the remote I'm eight quid down on top of my normal digital fee and I've only missed the first minute's play.

The big worry is that Repka is suspended, but Roeder has compensated with a tactical surprise, not just simply replacing Repka with Hayden Foxe, but also bringing in Scott Minto – confounding Joe's prediction that he'd never play for us again – to help Nigel Winterburn on the left of defence. Playing five at the back should at least ensure we don't concede seven again.

After two successive victories it's immediately apparent that there is confidence flowing through the side once more. After Kanouté heads over from Schemmel's cross, another flowing move midway through the half leads to Paolo Di Canio striking the ball home after Don Hutchison's fine turn and flick. Nicola and the kids have gone to the park and alone in my living-room I leap from my armchair and punch the air. Di Canio has started the day by demanding in the *News of the World* that the board give him an 'honest answer' as to why they will not talk to him about an extension to his £25,000 a week contract, which expires in 18 months' time. He says that the 'famous claret and blue shirt has become my second skin' and he wants to stay at Upton Park for the rest of his career. 'My agent asked West Ham if they would give me an extension to the current deal. They declined. This is very strange. I've proved my worth to the club again and again.' Understandably, the club felt that, with 18 months of the contract to run, it was too soon to offer a big-money contract extension to a 33-year-old. Will he be the same player at 35? But Paolo's goal today is a useful negotiating point and neatly answers all those critics who say that he can't play away. The travelling West Ham fans launch into their familiar Paolo aria.

It takes two fine saves from Shaka Hislop to keep the Hammers in the game, brilliantly tipping away Reuser's free-kick and then clawing away Makin's effort. There's a much better team ethic this afternoon, with everyone supporting each other and Foxe not scared of making agricultural clearances when needed.

After the break Kanouté misses a good header chance following another splendid dribble and run from Sinclair, who seems to be playing better rather than worse since he's demanded a move. Then it looks like it's all going to slip away again. Just as it seems that Hislop is playing so well he'll keep even a fit David James out of the side, the Hammers keeper punches Venus's free-kick straight to Hreidarsson, who volleys home.

Roeder has spent the game with his arms folded, only now he's occasionally unfolding them to make lifting gestures as if he's auditioning for a French mime company as a man lifting imaginary dumbbells. But West Ham are still playing neat, incisive football. On 65 minutes Michael Carrick wallops a superb long-range effort against the Ipswich bar. Seven minutes later Don Hutchison, enjoying his best game yet for the Irons, makes a surging run from the halfway line towards the Ipswich penalty area, plays the ball inside to Kanouté, who turns and shoots, the ball deflecting off an Ipswich defender into the net. '2–1 to the Cockney boys!' chant the away fans.

'Will this be West Ham's first away win for eight months?' asks the commentator. To my surprise, it really is that long since we won an away game; at Bradford on 24 February. Paolo Di Canio does a sensible job for the team helping to run the clock down by the corner flag. In the 88th minute he is replaced by Jermain Defoe. Yes, Paolo Di Canio has been substituted, and without any hint of a tantrum, surely a sign that he and Roeder enjoy mutual respect.

Defoe – who has bizarrely taken the captain's armband off Di Canio – will simply be asked to hold up the ball. He wins a free-kick by the corner flag and the Hammers waste some more time. Then in injury time it gets better. Carrick's through ball leaves Defoe clear of the Ipswich defence and, showing the composure of a born goalscorer, he side-foots the ball home as if it were a practice match. It's his first league goal, but we'll surely be seeing many, many more.

'Jingle bells, jingle bells, jingle all the way, oh what fun it is to see West Ham away!'

Matt Holland pulls a late goal back but it can't prevent a Hammers win. At the final whistle the subbed Di Canio hugs Glenn Roeder. The unemotional boss, as ever, looks a tad embarrassed at this Latin exuberance. PDC then embraces his prodigy Jermain Defoe as the lads salute the fans.

After the ad break the cameras show Paolo presenting Fredi Kanouté with the man of the match award. He uses it as an opportunity to deliver a garrulous mini-manifesto, stating that he did not 'blast his teammates', he criticised everyone including himself but 'the press do not report this in a good way'. He reiterates that 'we win and lose as a team' and dedicates the victory to reserve keeper Craig Forrest, who is recovering from an operation for testicular cancer.

Then he remembers that he has to present an award. 'Kiss kiss, ciao ciao,' he says, handing a bottle of champagne to Fredi and kissing the bemused striker once on each cheek.

'Never expect the orthodox from Paolo Di Canio,' gushes the anchorman in Alan Partridge style.

West Ham have won three games in eight days and are now up to eleventh – surely enough to give Jeremy Nicholas a hernia as he watches at home. How football can change. Fortune is no longer hiding and the next day's *Guardian* sums up the transformation nicely with a picture of Roeder and Di Canio about to embrace and the headline: 'Name: Glenn Roeder. Title: West Ham manager. Job Prospects: Excellent.'

10. WALKING IN A KITSON WONDERLAND

West Ham 0 Fulham 2 – 3 November 2001
Charlton 4 West Ham 4 – 19 November 2001

'Those bastards! We haven't got anything to moan about now!' jokes Joe, as we meet in Ken's Café before the Fulham game. Reno has decided to sample the authentic football experience again and I've found him eating a full fried brunch with his brother. The real problem, though, is that Americans are so enthusiastic. If they decide to do something they take self-help classes in it until they're perfect. My soon-to-be 20-stone pal is now overdosing on fried food, drinking pints of lager before and after the game, and has learnt how to decline 'fucking wanker' in all its footballing tenses.

We discuss the amazing three victories in the week and Roeder's request for the players to show some old-fashioned East End bottle.

'Some of our players probably thought he said "go on the bottle!"' quips Joe.

A home match against newly promoted Fulham is the first match of November and the sort of game we must get a result in to consolidate those three victories and get an unbeaten run going. A few years ago I saw Fulham playing in division three; now, aided by Mohamed Al Fayed's millions, they are a bigger club than West Ham, spending £12 million on just one player, striker Steve Marlet. In fact Fulham almost signed Fredi Kanouté in the summer. In the morning papers Fredi admits that, 'I was confused in the summer because Harry Redknapp and his assistant left and Frank Lampard went to Chelsea. I really thought West Ham was a sinking ship and that's why I said I wanted to join Fulham.' It's a testament to Glenn Roeder that after talks with the new boss Fredi decided to stay. 'I owe it to Glenn and I'm not disappointed,' adds our favourite personal stereo-wearing hit man.

'Welcome to Fortress Upton Park!' booms Jeremy Nicholas. 'Shut up!' we all say, fearing the force of the footballing jinx. But the side start off in lively form and Reno, impressed by Schemmel and Paolo, is now very effectively using the expression 'wanker!', an alien term to Americans.

WEST HAM

Repka is still missing through suspension, and Roeder reverts to a flat back four with Hayden Foxe partnering Christian Dailly in the middle of defence, and Laurent Courtois on the left of midfield. Hammers start well and Hutchison has a powerful shot saved in the first minute. The key moment in the game comes after 13 minutes when Fredi Kanouté goes one on one with Fulham's keeper Edwin van der Sar but curls the ball against the post.

There's a brief diversion for a bundle, when Foxe and Hayles start pushing each other on the halfway line, joined by several other players from both sides, and both men are booked. Reno gets to perfect his 'Hey, you fucking wanker!' once again. From then on Fulham improve and the diminutive and superbly named Steed Malbranque, surely a man who should be starring in a remake of *The Avengers* rather than the Premiership, begins to dominate midfield. With Hislop stranded Barry Hayles mishits the ball and Hayden Foxe makes a great saving tackle just in front of the goal-line. The 44th minute is normally the time West Ham give away a soft goal before half-time and it duly arrives from Malbranque's corner, when Legwinski thumps home a header, easily climbing above Winterburn with Hislop apparently superglued to his line. We've just made Jean Tigana's half-time team-talk a lot easier.

After 65 minutes the game is effectively over. Di Canio is brought down on the edge of the Fulham penalty area by Malbranque, but instead of giving a free kick, referee Barber waves play on and Di Canio adopts his demented traffic cop pose and is left making wild gestures to the gods. Fulham sweep down the field for Malbranque to leave Hislop helpless with a powerful rising drive. 'Hey, what is it with this referee?' exclaims Reno as he completes his West Ham education.

Defoe is on for Courtois, but it's Fulham who go close with Hislop making a great stop from Malbranque again. Fulham stroll to their first away win of the season as Fortress Upton Park is breached with ease.

After the game Roeder complains that the Hammers should have had a free-kick awarded before the second goal ('It looked a clear foul on Di Canio'). Trevor Sinclair reveals that 'Paolo said he's never had a good relationship with that referee. You could say that about most of them I suppose, but that was definitely a free-kick.'

Hayden Foxe accepts praise for his performance but admits: 'I'd rather play like poo and win.' Interestingly, Sebastian Schemmel seems to think he played like poo. The hardworking full-back, who has been caught out of position defensively during the game, appears to be verging on chucking himself off the Beckton Alps as he admits: 'The manager was very angry with me. He said I didn't respect his tactics and it was my fault. He said I played very badly and the team played very badly, because I have a big influence on the team, so the team had to play with ten players today. It's true that it was my fault.' If only other players were so willing to accept responsibility.

WALKING IN A KITSON WONDERLAND

The final postscript to the game comes when the Sunday papers print pictures of Paolo Di Canio with his hands around Barry Hayles's neck, apparently trying to take the game by the throat. This is too much for West Ham's leader, who takes the unusual step of phoning Sky Sports to say that he was simply calming the Fulham player down: 'I never had the intention to strangle him. If you look at my face I have a very relaxed face and that is unusual for me in a game, so this proves that I had no bad intentions.'

And just to prove that he doesn't have a persecution complex, Paolo adds: 'I can't accept this any more. I intend to take legal action because they [the press] are absolutely bad people.'

In the two-week hiatus between Premiership games, while England play Sweden, there are significant political events at West Ham. The chairman's annual statement to shareholders contains, for West Ham, an unprecedented level of bloodletting. This is getting like *The Sopranos*. Chairman Terry Brown announces a pre-tax loss of £4.7 million, this despite a six per cent increase in turnover. Most notably, Brown implies that the real cause of his friction with Harry Redknapp was 'Arry's high turnover of players, with all their associated costs. 'There is a misconception that the club has made substantial profits in the transfer market but the truth is very different,' writes Brown. 'During the last seven years we bought and sold a total of 134 players, virtually the equivalent of buying and selling a team every season. The net deficit from this player trading was £34 million (£5 million per season) before accounting for the Rio Ferdinand transfer fee – £16 million after that receipt (£2.3 million per season). During the same period our annual wage bill rose from £5.5 million to £28.1 million.'

Brown praises Redknapp for keeping the club in the Premiership, finishing fifth in 1998–99 and qualifying for the UEFA Cup via winning the Intertoto Cup, but implies that the club has not made lasting progress: 'It has to be said that the team Harry took over from Billy Bonds had just finished 13th in a 22-team Premier League with 52 points and after a seven-year roller-coaster ride, he left us with a team which finished 15th out of 20 teams with 42 points.'

West Ham have the eighth highest wage bill in the Premiership and the chairman, unusually for a traditionally secretive club like West Ham, mentions some of the massive wages paid to underperforming players. He cites the case of one 'free' transfer player [Davor Suker] who last season started only eight games, but whose wages amounted to almost the entire revenue of the East Stand for the whole season; another loan signing who played just 86 minutes [Christian Bassila] cost £720,000 in wages and loan fee; and a signing [Gary Charles] will cost the club £4.4 million in fee and wages but has only started a game three times in two years.

You start to suspect that Terry Brown might just be the secret half-brother of Gordon, such is his emphasis on prudence. However, it's hard to dispute

63

his business logic that TV money has simply been squandered on inflationary and unsustainable wages to players and we need to be more selective in making quality long-term signings.

'Television rights have brought massive funds into Premier League football (in excess of £240 million in 1999/2000) but the growth of digital subscription television may be slowing and television viewing figures are at best steady,' continues Brown. 'The Deloitte and Touche Annual Review of Football Finance for 1999/2000 discloses that the 20 Premier League clubs generated a total operating profit of £53 million on turnover of £772 million . . . Rapidly rising revenues which do not lead to rapidly rising profits should be a warning to us all. Borrowing excessively against future revenue streams or selling share stakes . . . and ploughing these capital receipts into revenue expenditure can not be justified by the pursuit of league and cup success, which can only be achieved by four or five clubs. Or even by the avoidance of the Sword of Damocles in the form of relegation.'

Brown, clearly a student of Mr Micawber's axiom of 'annual income £20, annual expenditure £20 ought and six, result misery', goes on to emphasise: 'Such expenditure cannot be justified and we will make no apologies for approaching future transfer negotiations in a far more structured and considered way. In this context I have been greatly encouraged by Glenn Roeder's diligent approach to contract negotiations. The danger in failing to control costs should be obvious to everyone. We do wish to win trophies and appear in European competition, but we will not pursue those ambitions recklessly at the expense of future generations of supporters nor, indeed, at the expense of the club itself.'

In Redknapp's defence it should be pointed out that the board sanctioned every one of his signings. Harry himself is understandably not at all happy with this public criticism, published in both *Upton Park News* and the club programme. Now Director of Football at Portsmouth, Redknapp points out that, with the Frank Lampard sale, his transfer dealings are only £5 million down over seven years and asks: 'Surely all those years in the top flight are worth £5 million?' He goes on: 'It sickens me to hear all this just a year after I was being described as the most successful manager in West Ham's history at last year's AGM. This is personal, he is trying to dump over me . . . It makes me so fed up and it really hurts to get rubbished like this.'

There might not have been a game for two weeks, but just in case the fans are bored, the internal politics at West Ham is starting to resemble a rumble down the Old Vic. Away from club finances, Trevor Sinclair plays for England and earns a penalty, despite claiming that he wants to leave West Ham to enhance his England prospects. Di Canio accuses the press of twisting his words (erm, so maybe you just keep quiet then, Paolo?), and Tomas Repka is sent off for playing for Czechoslovakia, so there's no change there. Robbie Fowler goes to Leeds for £11 million, and the Yorkshire club have now spent

WALKING IN A KITSON WONDERLAND

£97 million under David O'Leary – the sort of figure which would horrify Terry Brown and would probably buy us ten sides and every supporter a lifetime of lunches at Ken's Café. Meanwhile Fredi Kanouté responds to rumours that Liverpool are interested in him by saying that he likes to end the season at the club he started with, which is very good of him.

Sixteen days after the Fulham defeat West Ham travel south to Charlton. It's hard to dislike Charlton, the club that almost died when they left the Valley only to make an emotional return. The programme sellers smile and so do the stewards, there's a friendly air to the whole place and in general the club listens to its fans, something West Ham could learn from.

For example, upon arrival there's the simple idea of having a separate coffee kiosk so you avoid queuing up with everyone who wants a pie or burger as well. Nigel and Matt spot me by the said coffee kiosk and Nigel produces some holiday snaps of himself and Gavin on the Giant's Causeway wearing Hammers hats, and is talking bets on the order we'll arrive in. He has correctly predicted that Fraser will be next followed by the perennially tardy Gavin; who arrives a minute before kick-off having forgotten to take his ticket to work in Wapping and consequently having had to rush home to Blackheath.

We then discuss world politics and particularly the fact that, while the US bombs Afghanistan, in last weekend's *News of the World* Osama Bin Laden was outed as an Arsenal fan, having watched George Graham's Gunners in the Cup-Winners' Cup in the early 1990s. 'Just imagine if he'd supported West Ham, he might have ended up as a real nutter,' I quip.

Our seats are in the back row of the South Stand so we can stand with impunity all game among the agreeably raucous away fans. The team announcement is greeted by cries of derision. Kitson is up front, which we all think is a very strange decision, even if Fredi is injured, as despite a few substitute appearances this season he hasn't started a first-team game for 21 months and his last goal was while on loan to Charlton in March 2000. Supplanted by the maddeningly mercurial Paolo Wanchope, Kitson's last goal for the Irons was a Worthington Cup effort halfway through the 1999–2000 season. Minto is in for Winterburn and both Dailly and Foxe are playing alongside Repka in a five-man defence.

Incredibly, after three minutes West Ham are a goal up and it's Kitson, yes Kitson, our forgotten striker. Di Canio plays a lovely ball inside with the outside of his foot and Kitson strikes an improbably crisp shot which goes in off the post. What a moment for him. It's his first goal for 18 months and you can imagine him mentally sticking two fingers up at Harry Redknapp, the manager who had exiled him for the last two seasons. In fact Kitson is looking hungry and holding up the line well. Another delightful one-two between Di Canio and Sinclair leads to Kitson shooting against Kiely's legs.

65

WEST HAM

'I'd have felt more confident if we were 2–0 up,' I tell Nigel.

'Remember we lost to Wimbledon after going 3–0 up,' he chides.

'OK, make that 4–0 up.'

'Any side with Jason Euell up front can't be up to much,' says Nigel with unusual confidence. Even though Nigel went to an independent school and is a man of some footballing expertise, this opinion is somewhat strange, as Euell was a very promising youngster at Wimbledon. Charlton grabbed Euell and Luke Young in the summer – the sort of players West Ham should have been in for had they not been floundering in their aeon-long search for a replacement for Redknapp.

As ever, our pessimism proves well founded. After 21 minutes an innocuous high ball glances off Christian Dailly's head, catching Shaka Hislop off guard. He flaps at the ball and palms it into the path of Jason Euell, who cannot miss. Charlton have scored with their first attack.

'Any side with Jason Euell in it can't be up to much!' four voices repeat to the chastened Nigel.

It gets worse. Seven minutes later Tomas Repka shows the first touch of a cement mixer. Instead of doing the simple thing and hoofing the ball into touch, he tries to dribble clear and plays the ball straight into the path of Euell. The former Wimbledon striker then slides the ball between Hislop, who has gone to ground in the manner of a man falling over on an ice rink, and his near post.

'David James will be pleased with that,' I mutter darkly, referring to the recovering England custodian who's on the bench tonight. It's harsh on Hislop, who made two superb saves to win us the game against Chelsea, but as Trevor Brooking might say: 'I don't think the lad will be too happy with those goals.' Nor is Repka, who, after his terrible error, collapses on the ground with his head in hands.

Then, West Ham being West Ham, they sweep upfield in a glorious move and equalise. Di Canio, surrounded by three men, somehow plays a delicate pass out to Minto, who races with surprising speed down the left wing and plays a perfect ball into the area for Kitson to thump home. It's the best example of counter-attacking football you could ever wish to see and another vindication for Kitson, who is resurrecting his career in one match. Sky will be loving this; half an hour gone and four goals.

West Ham's defence, inspired by such a great goal, proceed to play like men in clogs running around a sodden quarry from *Doctor Who*. Any ball in the air causes problems. Then Hislop races from his line with the panic-strewn features of a man with an untrimmed beard running from the Taliban's vice and public virtue committee, and clatters Chris Powell. The ref fails to award a free-kick to Charlton, perhaps influenced by the mitigating circumstances of Shaka's look of absolute terror, but many officials might have regarded this as both a foul and a red card offence as Hislop was the last man in defence.

66

WALKING IN A KITSON WONDERLAND

There's another terrible moment when Euell is given a completely free header with three defenders around him. Luckily Shaka fumbles the ball round the post. Hutchison, Foxe and Repka are statuesque, looking at each other with the puzzled expressions of men who have just been given a detailed map outlining all the tribal factions, Al-Qaida bunkers and hidden caves within the most mountainous regions of Afghanistan.

Mercifully half-time arrives with the score 2–2 and the away fans buzzing with a mixture of pain and exhilaration. It's all been hugely entertaining and my £25 ticket feels like a bargain. But Charlton score again within six minutes of the restart, easily slicing through the Hammers defence, as Johansson runs behind Foxe to slot home the third. Bizarrely, the Hammers equalise again on 64 minutes. The indefatigable Di Canio chips in a cross which skims off Mark Fish's head. At the far post Sinclair knocks it back and Kitson – yes, useless, knackered, injury-prone has-been Kitson – completes his hat trick. He is mobbed by his teammates in front of us, with Paolo leaping on his shoulders.

The Hammers end breaks into a chorus of 'Walking in a Kitson wonderland!' And it's not ironic.

'What odds would you have given on the way here that we'd be singing that?' asks a bemused Nigel. Probably about 10,000–1. Kitson hasn't played so well in years and it's been good management by Roeder to bring him back. From the outset of the season he has made it clear that Kitson is in contention again and he's often been on the bench. It's not just the goals that have impressed tonight, he's held the ball up and worked tremendously hard at closing down defenders.

In fact, he's playing like a man with a terminating contract. Kitson has certainly been injury prone, but why ignore an asset that cost the company £2.3 million? When alongside Hartson he'd kept us up and looked a quality player. Redknapp had fallen out with him and any fans who met him last season were genuinely surprised that he was still at the club.

After the game Kitson admits: 'I was pushed out, shipped out on loan here there and everywhere . . . I have been disappointed with the way I have been treated but that is in the past, Harry has his views and that was that . . . My face fits more now and it has been much better. Glenn Roeder has been honest with me and said I would get chances. Getting involved and being on the bench has given me a buzz since he took over. I have tried to do my best for him because he gave me a chance.'

West Ham's defence continues to look more nervous than a manager receiving a vote of confidence from Doug Ellis, and we're badly missing the experienced Nigel Winterburn. Roeder brings on Lomas and Cole for Hutchison and Minto. Cole immediately makes a typical run, skilfully beating three defenders before being tackled. Lomas should add the defensive shield in front of our back five that has been so sadly lacking, with the underperforming Carrick and Hutchison both looking better going forward.

Lomas immediately launches into a couple of ugly but fair tackles, which is exactly what we need.

'I can just see Kitson scoring a hat trick and us still losing,' I mutter gloomily a few minutes later, as our defence still looks like a black hole waiting to suck in all known matter from the Charlton forwards' boots and implode to a density where Christian Dailly's knee will be the heaviest object in the known universe.

On 77 minutes Roeder substitutes hat trick star Kitson with the 19-year-old Jermain Defoe, another ex-Charlton player. He is greeted with boos and cries of 'Judas' from the home fans. Defoe was with Charlton until he was 16, when he decided to join West Ham 'to further his career' (and not a lot of people have said that). Charlton received more than a million pounds in compensation, but this still rankles with boss Alan Curbishley who believes that England Under-21 star Defoe, who scored 18 goals in 29 games while on loan with Bournemouth last season, will go to the very top. We'll soon knock that out of him. Clearly Curbishley has forgotten what West Ham did to prospects Kevin Lock (the next Bobby Moore), Mervyn Day ('England's goalkeeper for the next ten years'), Alan Dickens (the next Trevor Brooking) and Stuart Slater (a certainty for England greatness).

Mind you, the boy Defoe looks as if he could defy all known Hammers precedents and fulfil his potential. With three-thirds of the ground booing him you just know he's going to score. Christian Dailly, who has looked lost in a three-man central defence, is now playing at left-back, and let's give credit to the Scot, he's showing great character by sticking at his role and making a penetrating run up the left. He's obviously going to give the ball to Di Canio but no, he takes the ball away from the feet of the astounded Hammers captain and chips a good cross into the box. It's half-cleared to the edge of the area and met by Defoe with an instant volley into the corner of the net. Cue pandemonium in our end as the players leap on top of each other and Di Canio shouts his usual imprecations to the delirious crowd. 'There's only one Defoe!' is joyously chanted at the Charlton fans.

There are only seven minutes left and Defoe's goal has surely won it. We all agree how good it would be to wind up the Charlton fans with Defoe scoring the winner. I start making mental calculations of how far up the table three points would place us. But this is West Ham, who never look less secure than when defending a one-goal lead.

The 90 minutes are up, but then Joe Cole on the left tries to pick someone out with a fancy 40-yard pass when we're yelling at him to keep possession. Charlton race down the field and win a corner off Repka who, on the plus side, has at least lasted 90 minutes on the field. Although all three centre-backs could have been sent off without us defending any worse. Charlton then win two headers in our box and Johansson reacts quicker than Lomas and scores with a fine overhead kick. Oh God. The Valley goes crazy. The final whistle blows, but the disappointed Irons' fans still applaud the lads off. Should we be pleased with a point and a marvellous game with eight goals, or sick at losing two points and worried by a defence which looks slightly less secure than Osama Bin Laden's life insurance policy?

Whatever, the sheer glorious elation and unpredictability of it all seems to encapsulate all the emotions of being a West Ham supporter. Gavin – the beer hunter of Upton Park – produces his CAMRA guide and guides us to a pleasant local boozer which serves a most palatable pint of Greene King IPA. We gaze up at the TV monitors and watch Andy Gray attempt to make sense of it all, scribbling furiously with his decidedly overworked marker pen. None of it makes any sense.

The next morning I rush out and buy the tabloids and the *Standard* for their verdict on 'Valley of the Goals' and 'Kitty Kitty Bang Bang'. I feel proud to have my side associated with such a game.

A slightly more sober analysis comes from Joe who, on the phone, comments: 'Did you see it, it was awful! What other side scores four goals away from home and doesn't get three points?'

11. ON THE ROEDER NOWHERE?

West Ham 0 Spurs 1 – 24 November 2001

Five days after the thriller at the Valley we're at home to Tottenham. During the week Rigobert Song has been loaned to Cologne with Roeder again using his strangely dated vernacular to describe Rigobert as a 'good fellow'.

There has been no other activity on the transfer front, although presumably, like Arthur Daley, Roeder must still be desperately trying to shift a made-in-Guinea dodgy Camara and a one-gear Bulgarian Todorov from out of his Doctor Martens-sponsored lock-up.

Mike Pattenden, one of my fellow founder-editors of the old fanzine *Fortune's Always Hiding*, sends me an e-mail entitled 'Part-timer alert': 'Just been offered a ticket to watch the Hamsters play the Cockadoodles tomorrow. Shall I book a table at Kenneth's Bistro in West Hampstead? 2.00 p.m?' I reply to confirm our booking and add that I hope he's looking forward to his free-range egg on a bed of French fries drizzled with tomato sauce.

After the said rendezvous in Chez Kenneth's we trek up to the East Stand Upper. Finally the lower tier of the new Doctor Martens site is open, with the wraparound sections still to come, and today the ground contains nearly 33,000 fans, a post all-seater stadia record. The new stand is still a long distance from the touchline, but the pitch itself is going to be removed over the winter to keep Upton Park's traditional tightness. Those transparent continental-style dugouts have been ripped out too and have, bizarrely, been replaced by a set of plastic seats.

'They've just been round to Ken's and asked for some spare chairs,' suggests Mike.

'Carol will be out there soon shouting, "Number 63, sausage, chips and beans!"' I add.

The seating arrangements make no difference to Glenn Roeder who, as ever, stands up in his black undertaker's suit with his arms folded, pacing the

71

edge of his technical area like a man with a severe haemorrhoid problem.

West Ham's line-up is a severe disappointment. Kanouté and Winterburn are still out, Carrick has gone too and, mysteriously, Di Canio is missing. This is a surprise and, as the Italian maestro has been complaining to the press about not being offered a new contract, we wonder for a moment if Paolo has called someone on the board an 'ugly penis face!' (as he memorably did to his boss Fabio Capello in Italy) and walked out of the club.

But no, all four players are the victims of hamstring strains. With all that twanging at Chadwell Heath, West Ham could probably produce a country album. Perhaps there is some kind of gypsy hamstring curse upon the club, which can only be erased by Glenn Roeder sacrificing a goat in the centre circle and then urinating on each corner of the pitch, Barry Fry-style.

'When did we last win a game when Di Canio and Kanouté weren't playing?' asks Big Joe. None of us are sure, although Nigel thinks it was probably Bradford away last season.

Shaka Hislop has been dropped for the returning David James and the sheer size of the man is a reassuring presence in defence. Repka is back from suspension to partner Dailly, who was presumably slightly less bad than Foxe at Charlton. Defoe is starting his first full game up front alongside Kitson, but is finding it difficult against Spurs's three centre-backs.

'It's a bit different to playing Charlton, Kitson!' hollers Mike as the hat trick star of the Valley struggles to find a way past the towering Ledley King.

The first half is messy, but after Charlton it's a relief to at least have a clean sheet at half-time. Mike is soon shouting, 'This is shit, West Ham! . . . Ah, just like old times, isn't it?' Still, after Charlton, an ugly 1–0 victory will do fine. Anything really. The half ends with Sheringham whacking the ball against the bar and it's increasingly apparent how much we struggle creatively without Di Canio, hard as Joe Cole is trying.

Soon after the restart, though, we're a goal down. On 50 minutes Spurs are allowed too much space on the left, where Cole is often drifting inside, and when wing-back Simon Davies's cross comes in, James makes a brilliant save from Poyet's header – but the 34-year-old Les Ferdinand dives to bravely head home. Undone by a geriatric who has scored his first away goal of the season for Spurs.

Bizarrely, the goal celebrations are interrupted by an injury to the prone Poyet, who has collided with Trevor Sinclair and may have concussion. Poyet staggers to his feet and does a passable imitation of Basil Fawlty not mentioning the war. The concussed Uruguayan is appealing for a corner and then, we later learn from Ferdinand, attempting to order food. Surely not from West Ham's abysmal catering outlets we hope, and if he's dining at Ken's then where is his numbered ticket? 'Gus was away with the fairies . . . but then again, he usually is,' adds Sir Les. Eventually Poyet is shepherded off but, bizarrely, Trevor Sinclair has gone down the tunnel too.

'That's it, he's had enough, he's getting the laptop out, and he's putting a stamp on that letter to the board now,' I speculate. The players point out to the ref that they only have ten men and eventually Sinclair returns from the Doctor Martens Stand with a new pair of boots – or is that a pair of high-leg DMs? Things don't improve. Christian Dailly is a much improved player at home and is actually holding us together at the back, making a fine saving tackle from Ferdinand. Substitute Leonhardsen rattles James's post and then Sheringham hits the post for the second time in the match. It could have been 4–0.

Apart from the odd moment of hope from Joe Cole on the left, West Ham look clueless, slipping into an indecisive midfield muddle. 'This is where we miss Frank Lampard, no one to shoot the ball straight into the wall,' I tell Mike as another free-kick ends in ignominy. Poor Steve Lomas has tried hard in midfield, but having been injured for nearly a year before his return at Charlton, the man with the ginger bog-brush haircut is helped off the pitch with a broken toe – destined to be out for a further six weeks.

Substitute John Moncur takes an unusually long time before he collects his obligatory booking, but first produces a fine save from Sullivan with a rasping shot – West Ham's best and virtually only chance. The defence is marginally better than at Charlton. Repka, Dailly and James look like they might become a solid unit at the back, but what hope is there if our squad can't survive three injuries? The game ambles to a close with an easy three points for Spurs in what is normally a hard-fought local derby.

As Jeremy Nicholas reads the other final scores Nigel mocks, 'We go below Middlesbrough! We go below Sunderland! Crisis, what crisis?' West Ham are now in the bottom six, seven points from the relegation zone, with Man United, Arsenal and Liverpool to come in December. Those three straight wins in a week in October seem like a long time ago now.

Spurs's manager Glenn Hoddle makes a damning comment when he mentions: 'We never got out of third gear.' Although he does offer support to the other Glenn by adding: 'He'll do well here in the long run.' When Hoddle was England boss he employed Roeder as one of his coaches and the two have remained close since. After the game they are planning to go out to dinner, although even born-again St Glenn accompanied by Eileen Drewery might struggle to resurrect Roeder's West Ham career if there are more home defeats like this. Roeder himself tells the press: 'I would never use injuries as an excuse.' Before, erm, using injuries as an excuse, complaining: 'It didn't help being without Paolo, Freddie and Michael. Our small squad just can't cope with those kind of injuries.'

Dan, Joe and myself walk to East Ham station to avoid the ever-larger queues at Upton Park tube. Dan heads back to Upminster while on the westbound train Joe and myself are in despondent mood.

'They'll have to get rid of him when they see how much money is at risk,' says Joe. 'I'd get in Graham, at least his sides would know how to defend. They wouldn't score four goals away from home and not win.'

My view is that Roeder, apparently a decent man doing his best, should be given a season to prove his aptitude for the job, but then perhaps I'm too nice to run a football club; if we're in the bottom three by Christmas then the Graham option will sound dangerously appealing.

The only encouraging feature of the game has been the return of David James, much sooner than expected. After the match he reveals that he's been helped by a sports psychologist: 'He gets me focusing on what you need to do and made me more confident after the injury,' says the giant keeper. 'When you're out for a long time your mood goes up and down and these days you need to be prepared mentally as well as physically and technically. You need mental training.' Particularly to be a West Ham supporter.

I await the obligatory call at home from my Spurs-supporting chum Mark McCallum. 'Your goal is like the Tardis in reverse, it's bigger on the outside than in, which is why our shots kept bouncing out. I shall leave you to ponder what lies ahead for the rest of the season . . .' he tells me cruelly. Thank you, Mark, and may Chas and Dave songs haunt your consciousness for evermore.

12. PAOLO AND THE PONCY PENALTY

Sunderland 1 West Ham 0 - 1 December 2001
West Ham 1 Aston Villa 1 - 5 December 2001

December begins with a daunting trip to Sunderland. Perhaps because little is expected of them, West Ham play well and have enough chances to win the game. In the first half Sinclair sets up Defoe who rolls the ball across goal when he should have hit the target. Don Hutchison, captain for the day and booed by the home supporters whenever he touches the ball (the same fans who voted him player of the year last season), responds with one of his best games since returning to Upton Park.

In the early stages of the second half West Ham have three excellent chances: Sorensen palms away a rasping shot from Cole and then produces a superb double save, first from Defoe and then turning Carrick's strike from the rebound on to the bar. Then Hutchison glides past two defenders only to roll another effort across goal.

With five minutes to go it seems that West Ham will have to settle for one point rather than the three they deserve. Only then Arca breaks down the left and sweeps a cross into the middle. Kevin Phillips runs into the space between Repka and Dailly and, beating James to the out-swinging cross, volleys home a typical predator's goal to send the Irons home pointless.

It's a sickening moment for Roeder, but he sensibly refuses to condemn Defoe for missing two good chances, saying that he got into good positions and is gaining in experience, 'but today was not to be his day'. He describes it as West Ham's best away performance of the season: 'We should have been out of sight by the time Phillips scored . . . The disappointing thing is that our centre-halves handled him so well . . . Maybe I should have left him at Baldock.'

The final comment is a reference to the fact that it was Roeder who first spotted Phillips at Baldock Town and 'thought he was worth a punt' of ten grand of his chairman's money at Watford, and privately, despite defeat, Roeder could reflect that his judgement has been more than vindicated by

75

WEST HAM

Phillips's 103rd goal for Sunderland.

The other point of note is that the West Ham gaffer has accommodated the cold north-east winds by donning a navy-blue Fila anorak over his suit as he glowers on the touchline. Now he looks less like an undertaker and more Man at C & A.

With games against Man United and Arsenal coming up and the club fifth from bottom of the Premiership, three points are essential from the following Wednesday night's fixture against Aston Villa. Which is why West Ham concede a goal after 60 seconds. David James fluffs a kicked clearance, Barthez-style, which skews to Steve Stone on Villa's right. The slaphead winger beats his man and gets in a cross which should still be dealt with. Only Tomas Repka, introduced a few minutes earlier as 'Tomas "The Hit Man" Repka!' by DJ Jeremy Nicholas, is apparently not yet tooled up. The non-bouncing Czech allows Dion Dublin to get on the wrong side of him and head an easy goal. Groans of disbelief echo around Upton Park.

Nigel and Matt have both arrived late and missed the goal. Upon being informed of the first minute catastrophe, Nigel replies succinctly: 'We're going down.'

Villa are wearing horrible silver away shirts, reminiscent of Manchester City's abomination of silver shirts and luminous lime-green socks worn last season, and look as average as their kit.

Yet West Ham are almost sublime in their awfulness in the first half. Sebastian Schemmel is showing an uncanny ability to slice the ball into touch and unerringly rifle the ball to the opposition – and sometimes towards the northern coast of his native France – unrivalled since the days of Ray Stewart.

Hutchison has disappeared. Di Canio overelaborates and refuses to play the simple ball and even he, the great PDC, elicits previously unthinkable groans from the increasingly impatient fans. Joe Cole always tries to play the same killer cross-field ball which never hits its man.

Repka, an international centre-half with Czechoslovakia, has lost all confidence and is fluffing simple passes and clearances. Any primitive high ball lofted towards Dion Dublin causes huge problems in the Hammers' defence, which looks almost scared to mark the ageing centre-forward. Another Dublin header is pushed onto the bar by James and in the ensuing goal-line scramble looks like it might have crossed the line and is then somehow booted off for a corner.

I'm tempted to shout out, 'Come on Hammers! Really pep it up and make it mediocre!', a classic cry which I heard in the 1970s.

The Upper East Stand starts to sound like a convention for Tourette's Syndrome sufferers. 'Fucking Schemmel! . . . Fucking hell West Ham! . . . Fuck me! . . . Hutchison you fucking tart! . . . You fucking tossers! . . . Play the fucking simple ball Di Canio . . . Fuck off! . . . This is fucking shit West Ham!'

PAOLO AND THE PONCY PENALTY

The man sitting behind me is more reflective: 'It might sound silly, but I'm gonna die without ever seeing West Ham win a trophy . . .' If he feels like the rest of us, his demise might come sooner than he expects. West Ham are playing like a relegation side. No one is launching any crunching tackles in midfield to fire up both team and crowd. It's left to the ageing but spirited Nigel Winterburn, age 38, to charge into three crunching tackles, which result in huge roars of 'Come On You Irons!'. Ironically our worst home performance is generating the best atmosphere. The 28,000 fans have been pushed too far and through some kind of collective kinetic energy are attempting to will an improvement.

The West Ham crowd are always at their best when all hope is gone. Like the time when we were 4–0 down at half-time at Highbury and a huge chorus of 'We all agree, Dowie is better than Bergkamp!' went up. Or the legendary FA semi-final against Nottingham Forest when, while being thrashed 4–0 and attempting to persuade ourselves that George Parris was really a top-class midfielder in the Brooking mould, the West Ham fans spontaneously chanted 'Billy Bonds's claret and blue army!' for the final half-hour of the game.

Mercifully half-time arrives with us only 1–0 down. 'Well, that was all right, wasn't it?' beams Joe with mock enthusiasm as we huddle beneath the stand, battle-shocked, having been subjected to the footballing equivalent of mustard gas. Bewildered supporters queue for the latrines, sorry, gents, muttering in disbelief. If the lads have any character at all, they need to show it in the second half.

In fact Glenn Roeder may well have called them something worse than 'fellows' for once, as West Ham really come at Villa after the interval. He's definitely not a teacup thrower, but perhaps Roeder has at least flicked a wet tea bag at his men.

There's been a transformation. The diminutive Defoe is causing numerous problems for the large Villa centre-backs. Carrick blasts over from a good position and Staunton blocks Di Canio when he seems sure to score. Sinclair and Schemmel combine on the right and Schemmel does very well to square the ball in to Di Canio whose shot is saved by the legs of Enckelman (deputising for Schmeichel) who, like most keepers who visit Upton Park, is playing superbly. The frustrated Di Canio is booked for dissent and with typical theatricality holds his arms aloft, appealing to the heavens.

Then comes our chance. Defoe is bundled over by Mellberg and the ref points to the spot. Yet I don't feel confident as Di Canio walks up to take it. His game thrives on praise and he's now in a struggling team and has just missed two chances.

Di Canio steps up and, in dreadful slow motion, seems to play a limp back pass to the keeper. Was he trying to chip it? It is one of those moments when the normal laws of time appear to no longer apply and you know for certain that there is no God. Captain Ahab probably felt very much the same at the moment the white whale emerged to bite off his leg.

77

Had Paolo tried to make the goalkeeper go the wrong way and gently roll the ball in the other corner? It is possibly the worst penalty ever seen at Upton Park.

Dirty Den, unable to visit Upton Park on Saturdays due to work commitments, goes into thermonuclear meltdown mode. This is a man who has seen too much. His face becomes a bright shade of puce and the Ferguson hairdryer seems almost a pleasant prospect compared to Denis's imminent tirade. No one is a bigger fan of the maverick Italian Paolo Di Canio, which is why his faults hurt him all the more. As Prefab Sprout might have put it, this is when love breaks down. It's like watching a horrible domestic row in your street, in which you feel powerless to intervene, as Dirty Den stands up and hollers:

'DI CANIO GET OFF THE BLOODY PITCH THAT IS A FUCKING DISGRACE WHAT'S MORE FUCKING IMPORTANT WEST HAM GETTING A POINT OR YOU SCORING A FUCKING PONCY GOAL!!!!'

'At least Denis is enjoying it,' I venture.

He's right though, Paolo has surely cost us the game. Di Canio holds his head in his hands. The time for showmanship is not when you're being sucked into the relegation mire. As Nigel says, Di Canio still shows glimpses of his sublime skill, but that's it, just glimpses. He's the best player seen at Upton Park since Trevor Brooking, but he's 33 and a half and not quite the player he was. For the second half of last season he was woefully off form, blaming his problems on sinus and Achilles tendon injuries. But for almost a year now, although still influential, he hasn't looked the invincible player of old.

'Will Roeder be brave enough to take Di Canio off?' asks Nigel.

'If you substitute Di Canio it means he's leaving the club,' counters Matt.

The chastened Di Canio at least sticks to simple balls for the next few minutes. Sinclair races on to a through ball from Joe Cole and screws the ball narrowly wide of Enckelman. The decibel level is encouragingly high and it's almost like Fortress Upton Park used to be for games under the lights.

'This will be the third game in a row we've lost 1–0,' I reflect ruefully.

Denis, now somewhat calmer after his domestic with Di Canio, is a creature of rigid footballing habits, and tries to persuade those of us tubing it to leave in injury time and jog for the Silverlink train from West Ham. No one will go. Personally, I don't believe in ever leaving a match early. With West Ham anything can happen. We even stayed up once in 1996–97 after an unbeaten run was started by Tony Cottee scoring twice against Everton in the last few minutes to snatch a 2–2 draw. As we used to say to former *On A Mission* editor Shane Barber: it's never over until the fat bloke leaves.

We are in injury time. As Denis gets up from his seat, Joe Cole jinks the ball through to Defoe on the edge of the area, sideways on to goal and surrounded by defenders. Yet somehow he manages to swivel and strike a sumptuous cross shot into the far corner of the Villa net. YEEES! I smack Denis on the back. We've equalised and, even better, we can berate Dirty Den for being a part-timer. 'Shouldn't you be off getting the Silverlink?' we mock.

The final whistle blows and Jeremy Nicholas plays 'Cum On Feel The Noize' by Slade as the relieved masses file out.

'Not good enough,' mutters Joe, deeply unimpressed by our struggle to snatch defeat from second half domination.

Still, it was a fantastic strike, and that Defoe goal might be more than a point in terms of boosting our confidence levels. Three defeats in a row with no goals scored has the look of a side destined for the bottom three. And Kanouté will be back to face fading Man United at Old Trafford, who have, though, tonight just beaten Boavista 3–0 in the Champions League, and will probably wallop us 5–0.

After the game Roeder announces in his peculiarly antediluvian fashion that 'the little fellow was magnificent and deserved his goal' (that's Jermain Defoe), speaking of him as if he's a guest at a meeting of the Royal Geographical Society rather than a top young striker.

The manager says with some understatement that Repka was 'caught out' for the Villa goal and that the side 'played nervously' (presumably that's manager speak for 'crap') in the first half, but that at half-time 'I asked the players to take more responsibility'. He adds that the Irons could have had six points from the last two matches, but instead have one, and now face their toughest month of the season.

Will Di Canio still be taking penalties? Roeder is not about to turn on his captain. 'I would never criticise anyone for taking a penalty. You have to have bottle to take one in the first place,' he emphasises. 'He will still take penalties for us – just try taking the ball off him.'

At least West Ham's storming revival in the second half offers some hope to the fans, but as the *Guardian* match report puts it, the side 'need a win sooner rather than later'. And it's surely not going to come in Saturday's trip to Old Trafford.

13. CAN WE PLAY YOU EVERY WEEK?

Manchester United 0 West Ham 1 – 8 December 2001

'Don't even think about it! When did West Ham last beat Manchester United twice in a row at Old Trafford?' asks Big Joe, just in case I'm feeling optimistic as we meet in the bar of the North Stafford Hotel in Stoke.

Manchester United have already lost four games this season – which should mean they thrash us 5–0 and everyone then says: 'What crisis at Old Trafford?' No West Ham fan will ever forget the 1–0 victory in the FA Cup last season, with Di Canio poking the ball past the taxi-hailing Fabian Barthez and then running to the corner flag in front of the West Ham fans and telling the cameras: 'I can play away!' Sadly I missed the game due to the imminent birth of my second daughter Nell, but can still recall madly jumping off my sofa and hugging my older daughter Lola in sheer disbelief when the final whistle blew and chanting 'Paolo Di Canio!' at my bemused Highbury neighbours.

But West Ham have just played terribly against Aston Villa and United will want vengeance. Since winning three in a row in October the Hammers have taken only two points from the last fifteen, drawing two matches and losing three. The day has started badly, too. My would-be companion Gavin has been taken ill after a night out with Nigel at a Uriah Heep concert (his ailment is unconnected to the music). I try to raise his spirits by saying that at least he'll escape seeing us thrashed.

Now there's a ticket to shift. On the train to Manchester I make several mobile calls to Joe, who is travelling to the game from the Midlands, and arrange to meet him at Stoke station where he'll drive to the game with his brother-in-law and shift Gav's ticket to his brother-in-law's son. Phew. Talk about lastminute.com.

On the drive to Manchester Joe fields more mobile calls, one from a Manchester United fan. 'Nah, mate, you'll win 5–0. Van Nistelrooy against Dailly, it don't bear thinking about.' As someone who manages comedians he is inured to chaos and disappointment. His acts can fail to turn up at gigs, bungle

81

simple arrangements, disappoint and elate and sometimes make you laugh. It's pretty good preparation for being a West Ham supporter really.

The air in Manchester is crisp and the sky clear as we walk to the ground. A call from my old schoolmate Paul Garrett, munching prawn sandwiches in an executive box, reveals that David James has orange hair and United have rested Van Nistelrooy and Veron while Beckham is only a sub. So at least there might be some hope.

Old Trafford has the loudest PA in football and it's thereafter impossible to make a mobile call. Blimey. Just imagine Jeremy Nicholas at this volume; it could result in psychiatric disorders and suicide attempts all over East London. The 3,000 West Ham fans are inspired by the biggest fixture of all though, noisily singing 'Bubbles' and waving one arm in the air as they holler: 'Let's all do a Barthez!'

From the kick-off something is very, very strange. Cue *X-Files* music. West Ham, who have taken just two points out of 15, keep the ball and dictate the tempo of the game. Roeder shows his ability to make innovative tactical changes by moving Hutchison out to the right, Sinclair to the left and playing Joe Cole and Michael Carrick in the middle. With Defoe a wriggling nuisance up front and Di Canio holding the ball well and clearly up for the big occasion after last Wednesday's penalty débâcle, it works beautifully.

More encouragement comes from the fact that Carrick and Cole – whom no one thinks are disciplined enough to play in central midfield – match Keane and Butt for tackling. Scholes has one wicked shot beautifully tipped over by James and the Hammers keeper gives a Schmeichel-style rollicking to his defence for backing off. But United are not pressing with anything like their usual intensity. United's promising young centre-half O'Shea is booked for clattering Jermain Defoe. Roy Keane, definitely in one of his snarling moods, is booked for abusing the ref as he books O'Shea and is then lucky to escape dismissal when he clatters Cole way after the ball has gone.

Don Hutchison looks much better on the right of midfield, keeps the ball effectively and skilfully, and nearly scores with an instinctive long-range drive that Barthez tips around a post. At one point West Ham have so many passes that the Hammers fans cheer every successful delivery. As the United fans lapse into silence the Hammers contingent taunt them with a mass 'Shhh! and then a suggestion of 'Shall we sing a song for you?'.

Half-time arrives and the wife and son of the late Les Sealey, the former Hammers and United keeper who sadly died of a heart attack in the summer, lay a wreath in the goalmouth. A special record is dedicated to Les, which the United PA system then ruins by crassly playing a safety announcement in the middle of it.

The second half brings greater United pressure, with the United fans claiming a penalty when Hutch chests the ball down dangerously close to his arm in the area, but referee Paul Durkin waves play on. Beckham replaces

Chadwick and it all begins to look ominous. Glenn Roeder is on his feet at the edge of his technical area from the start of the second half.

But then on 64 minutes comes definitive proof that there is a benevolent deity who understands human frailty but also rewards the meek in the kingdom of merchandising. It's a classic West Ham passing movement. The ball is shifted quickly from Cole to Hutchison to Defoe to Di Canio and then back to Cole, who shimmies past a United challenge and finds Schemmel wide on the right. The tireless French full-back plays a low cross into Di Canio who swivels brilliantly and chips the ball across goal to Jermain Defoe who rises above the entire Man United defence to get in a header. Clearly it's gone wide. But no, Defoe is on the ground being mobbed by Trevor Sinclair and co. Everyone around me is going absolutely mental. It can't be. YEEEEES! HA! WAHEY! The West Ham players rush over to celebrate in our corner. The impossible has happened. We're ahead against Man United.

'Right, only 26 minutes to hold out,' I tell Joe.

'Don't think about it,' cautions Joe. He's right. Us pessimists aren't going to allow a trifling goal to give us any hope of winning at Old Trafford.

Andy Cole comes on for Butt and the feared United onslaught materialises. They seem to force countless corners but the heroic James plays like a man determined to prove that he should be England's keeper in the 2002 World Cup. His new barnet might resemble Harpo Marx, but he dominates his area, smothers the ball at Neville's feet and then makes a stunning save from Silvestre's close-range header. Repka is making crucial blocks and Christian Dailly, yes dear old lovable useless Christian Dailly, the man everyone said was one of Harry's bad buys, whom we should shift as quickly as possible, is rewarding the faith of Glenn Roeder by suddenly resembling a footballing colossus at the back.

Then West Ham break, Defoe wriggles inside three defenders on the right and wins a free-kick after a crude challenge from Gary Neville, who is yellow carded. As West Ham win a throw-in in front of the away supporters, Paolo Di Canio runs over to retrieve the ball while making strange gestures around his genitals. He appears to be miming 'big balls' – either that or he's a fan of *Viz*'s Buster Gonad and his unfeasibly large testicles.

Joe and myself join in the hugely enjoyable choruses of 'Can we play you every week?'. Joe Cole shows brilliant skill to twist out of an impossible position when surrounded by three defenders and hare into the United area. He is then felled by a Roy Keane forearm smash across his face. Astonishingly, referee Durkin fails to award either a penalty or a free-kick.

The PA announces today's attendance of 67,582, which is greeted by an immediate chant of: 'Is that all you bring at home?' Meanwhile, Roy Keane is engaging in a one-man campaign to be dismissed by the most lenient ref in history. As Repka helps the ball off for a corner the graceless United skipper whacks him across the back of the head. United's poor form has clearly got to

Keane and for a world-class player he is showing an alarming lack of discipline.

'We love you West Ham, we do! We love you West Ham we do! Oh West Ham we love you!' sing the disbelieving Londoners as the impossible edges closer. Two seasons in a row? Barthez has now joined the United attack as the game moves into Ferguson time. The ball moves out to Di Canio – who picks it up and jumps up and down. The ref has blown! The West Ham players rush over and Paolo gives Defoe a piggy-back. Wantaway Trevor Sinclair looks as pleased as anyone. James throws his gloves into the crowd. This just isn't meant to happen.

YEEEEEES! Sir Alex Ferguson, your boys took one hell of a beating! The best part is going to be hearing Fergie's excuses. He obliges us by ignoring the fact that Roy Keane should have been sent off and West Ham awarded a penalty, and then berating the ref Paul Durkin for not giving a penalty against Don Hutchison, churlishly commenting: 'He never gives us a penalty kick no matter what the situation. I was disappointed with him. I used to think he was a good referee but not now.'

Outside the ground it's hilarious to listen to the United fans moaning on the way back to Manchester Piccadilly station. 'I've been coming here for 30 years and that's the worst football I've ever seen,' complains one. They lose two home games in succession and you'd think that the entire team had committed hara-kiri.

On Piccadilly station I phone Gav to tell him he's missed a superb victory and he sounds doubly depressed; then Nicola at home to tell her the incredible news. Next it's a call to Paul, still celebrating among his prawn sandwiches. We decide that our fellow school friend Nick, a lifelong Red, is now hiding out in a cave complex in Bermondsey, Osama Bin Laden-style, surrounded by a few diehard fanatics, refusing to believe that the hated Ferguson regime is over. I leave a message on Nick's mobile telling him: 'I think you're too good to go down.'

Even the late-running train to London Euston doesn't matter. At Stockport a disgruntled Red gets on the train who is clearly dismayed by the West Ham fans doing a conga down the packed train. 'They'll probably lose 4–0 next week . . .' he mutters.

'We don't care, we know we're shit!' responds a West Ham fan.

The bar has been drunk out of cans of beer and I'm reduced to purchasing two cans of cider. But nothing can take away the inner glow, not even Virgin Trains regretting our late arrival in Euston. Glenn Roeder is a football genius. Christian Dailly is the new Franz Beckenbauer. And we've won at Old Trafford. Twice.

14. ALWAYS BELIEVE IN . . . JOEY COLE!

West Ham 1 Arsenal 1 - 15 December 2001

After the euphoria of Man United comes another easy game against Arsenal. In that morning's *Daily Telegraph* Glenn Roeder gives an encouraging interview. Speaking from a position of some strength after the win at Old Trafford, he admits: 'Of the 22–24 players in our squad, between 6 and 8 are sub-Premiership standard.'

In an implicit criticism of his predecessor, Harry Redknapp, he says he believes that Alan Curbishley looked at the squad, thought 'Right club wrong time' and turned the manager's job down. He continues: 'The players who came in after Rio Ferdinand was sold to Leeds have fallen short of the class we want, but unfortunately they are on three- or four-year contracts . . . The board understand the squad situation. Probably that was what led to the downfall of Harry, because they could see the quality was not being brought in that should have been. If I can survive long enough I can flush those players out of the club as their contracts run out.'

Roeder also mentions 'top dollar' salaries and it's rumoured that some of Redknapp's post-Rio signings may be on up to a million pounds per annum. From the Undertaker's remarks it might be deduced that Titi Camara, Rigobert Song, Svetoslav Todorov, Raggy Soma and Hayden Foxe are in danger of moving on to a better place, while the overpaid and under-utilised Gary Charles, another disastrous signing, would surely be sold to anyone who will take him.

Then there are squad players like Scott Minto, Paul Kitson and Shaka Hislop who must be at risk. Of the post-Rio signings perhaps only Christian Dailly is safe. He has appeared in every game so far this season (one of my companions jokes that the Scottish defender must have some very incriminating photographs indeed of Roeder) and was one of the stars of the win at Old Trafford.

Another interesting facet of Roeder's interview is the fact that because of his fear of flying, Paolo Di Canio shared a six-hour car journey back to London in the manager's car after the Blackburn defeat. You wonder what effect this must have had on Roeder's mental state, although it seems he survived the experience: 'It was an interesting six hours. When I got this job some managers said to me "Di Canio is unhandleable", but I haven't found him the monster everyone told me he would be. Paolo is so passionate about football and doing well. He knows how high my standards are. What drives Paolo mad is when players' standards do not match his.'

Before the start of the Arsenal game I walk down Green Street to view the imposing edifice of the huge new Doctor Martens Stand. It almost looks like the home of a proper football club. Walking from Ken's Café to the East Stand I mention to Joe and Dan that the new Dr Martens Stand looks impressive now that the twin castles by the main entrance are in place, with the main doors fronted by four Chigwell-esque columns.

'They haven't put the mock-Tudor effect on yet then . . .' suggests Joe.

'And there's the huge pair of lions on the gates to come,' adds Dan.

The new stand is looking better from inside the ground too, the wraparound sections in the corners are almost completed and there's a gate of 34,523 today, nearly 10,000 up on the previous capacity. Kanouté is in for the rested Defoe, but otherwise it's the same side which won at Old Trafford. It's immediately apparent that Joe Cole is having another fine game in the centre of the Hammers midfield. Gone is the playground football where JC beats several players with no end result. Just as at Old Trafford he's dominating the game. There are delightful one-legged pirouettes ('someone's gonna break his leg if he keeps doing that' suggests one pessimistic fan) as he navigates his way through a crowded midfield and gets the ball out wide. Patrick Vieira clatters him for his impudence and is rightly booked, but, encouragingly, JC comes back for more.

'Cole! Cole! He's indestructible! You've got to follow your soul, Cole!' chant the Bobby Moore Stand to the tune of 'Gold'. This is surely the only recorded use of a Spandau Ballet song in football chant history and, indeed, several thousand fat blokes in claret and blue nylon shirts make unlikely New Romantics.

Only what sort of person still has Spandau Ballet records and, even worse, spends long evenings trying to adapt them into a football song? Changing the lyrics of the Pet Shop Boys' 'Go West' to 'You're shit and you know you are!' must have been relatively easy, but presumably there are fans still poring over albums by Duran Duran, Ultravox and Visage, desperately trying to invent a new song. And just imagine the nerve-wracking moment when you holler your new song at maximum volume hoping that the other fans join in. No wonder the originators of football chants keep quiet, as for every success there must be ten rewritten versions of 'To Cut A Long Story Short' that only get a four-letter word response.

ALWAYS BELIEVE IN . . . JOEY COLE!

Cole, who probably thinks Spandau Ballet is something Graeme Le Saux watches at Sadler's Wells and regards New Romantic fans in the same bemused way my generation thought of the sad old gits who still liked rock and roll, is looking much stronger this season. In the early minutes he shrugs off the nasty, tall and brutish Martin Keown to fire just wide of Taylor's far post. He even wins a tackle with Grimandi on his own dead-ball line before spraying a pass out of defence to Di Canio.

Many West Ham fans worry that being so over-hyped in his early career might result in Joey going the way of Stuart Slater, Kevin Lock, Ade Cocker, Alan Dickens and a myriad other Hammers' prodigies turned journeymen. Lock was 'the new Bobby Moore', and poor old Alan Dickens went from being 'the new Trevor Brooking' to drifting out of the game in his early 30s and becoming a London taxi driver.

Last season Michael Carrick looked a better team player than Cole, and is again helping to quietly dominate the midfield against the Gunners through his ability to play the ball short or long with either foot. Only today I'm a Cole convert too. On this form, the boy can do anything he wants to in the game. Hopefully while with West Ham.

Hutchison is continuing to play better on the right (which makes it increasingly bizarre that he left Sunderland because they played him on the right and he wanted to play in the middle) and plays a delightful through ball with the outside of his right boot to Di Canio in the area. PDC tumbles, there's a huge shout for a penalty, but referee Alan Wiley books Di Canio for diving. Paolo immediately adopts his wronged man in silent film melodrama posture, waving his arms in the air, holding his head in his hands and imploring the gods to remonstrate with these fallible mortals. Looking at the slow motion replay on *The Premiership* that night, though, it appears that Wiley might be right, although Di Canio still vehemently refutes the claim.

On 36 minutes we take the lead. There's a lovely intricate move on the right with the ball pinging from Cole to Schemmel, who nutmegs Ashley Cole and passes to Di Canio, in to Kanouté, back to Cole, out to Schemmel, on to Di Canio, whose attempted pass then bounces off an Arsenal defender into the path of Sebastien Schemmel almost on the Arsenal dead-ball line.

Matt, sitting next to me, clearly has little faith in the flying Frenchman's crossing abilities and favours letting the ball run out for a corner. He hollers: 'Don't cross it, Schemmel, you TWAT!' Only Schemmel does cross, hard and low, and Kanouté hammers the ball into the net. There's uproar around Upton Park and mass taunting of Matt from our party. Even better than a goal being scored is the chance to bait a fellow fan who gets it so abjectly wrong. Of course, we've all done it. I remember saying that 'Ian Rush isn't the player he used to be' when he played for Liverpool at Upton Park. In the same millisecond he turned and thumped a sumptuous volley into the roof of the Hammers' net.

87

Surely we can't beat both Man United and Arsenal in the same week? Erm, no, we can't. The Irons have not lost their timeless ability to concede an easy goal within minutes of scoring a good one. Pires – who, with his shambling gait, lank black hair, wispy black goatee beard and red boots which appear to be modelled on a pair of velvet slippers, looks like the sort of stereotypical French bohemian character who would be found inhabiting that group of run-down holiday chalets at the start of *Betty Blue* – begins a move on the right, switching play to Lauren on the left. Lauren crosses, Schemmel momentarily loses Ashley Cole and the Arsenal left-back equalises. There's still time for Henry to leave Dailly on his posterior (who otherwise is having another good game) and cross for Wiltord to head over before the interval.

After the break Henry continues to mesmerise with his speedy dribbles on the left and Grimandi bangs a fine chance against the Hammers bar. Cole is still challenging for every tackle with Vieira. Meanwhile, the Bobby Moore Stand amuse themselves with Desmond Morris-like theories, singing 'Keown! He's got a monkey's head!'.

A Sinclair flick from a Di Canio corner is almost headed in by Dailly. Pires is booked for diving, and then Kanu releases Bergkamp into the space vacated by his former teammate Nigel Winterburn and the Arsenal striker bangs the ball against David James's bar again. In turn, the Hammers have a penalty appeal turned down when Sinclair's flick from another Di Canio corner is clearly handballed by Vieira, whose sheepish face betrays his guilt. At the end there's still time for Don Hutchison to swipe at air in the Arsenal box and miss a good chance that would have won the game for West Ham.

Still, a draw is a fair result and, if anything, West Ham have been lucky that Arsenal hit the bar twice rather than scoring.

'I'll settle for four points from Man United and Arsenal,' I say at the final whistle.

'Course, it goes without saying that we'll lose to Leicester,' says Joe and we all concur.

'Plus they'll still be hungover from the Christmas party,' I joke. At least those days are over. This week the Woodgate and Bowyer trial has dented football's image and we can be assured that no group of players – certainly not with a sports scientist at Chadwell Heath – will be stupid enough to get bladdered at their Christmas party.

15. I'M DREAMING OF A WET CHRISTMAS

Leicester 1 West Ham 1 – 22 December 2001

'WEST HAM ANIMALS' screams the front page of the *Evening Standard* of Thursday, 20 December. Nicola has just relayed a cryptic message from Big Joe suggesting that if I buy the *Standard* I might find it interesting. Inside the newsagent I find myself laughing and shaking my head in disbelief. Like most West Ham fans I greet the story with a mixture of incredulity, enjoyment and shame. 'Star players vomit and urinate on bar in orgy of drunkenness at London nightclub Sugar Reef' adds the strap-line, helpfully placed next to the club badge.

Just a few days after the Bowyer and Woodgate trial even the most pessimistic of Irons fans didn't think the lads would be stupid enough to get bladdered and then misbehave with the nation's press waiting for any slip.

Typically, this being West Ham, the offence that has caused most outrage is suitably surreal. After the players' Christmas meal at TGI Fridays on Tuesday, 18 December, they moved on to Sugar Reef in the West End, a trendy haunt of Posh and Becks's. Here, one of the players stood up and 'urinated over the bar' in front of disbelieving customers, resulting in the whole party being thrown out of the club. According to the *Standard*'s marvellously strait-laced account, a blonde female guest had shouted, as one might, 'Oh, my God, he's weeing on the bar!'

Clearly following the club's new-found emphasis on sports science, the 18 players, who did not include wowsers Paolo Di Canio and Fredi Kanouté, had allegedly run up a bar bill of £1,800 on isotonic and vodka Red Bulls during their stay. In another incident a reserve team player had vomited over a table – all this despite the fact that West Ham had sent seven bodyguards to keep the players out of trouble.

West Ham responded to the incident by going into *Pravda*-speak. An official statement worthy of *Yes Minister*'s Sir Humphrey emerged, admitting: 'Unfortunately a minor incident occurred after the majority of players had left for home and following this incident it was decided that the party should leave the club. The team manager will deal with the player involved in the appropriate manner.'

For the first time ever, the word urination is mentioned on Ceefax as it's announced that the mystery urinator will be fined two weeks' wages by the club. Glenn Roeder ventures into sociological territory and starts to sound like one of those pensioners standing at Stratford bus station who insist that everything was much better 30 years ago. He announces: 'We live in a society where anything goes and it's sad. Footballers do have a great responsibility because of their position in society, but in society we are at an all-time low.'

The next day *The Sun* names the culprit as defender Hayden Foxe. Still, there are mitigating circumstances – well, he is Australian. At least we now know what those special talents were that encouraged Harry Redknapp to wait so long for his work permit to come through.

Glenn Roeder is understandably exasperated by his miserable wet Christmas and goes into his shocked headmaster routine, pointing out that one player has ruined the night for the other 24 and possibly threatening to haul Foxe up before the assembly every Monday morning to apologise for his wee mistake. Justifiably, he points out that he told the players to be on their guard and not get as pissed as footballers. He also sent along seven bodyguards, so there was little else the club could have done.

'You see all sorts of people in back alleys and streets tiddling up walls and it's not acceptable,' continues Roeder, using more of his strange old-world vernacular, and making most West Ham fans wonder when was the last time they heard anyone using the word 'tiddling'. This is, after all, coming from a man who once acted as Paul Gascoigne's minder. You suspect that tiddling up back alleys was probably one of Glenn's lesser worries with Gazza rampaging around Toon.

Maybe us fans shouldn't be surprised. There's been a long and infamous tradition of festive shenanigans at West Ham. Legendary lad done bad Frank McAvennie famously punched West Ham's then commercial manager Brian Blower in a row about admitting Frank and his guests to Blower's private party back in December 1989. That same year Hammers players were involved in New Year's Eve 'high-jinks' – they were shopped by the chairman of Hartlepool whose side were staying in the same hotel – on the eve of a match against Barnsley on New Year's Day 1990; an incident which may have hastened the departure of manager Lou Macari. Following Foxe's wee misdemeanour, former Hammers midfielder Mike Marsh recalled the time under Billy Bonds and Harry Redknapp's reign in 1993–94 when 'we used to run amok in Bournemouth and it was absolute mayhem. Social-wise the place was up the wall and on one Christmas party we needed two buses because one of them got wrecked on the way out.'

I'M DREAMING OF A WET CHRISTMAS

As recently as 1999 Trevor Sinclair was fined £250 for running over the roof of a car driven by beauty therapist Belinda Knowles after a boozy players' Christmas party in Romford. A wing mirror was broken and an aerial and windscreen-wiper were damaged in the incident. The players had just come out of Yates' Wine Lodge when Knowles's Mini was stopped by a 'loud and boisterous' group of men in fancy dress costumes of skin-tight sparkly body-suits and wigs. Then Tricky Trev jumped on the roof, rolled over the bonnet and lay in front of the car – and still he didn't get a penalty. Sinclair admitted criminal damage as Romford JPs heard how he had pretended to be hit by the car out of 'high spirits'. To be fair to Sinclair, he has virtually given up alcohol this season and now leads a quiet life with his family – 'I kept getting involved in silly little incidents and it was all down to the booze . . . I couldn't handle alcohol and it didn't mix with me,' he admitted to *Hammers News*. Maybe Foxey could learn from Sinc's example – or at least be given a club map of where the gents is in Sugar Reef.

After the pisser-gate incident, the game that Saturday at relegation-threatened Leicester, the last before Christmas, seems almost a distraction. West Ham emerge with a worthy point from a difficult match, maintaining a four-match unbeaten run. After trailing to a goal from Muzzy Izzet, the Hammers equalise on 70 minutes when Joe Cole is brought down in the area by Matt Elliott. Slow motion replays prove that it was a foul, but that doesn't stop the bellicose Leicester centre-half from furiously accusing Cole of diving, kicking and slapping the youngster during a 19-man flare-up and then headbutting Trevor Sinclair, who had come to Cole's aid. He is rightly red carded and after an interval of several aeons, Paolo Di Canio remains calm to score one of his poncy penalties, almost as a point of principle after his shocking failure against Aston Villa, chipping the ball into the centre of goal after Ian Walker has dived, and then, bizarrely, breaking into tears. His aunt has just died and Paolo has dedicated the goal to her. Cole is then singled out for some Room 101 treatment by Robbie Savage and Dennis Wise but manages to survive it all with some maturity.

In the post-match interviews more glimpses into Roeder's home life emerge; it seems he's too busy worrying about tiddling up alleys and declining moral standards to watch *EastEnders*. This must be the only man in Britain who doesn't know who Nick Cotton is. 'My wife tells me there's a nasty character in *EastEnders* called Nick Cotton. I don't know because I've not seen it myself, but Joe must have felt like him when he walked off with all the abuse he was getting.'

Hayden Foxe finally speaks about the Christmas party incident too. The cultured centre-back explains: 'I wouldn't go as far as saying that I was pissing at the bar in front of a thousand people. It was a discreet little quiet one.' Right, so that's all right then.

Just before Christmas he admits his embarrassment on the club's website.

'What I did was wrong and got blown out of proportion as if it were a huge, huge event. You do have a few drinks at the Christmas party – and I'm not saying that to promote drinking – but it was a case of the lads enjoying themselves. Some people are taking it light-heartedly and some are taking it the other way. I can't turn back the clock even though it's something I'm definitely not proud of. I apologised to the club and the players and, of course, it embarrassed my family because it got back to Australia as well.'

Hmm. Maybe Hayden wasn't so out of order after all. As one of my Chelsea-supporting friends put it: 'Weeing on the bar, isn't that considered to be a tip in Australia?'

WEST HAM BAD BOY XI

FRANK McAVENNIE: Admitted taking cocaine while a West Ham player and wishes a sub-*Neighbours* haircut, friendship with Peter Stringfellow and mock-Tudor mansion with page three lovely to be taken into consideration.

JOHN HARTSON: Attempted to play football with Eyal Berkovic's head during a training session, filmed by Sky cameras. Was fined and apologised for the incident. Also fined in court for using a plant pot as a football after a drinking session in Swansea.

HAYDEN FOXE: Same old Hayden – taking the piss. Failed to find the gents in Sugar Reef, urinated over the bar and became a Hammers bad boy legend.

THE BLACKPOOL FOUR: On the eve of an FA Cup tie at Blackpool in 1970, Bobby Moore, Jimmy Greaves, Brian Dear and the teetotal Clyde Best ignored a club curfew and went out to a nightclub for a lager or two. Moore and Greaves played for West Ham the next day with Dear as sub and they lost 4–0. Moore, Greaves and Dear were all suspended for two weeks and fined a week's wages by Greenwood.

TREVOR SINCLAIR: Fined £250 for damaging beauty therapist Belinda Knowles's car, after pretending to be hit and rolling over the bonnet, following a boozy players' Christmas party in Romford. And all while wearing a wig and fancy dress costume.

IAN WRIGHT: Responded to being sent off at home to Leeds with admirable equanimity. Wrighty stormed into the referee's dressing-room and smashed it up.

KEITH ROBSON: Manager Ron Greenwood had to go to court to plead for the wayward winger not to be jailed for driving the wrong way down a one-way street in a teammate's car while banned for drink-driving, claiming that he needed him to help West Ham's relegation fight. Robson was so crazy that even Trevor Brooking referred to him as 'Mad Robbo'.

JULIAN DICKS: Numerous red cards and not one of the club's greatest trainers. Admits several training ground walk-outs and telling Billy Bonds to 'eff off'. Bonds confessed: 'There were times we could have come to blows. I would love to have chinned him a couple of times and he would have loved to have chinned me.'

DON HUTCHISON: Admits late-night drinking sessions while in his first spell at the Hammers and thinking he was 'invincible'. Hid his wedding tackle behind a Budweiser label while at Liverpool and once had a plate of sandwiches thrown at him at half-time by Harry Redknapp for not tracking back.

TED MacDOUGALL: Fingered by Billy Bonds in his autobiography for being rude to waiters. He 'carried on as if waiters, receptionists and the like were just menial workers instead of ordinary, decent people doing a job'.

16. STAYING UP WITH THE CHRISTMAS DECORATIONS

West Ham 4 Derby 0 - 26 December 2001
West Ham 1 Liverpool 1 - 29 December 2001

Christmas Day Ceefax boasts news of the Queen's response to the terrorist outrages of 11 September and details of the bush fires sweeping Australia. Another item, perhaps less significant on the scale of global politics, reads: 'Foxe apologises over incident.' The Hammers defender is quoted in the Boxing Day red tops saying how much he regrets urinating over the bar at Sugar Reef. Perhaps they should have utilised his talents to help put out all those bush fires back in Oz.

On Boxing Day the Hammers play Derby at Upton Park in a noon kick-off. Everyone is half awake and there's a slightly unreal, hungover air to the proceedings. Jeremy Nicholas tries to ferment enthusiasm for 'Deadly Don Hutchison!', 'Tomas The Hit Man Repka!', 'Fredi The King Kanouté!', 'Paoooolo Di Caniiiio!' and, presumably, our secret weapon on the bench, 'Hayden The Urinator Foxe!'.

Dan has placed a bet on West Ham winning 4–1, having won £50 last year on Boxing Day when we walloped Charlton 5–0. Mind you, maybe after the Tuesday night Christmas party they really celebrated yesterday.

The programme contains a seasonal feature by the club chaplain Elwin Cockett in which my old pal Steve 'North Bank Norman' reminisces about a terrible trip to Spurs for an epic Boxing Day defeat. My personal low was attending an abysmal 0–2 home capitulation to Orient on Boxing Day. But for Steve it was driving a group of friends to see West Ham play at Spurs. First he discovered that he'd forgotten everyone's tickets, so they had to pay twice to get in. They arrived in the ground 25 minutes after kick-off when it was already 1–0 to Spurs. The Hammers went on to lose 5–0. 'I can't even remember if we stayed for the fifth, but angry, cold and in my case skint, we left for home with about 25 minutes remaining. In total I saw about 40 minutes and it cost me about £170!'

Things have improved in recent seasons, but this is the fixture that brings habitual seasonal dread to Irons fans – with the accompanying fear that we will, as the cliché goes, come down with the Christmas decorations.

With numerous of our number visiting friends and family around the country our seats are occupied by all sorts of friends of friends. 'Don't worry, this will go straight into the wall, we never score from these,' I announce knowingly to the two female footballing virgins sitting next to me as West Ham gain an early free-kick. We immediately score, even if the shot is, as I predicted, straight into the wall. Don Hutchison's effort is strong enough to go through the defenders on duty and be bundled in by Sebastien Schemmel for his first ever goal for the Hammers. No one deserves it more. He might get caught out occasionally at the back but his sheer energy has won over the Hammers fans and Seb has been one of the players of the season so far.

For the rest of the half we see a series of delightful back-heels and one-twos from the likes of Cole, Hutchison and Kanouté, and some sublime aerial flicks by Paolo, but little impact on the Derby goal. Di Canio has a shot beaten away and Carbone goes close for Derby and that's about it.

Finally we get the second after 73 minutes. A Derby defender on the edge of the box allows the ball to squirm to Di Canio, who scores in emphatic style. It's a moment of class reminiscent of his peak form two seasons ago. Another one for his aunt presumably, but this time there are no tears.

On a desperately chilly afternoon the second half is enlivened when Carbone is sent off for going in high on Repka, having been booked in the first half for diving. Carbone accuses Repka of diving.

'Fuck off, you black bastard – get back to the jungle!' shouts a staggeringly unoriginal racist a few rows back as County's Darryl Powell joins in the argument over Carbone's sending-off. Clearly, bigots don't have Christmas off, but it's always profoundly depressing to hear that sort of thing, even if there is much less of it than ten years ago. At least it's now a shock to hear such comments, which must be a sign the club is making progress. The last time I looked, James, Kanouté, Sinclair and Defoe were all, ahem, black, but this seems a point somewhat lost upon the, mercifully few, racist idiots left at Upton Park.

Meanwhile Carbone is going mental. The tiny Italian appears to want to fight Hit Man Repka and is finally led off by his old Sheffield Wednesday teammate Paolo Di Canio, arms around his neck, perhaps whispering his patented recipe for tiramisu into the irate Carbone's lughole. Strewth. What demons must rage within Carbone's head if PDC is a calming influence?

Hayden Foxe spends much of the second half jogging up and down the touchline. I'm reminded of that line from Ian Dury's Blockheads: 'Imagine one of 'em pissing in your swimming pool!'. Maybe this is the ultimate Roeder tactical threat – send on Foxe to piss all over the County defence. He never actually gets on but the psychological damage can be seen.

Kanouté goes close a couple of times and then in the 86th minute Sinclair scissor-kicks a glorious third – completely out of context with such a tepid game, its execution is reminiscent of the wonder goal Paolo Di Canio scored against Wimbledon two seasons ago. A Di Canio short corner from the right reaches Joe Cole, who volleys in a cross to Sinclair who scissor-kicks the ball into the far corner. The ball hasn't touched the ground in the whole move. 'You've just seen the goal of the month scored by Trevor Sinclair!' announces the never knowingly under-excited Jeremy Nicholas. Now just stay with us, Trevor.

Derby really start to crumble and have the look of relegation all over them. Ravenelli looks grey, overweight and dispirited, while the rest of the side struggle to get to know each other with Christie strangely left on the bench. Defoe goes close before Cole plays him in and he's one of those players where you know he just won't miss, as he cleverly toe pokes the ball home. That injury-time goal has made it 4–0, which has a very nice feel to it. Four–nil to the Hammers and the excuse for a few 'Boxing Day roasting' puns.

Jeremy Nicholas goes into overdrive: 'Ladies and gentlemen, we go above Charlton! We go above Everton! We're TENTH!' For a giddy three hours we are in the top half of the table, at least until the afternoon fixtures when we slip back to eleventh. Who knows what would happen to Nicholas if we ever made it up to an Intertoto spot. He'd probably spontaneously combust over his turntable and some poor Hammerette would just find a smoking trainer to remember him by.

Three days and several more Christmas hangovers later there's another home match against Liverpool, the last of 2001, and there's danger of optimism breaking out at Upton Park.

Paolo Di Canio is suspended, replaced by Defoe, and against last year's treble winners we play our best football of the season. Admittedly Liverpool have opted to keep Gerrard and Owen (ominously needing just one goal to score his 100th for Liverpool) on the bench, but it's still a quality line-up. Just as the first half against Aston Villa was one of those games where everything goes wrong, the game here is one to please Dr Pangloss, all is for the best in the best of all possible worlds, as an exhilarating West Ham display has the Liverpool players contemplating the thought that, as the song says, they might soon be signing on with hope in their hearts.

It's a solid team performance. Carrick is neat and Cole inspired in midfield, with Cole showing his tricks but also knowing when to play the simple ball. Sinclair is in rampaging form on the left, Kanouté and Defoe are effervescent up front. Perhaps without Di Canio's dominating influence the side are able to play a quicker game. West Ham are playing the sort of sharp, incisive two-touch passing football, all within the traditional 4–4–2 framework, which would have graced the best sides of Ron Greenwood and John Lyall. The crowd sense this and loud refrains of 'Bubbles' echo around the sold-out stadium.

'Watch Dudek, he's the best goalkeeper in the Premiership, he'll be as good as Schmeichel,' suggests Denis, here for a rare Saturday game while on leave from work. He proves a shrewd judge, as Dudek generally performs in the manner of a man wearing underpants outside his trousers.

Dudek makes a fine save from Hutchison's header, then another good stop after Defoe manages to roll away from Henchoz. Liverpool's only real chance falls to the rusty Nicolas Anelka, let in by Repka's missed clearance. The former Gunner twice fails to score as James makes an excellent double save.

On 38 minutes West Ham take the lead. Defoe makes a spirited run down the left, and from Henchoz's block, Sinclair crisply fires home from 20 yards out for his second goal in successive games. The lads then do a weird clucking chickens goal celebration routine, probably hoping to become a question on *They Think It's All Over*. Liverpool are being overrun, although you have to admire the quality of defensive blocks from Carragher, Henchoz, Hyypia and Riise – the Merseysiders have a title-winning back four. Defoe fires just wide after Sinclair leaves Carragher on his posterior and it's been a mightily encouraging first half.

At half-time Denis and myself mention that even Steve Rapport, over from San Francisco, won't have anything to moan about at this rate. The gents in the Upper East Stand is flooded and one fan, tentatively stepping over a sodden floor, exclaims: 'Blimey, Hayden Foxe has been in here!' Then a minute later someone else makes exactly the same joke. Hayden, you're now an Upton Park legend.

The second half continues with West Ham still dominating, although the introduction of Gerrard has stiffened Liverpool's midfield. Cole takes the ball off the better-placed Defoe's foot and shoots wide after Kanouté's fine cross. Kanouté crosses from the right again and as the ball is half-headed out Sinclair produces another spectacular overhead kick which is somehow pawed over by the perspiring Pool custodian. 'Sign on, sign on with hope in your heart . . .' taunt the Bobby Moore Stand. Dudek pushes the ball wide again from Carrick's long-range shot. There's a sublime move where Hutchison back-heels to Sinclair who crosses for Defoe to shoot and Dudek to claw away for yet another corner. Unless this is some kind of parallel universe, on this form we can take on absolutely anyone at Upton Park.

Caretaker gaffer Phil Thompson, who possesses less a Roman nose and more of a colosseum of a conk, is at the edge of his technical area and is clearly a very worried man as he brings on Michael Owen after an hour. 'Sit Down Pinocchio!' chants the Bobby Moore Stand, followed by 'You've got Pinocchio, we've got Jermain Defoe!'.

More Cole trickery wins a free-kick, which Hutch, having a fine game against his former employers, runs up to take. 'If he scores this I'll kiss you!' suggests Denis. Mercifully Hutchison's quick effort is turned round the post by Dudek yet again.

Liverpool have brought on Litmanen and are throwing four strikers at the Hammers rearguard. Litmanen shoots but James makes another good stop from his swerving shot. We're surely going to hold on for a great victory and people will then realise that Glenn Roeder really has turned the club around. Only then, on 88 minutes Jari Litmanen crosses, the ball is caught between Winterburn and Heskey's chests, there appears to be an inadvertent joint handball, Heskey pokes it back to the waiting Owen and he flashes a fierce drive into the roof of the net. Somehow you just knew he'd get his hundredth goal against us. Owen runs to the Liverpool bench. David James kicks his post in frustration. We've had eight good chances and only gained a draw.

But as the final whistle blows the Upton Park fans remember the quality of the performance and stand up to cheer off Glenn's glorious gladiators. The last performance of 2001 has been the best and this glimpse of the future gives everyone hope.

'It says a lot about us that they had four international strikers and only broke us down right at the end. There's a certain way you have to play football at West Ham and we are carrying on that tradition. We've got great team spirit and a good young team,' says a satisfied Roeder in a post-match interview.

Rightly he dwells on the form of Carrick and Cole. 'A lot of people said you can't risk Joe in a two-man midfield, but he is proving them wrong. I don't think Joe Cole has ever played better in a West Ham shirt than in the past five weeks since he came back from injury. I think he and Michael will end up true internationals, a stage where football can be a game of chess. They see the pictures. International football is often about one- and two-touch and that is Michael's forté.'

Now, as West Ham approach 2002, all we have to do is hold on to them.

17. NORTH BANK NORMAN RETURNS

If Paolo Di Canio was a West Ham fan he'd be Steve Rapport, aka North Bank Norman. Indeed now Paolo has shaved his head he looks not dissimilar to Rapport, who long ago tore out his hair on the Chicken Run watching David Kelly and Mike Small wandering offside. Like Paolo, Rapport is a perfectionist, and demonstrates similar impatience with various inept West Ham performers who do not share his dedication to the club.

Steve was famed among West Ham fans as North Bank Norman, editor of the passionate, award-winning West Ham fanzine that ran from February 1989 until May 1992. His bald cranium, black leather jacket and howls of exasperation were part of the fixtures and fittings of the old Chicken Run. After the fiasco of the board's Hammers Bond scheme and the relegation of 'the worst West Ham side ever', he could take no more, decided that 'you can't be funny about something that's breaking your heart' and emigrated to San Francisco, where he hoped to join a Mitchell Thomas Phobics support group. The Chicken Run was a much quieter place after his departure, and as his sister Hannah later pointed out, it was odd how the referees suddenly seemed much better when you were no longer standing beside Steve.

Only his addiction has proved beyond even Californian self-help groups. Born in Stepney in 1956, his life has changed greatly over the years, from being a law student at Warwick University, to a successful career as a music photographer, then a web innovator in the US and now another change of direction, he is the owner of the Hwa Rang Kwan Martial Arts Center in San Francisco, where he teaches tae kwon do and kick boxing. He's been married and separated and invariably taken new girlfriends to Upton Park – surely the ultimate test of their devotion.

For Steve is still unable to quite quit the Hammers. He's the co-moderator of an Internet West Ham fans' discussion group (hammers@ironworks.com) and consequently knows more about the intricacies of West Ham than most of us in England. This is a man who listens to games on-line and has been known to drive a car with a 'WHU' number plate around America's highways. Twice a season he returns to London to visit his mum and bases his visits around West Ham fixtures. He comes back all Californian and relaxed and invariably returns needing counselling. Not that he's a jinx . . .

'I told you I wasn't a jinx, it's a myth! We've beaten Derby 4–0 and we should have beaten Liverpool, I mean how many chances did we have?' exclaims Steve, as Dirty Den and myself join him in Ken's Café. 'What is it about West Ham and last-minute goals?'

Then, like the born-again Californian he now is, he gives us both a big hug. 'No, no, we don't do that here, we're English,' I tell him as he embraces both Denis and myself. 'Carol's thrown people out for much less, you silly hugger.' We nurse our disappointment at conceding a late equaliser over cups of strong tea and toasted cheese sarnies.

One of the few consolations of West Ham losing 7–1 at Blackburn was the thought of the comic possibilities of Steve reaching meltdown and causing another Three Mile Island-like panic in the States. His walk-outs at games are legendary (while 4–0 down at half-time at Highbury and while losing 5–1 at Anfield are two I'll always remember). So what was his reaction to the Blackburn débâcle? As ever, the artist formerly known as North Bank Norman is not short of opinions.

'Charlton was even worse than Blackburn!' he claims. 'I had the misfortune of watching both games at home on my 61-in. monster Hitachi TV, from the comfort of my Charles Eames black leather recliner, in my front room in sunny San Francisco. In the Charlton game I witnessed the worst defending from any football team I have ever seen, anywhere in the world, at any time in my 40-odd years of watching and playing football!

'And if we view the Blackburn game as simply a 90-minute exercise in ineptitude, then we can conclude that, at the end of 90 minutes, West Ham were indeed sufficiently inept to no longer need the exercise. I was so angry that I kept channel-surfing, and every time I turned back to the game, Blackburn immediately scored again. Of course, I missed the West Ham goal, which was just as well, 'cos it would only have made me even more angry. I mean, why bother scoring?'

Nor is Steve happy to hear the rumours in some papers that Paolo might be joining Man United, as it would invalidate his PDC screen-saver. He's reserving judgement on Roeder but believes that the time was right for Redknapp to depart. 'If being a diamond geezer wiv a cockerney accent and outlandish views on les continentals were the sole criteria for holding down the job of manager of West Ham, then 'Arry Boy could have been awarded the post for life. But let's be honest, Harry was way out of his depth as a Premiership manager. He probably thinks that tac-tics are those cute little mints that come in plastic boxes.'

After high tea at Ken's we take the bus to Manor Park, where we're all invited round to Steve's mum's for sandwiches. The Rapport family are there en masse and like Steve are all West Ham obsessives. There's Steve's sister, his cousin and Steve's mum, who despite her mature years is eulogising about Paolo Di Canio's autobiography. (What must she make of all those 'ugly penis face' comments?)

Steve's super-hospitable mum thrusts cups of tea, cheese sandwiches and quiche at Denis and myself as we carry on in the fashion of our *Fortune's Always Hiding* editorial meetings of the late 1980s, discussing West Ham trivia and pretending it's work. Steve is telling us that they sing 'I'm Forever Blowing Bubbles' in *The Sopranos* and that John Cleese is a closet West Ham fan and that's why there are all those Hammers references in Monty Python ('Karl Marx: The Hammers, the Hammers is the nickname of which English football club?'). Oh, and so is J.K. Rowling. Then Steve is on to *EastEnders*' actors Todd Carty and Nick Berry, who both support West Ham and grew up on his manor of Manor Park, as did Mike Read and Michelle Collins.

Free association abounds as Steve's sister starts to wonder what a certain striker's wife was doing with a knife by the bedside table, Steve reminisces about playing truant to watch West Ham play Hereford in a daytime FA Cup tie during the three-day week, Denis remembers Frank McAvennie's finest right hook (that's on the pitch) and we recall watching West Ham play Real Castilla in an empty stadium (Upton Park was closed as a penalty for crowd trouble in Spain) on the telly in 1981. Then, for some reason, we start selecting the worst ever West Ham side.

After an hour or so of this I remember that I wanted to ask Steve some serious questions, like, are you Paolo Di Canio in disguise?

'Yes. But it's not a very good disguise, and right-wing henchmen with thick Italian accents keep accosting me every time I go to North Beach, imploring me to come back to Roma and finish what I started. But I don't know what they mean . . .'

Does he still fret about the 'Burnley-isation' of West Ham?

'Yes, I worry about us ending up playing in claret and blue. Oh, wait. D'oh! Too late!'

Should we have sold Rio and Frank?

'We certainly shouldn't have sold Rio. Am I the only person who thinks that his replacement, Mr Repka, is a liability? Every time I read a description of a goal that we have conceded, it begins with the words "following a mistake by Tomas Repka . . ." As for Fat Frank, or EMMA as we call him (England Midfielder My Arse!), he can stick his blue flag up whatever orifice is most convenient . . .'

Time has mellowed Rapport a little though. He does admit that the board's obsession with being solvent might have some merit. 'The deeper in debt the big wads at the fashionable West London boutique Chelsea's of Chelsea (as the *Grauniad* likes to call them) get, the more I think that being a bunch of unambitious tight-wads has some long-term merit.'

And with that we go back to discussing Steve Potts's only ever goal for West

103

Ham (in the 7–1 thrashing of Hull City) and the time a great TV career nearly never happened. Our *Fortune's Always Hiding* cartoonist, then just Porky but now known as Phill Jupitus, almost expired running to the Norwich ground as we arrived 20 minutes late for a League Cup tie to find West Ham 2–0 down. (Every game Steve ever attended seemed to involve roadworks, gridlock, failed bids for parking spots and frantic dashes to away grounds.) Happy days. Phill was a great cartoonist, but sadly his career was all downhill after *Fortune's Always Hiding* folded.

Eventually, Denis and myself leave, kissing Steve's mum goodbye and receiving more Californian hugs from the man himself. We wish Steve a good flight in the morning and wonder if it's safe for a martial arts instructor to maintain this level of commitment to West Ham.

'Maybe it's best for everyone that I now live 6,000 miles from Upton Park, as I am a dangerous and highly trained warrior, able to kill a man by merely touching him with my death hand,' he reveals to his stunned Luke Skywalker-like pupils. 'How safe would Tomas Repka and Arfur Dailly have been, had I been in the vicinity of Ewood Park or The Valley?'

Yes, it's probably better that he maintains his distance from an environment that might produce memories of Trevor Morley and Sandy Clark and Derek Hales flashbacks. We leave Steve Rapport to return to his on-line Hammers Addiction Anonymous classes in that part of San Francisco which is forever blowing bubbles.

18. DON'T GO PAOLO

Leeds United 3 West Ham 0 – 1 January 2002

The New Year begins with the obligatory thrashing at Leeds. Mercifully, the lads don't mess about waiting until just before half-time to concede a soft goal or two. On a freezing, snowbound Yorkshire night, we get our ineptitude in first. West Ham are two goals down after seven minutes, thus ending all hope of extending our six-game unbeaten run.

After four minutes Smith runs clear of Winterburn and crosses from the right, Dailly and Repka (wearing a bizarre combination of gloves and short-sleeved shirt) feebly try to play offside and the unmarked Viduka fires past James first time. Three minutes later Danny Mills intercepts Winterburn's intended pass to Sinclair, shoots past the left-back and crosses for Viduka to just beat Repka to the ball and score with a classic diving header.

At least West Ham show some character by coming back into it for the rest of the first half, despite the absence of the injured Michael Carrick. A Repka header goes close, but after the rejuvenated Robbie Fowler chips a great third goal it's David James against the Leeds attack. At least the preposterously peroxide custodian – whose barnet is reminiscent of Poly Styrene of X-Ray Spex – has enhanced his World Cup prospects in front of the watching Sven-Goran Eriksson.

More worrying than the defeat is the absence of Paolo Di Canio. He was suspended for the Liverpool game and now apparently has a seasonal hamstring strain. Much has been written – most of it unfairly – about his penchant for missing away games, but this unhinted of absence seems more suspicious in view of recent newspaper headlines.

On the morning of the Leicester game the *Daily Express* ran a back-page banner headline 'Di Canio off to Man United' story, and claimed 'the player had told Ferguson he is desperate to leave Upton Park' and that Ferguson had 'informed Di Canio's advisers that he would pay any transfer fee necessary to prise the wayward star away from London'.

After Di Canio's tearful dedication of his penalty to his late aunt at Leicester the story seemed to be yet more fruitless tabloid speculation. But in the Boxing Day edition of the *Express* the story emerged again, claiming that Di Canio was a step closer to moving and this time putting the emphasis for the move on West Ham, claiming that Glenn Roeder was dissatisfied with his strike rate (only three goals in open play after that day's goal against Derby). It was repeated again on 29 December, with the claim that Di Canio 'begged to be allowed to leave when he learned of United's interest'. Importantly, if he signs before 19 January, he is eligible to play for United in the European Champions League.

After the Leeds game the Thursday edition of *The Sun* proclaims a 'Sunsport exclusive' (ahem) that 'United land £3m Di Canio' and claims that Di Canio's absence from the side at Leeds was not due to his hamstring injury but because he no longer wanted to play for West Ham.

It's depressing news as Di Canio is certainly the most skilful player to be seen at Upton Park since Trevor Brooking (and, let's face it, Trev was not exactly Mr Flamboyance) and is possibly our greatest player ever. But like most West Ham fans, I understand why Di Canio will be tempted by United's offer. He is 33 and a half and this is his last chance to win a possible Championship, Cup or European Champions League medal with a legendary side. I've often said to Man United supporters that if Di Canio was appearing at a stage like Old Trafford he'd be the next Eric Cantona.

Of course, he has come up with numerous quotes about how he will stay at the club for the rest of his career and how 'my West Ham shirt is like a second skin'. (Presumably the United shirt will be his first skin.) But then he probably never thought it likely that Fergie would come in for him. The manager who signed him has been sacked and Ferdinand and Lampard have departed. We have Titi Camara and Gary Charles in reserve, United have Giggs and Beckham on the bench. When push comes to shove, as it did with Paul Alcock, Di Canio has provided fabulous value for £1.5 million and numerous unforgettable memories for anyone who has ever seen him play in a West Ham shirt.

By Friday the story is in the broadsheets, giving it worrying credence. Glenn Roeder tries to wish the situation away by declaring himself 'in the dark', and rather disingenuously states: 'We are not in contact with Manchester United. I have a good relationship with Paolo but have not found it necessary to speak to him about it, nor has he spoken to me on the matter.' Right, so the fans' idol and your star player is rumoured to be joining Manchester United and you don't mention it to him while sharing a cup of isotonic Rosie Lea at Chadwell Heath.

There might have been no contact between the clubs, but it seems Paolo's Florence-based agent Matteo Roggi has been in touch with Old Trafford. 'Manchester United are involved in negotiations with West Ham and something will probably happen,' he tells the Friday *Guardian*, before adding, apparently oblivious to the homoerotic tones: 'Mr Ferguson has always been a Paolo Di Canio lover and people might think there is a vacancy because United have allowed Andy Cole to leave.'

Interestingly, one of the subscribers to the West Ham Internet discussion group – hammers@ironworks.com – is less impressed by the role of agents and suggests they are 'another breed who should be put up against a wall – after Hayden Foxe has had a skinful'.

By Saturday Roeder is backtracking and admitting the lure of Old Trafford: 'Manchester United are the one club where it's difficult to convince a player he shouldn't go, whether it's a teenager or someone in his 30s like Paolo. Put yourself in his boots or if you had a son in the same position. They are arguably the biggest club in the world.'

Surprisingly enough, Di Canio has a cold for the tricky FA Cup trip to Macclesfield on Sunday, 6 January, which conveniently means he won't be cup-tied should he leave. That night Roeder admits that the club did receive a faxed bid from Man United on Friday night – the first official approach – which was turned down. At least the club seems determined not to give Paolo away. It's thought United have offered £2 million and West Ham are holding out for £3.5 million.

Roeder is reported to be 'furious' – perhaps even angry enough to unfold his arms – with the way United are conducting themselves and declares: 'It's now up to people to ask Manchester United what the next step will be. I want this matter laid to rest one way or the other. Hopefully when this happens we will still have Paolo at West Ham.' He adds: 'I expect him to be fit to play against Leicester on Saturday,' not making it clear if this is a statement or a threat.

Di Canio is uncharacteristically silent. ('At the moment there is just nothing to talk about. When the time is right I will speak but only on my website and on television, so that my words cannot be twisted.') Although on the icons.com website he is able to lambast a *Sunday People* reporter in typically idiosyncratic style. The hack has rehashed old quotes about David Beckham into an 'I can't wait to join Man United' piece.

He fumes: 'I feel sorry for reporters that invent and recreate old comments to sell their newspapers. They have no real value of life and must be very lonely people without any real friends. I think they must have brains the size of a pea. When the truth does come out they will be made to look foolish.'

It seems Paolo is starting to hate journalists as much as Sir Alex Ferguson, who is currently refusing to talk to anyone other than MUTV. They'll surely get on well. As for the *Daily Star* columnist who suggested that when Di Canio kissed the West Ham badge it was false and that the next time he saw a player kiss his badge he'd be physically sick, Di Canio announced himself 'disgusted' and continued:

WEST HAM

'I've always been loyal to West Ham United and love the club and its fantastic supporters. That's why I kiss the badge and whether I play for West Ham, Manchester United or Macclesfield I will always kiss the badge because I love my job wherever I play and will always respect the people who believe in me. This reporter should go and buy a lot of sickness medicine because I will not change this. Even if I was to leave the club, that would not change my passion . . . It's like suggesting that if you're married and then get divorced, that you never loved in the first place.'

It's all starting to resemble an episode of *The Prisoner*. Glenn is the new number one, Di Canio may be the new number ten or indeed the old number ten, no one is sure, and no one knows who the new number one or two will be at Old Trafford. One day Di Canio will feel gas seeping through the door of his Chingford home and wake up in the Village surrounded by inanely smiling people from Surrey in red shirts. It would be no surprise to see Paolo being chased along the beaches of Portmeirion by a giant bubble.

Number 10: 'What do you want?'

Number 2: 'We want information.'

Number 10: 'You won't get it! You will twist my words, you think can push me around, you want to see me leave the Village . . .'

Number 2: 'You number 10, are unmutual.'

Number 10: 'I will not be stamped, filed, indexed, briefed, debriefed or numbered! I will take all your penalties, corners and free-kicks and you will love me. My life is my own! I will not resign!'

Among the fans, opinion is split as to whether the club is secretly grateful to unload the 33-year-old Di Canio for a good price and is playing a clever PR game, or if Paolo has simply succumbed to the lure of the Mancs. Above all, it seems to be forgotten that Di Canio is under contract and according to Premiership regulations clubs are not allowed to approach or 'tap up' other team's players.

The day after the Macclesfield win Di Canio is photographed arriving at training in Greta Garbo style, wearing shades, a sheepskin coat and a huge orange hat and scarf. The combination of Di Canio's sartorial skills with Becks's sarongs and Al Capone suits makes me think that perhaps Paolo and United deserve each other. After the events of the last week most fans are simply left to wonder if Savo Milosevic really is being lined up as a replacement or whether Di Canio's fellow Italian Machiavelli is being drafted in.

I reflect that it's just over a year since Paolo scored the winning goal in West Ham's epic FA Cup third-round victory over Man United at Old Trafford, calmly slotting the ball past Man United's taxi-hailing keeper Fabien Barthez. Before the game Di Canio declared that: 'I want the West Ham fans to know that before I finish my career we are going to win something, otherwise I'll kill myself.' If his on/off transfer saga goes on much longer many Hammers fans may indeed expect him to dive on his sword.

19. THREE-NIL IN YOUR CUP FINAL!

Macclesfield Town 0 West Ham 3 – 6 January 2002

'KEEEEEEEEN! FOR FUCK SAKE PUT 'IM UNDER!! PUT 'IM FUCKING UNDER!!!!!!! CLOSE 'IM DARN! CLOSE 'IM FUCKING DARN! OI! KEEN! YOU GET OVER HERE!!! HOLD THE FUCKING LINE!!!! HOLD THE FUKKING LINE!!!!!'

My memories of Kevin Keen are indelibly linked to a bombastic red-faced character called Lino who used to stand on the Chicken Run. Back in the late '80s he was a Harry Enfield-esque character who would arrive at each game wearing an immaculate suit and then proceed to holler all manner of obscene abuse at anyone who ventured near the touchline. Lino was the best manager West Ham never had and now sits in the Lower East Stand, where those around him refer deferentially to him as 'Coach'.

Linesmen were a particular bête noir and led to Lino's monicker; every game he would exclaim in the manner of Harry Enfield's Frank: 'Oi!!! Lino!!!! No!!!!!! That was never fucking offside!!!' Even policemen would suffer, with one PC looking at the crowd being informed: 'Turn round, you get paid for watching it!'

But it was Kevin Keen, playing on the right wing, who was the favoured target. You could see the 12-year-old Keen (at least that's how old he looked) trying to sneak infield, only to be upbraided with a cry of 'Oi!!!! Keeeen! Get over here on the fucking wing! Put 'im under! Put 'im fucking under!!!!' Keeny would then shuffle back to the right wing, again in worrying proximity to his red-faced Nemesis.

And now, like the ghost of Christmas past, Kevin Keen has returned to haunt my dreams. Yes, Keen is playing for West Ham's third-round FA Cup opponents, Macclesfield Town. I can still picture the young Kevin Keen racing down the wing, slicing the ball and falling over in front of the Chicken Run. Still, Keen was always a trier. He played for West Ham during nine of our worst years, from 1984 to 1993, and, although never quite Premiership class, he was a good division one player and, indeed, during the promotion year of 1992–93 he was possibly West Ham's best player.

Typically though, West Ham lost Kevin Keen through a lack of ambition. Before the Macclesfield tie, the 34-year-old Keen revealed that 'leaving West Ham was a horrible, horrible decision. I loved the club but I had just had my best season and felt the contract they offered me was a massive kick in the teeth. I was in the office with Billy Bonds and was nearly in tears when I said I was going to Wolves.' Such a story will be familiar to many fans – the club was not even ambitious enough to keep Kevin Keen.

The trip to third division Macclesfield is, of course, the stuff of cup nightmares. If there was a real upset West Ham might win. In the past 30-odd years the Irons have suffered metal fatigue against the lower orders, losing to Hereford, Newport, Wrexham (home and away), Torquay, Grimsby, Swansea and Tranmere. Not to mention League Cup defeats to the likes of Stockport, Northampton and Reading. Even Farnborough took us to a replay and Emley Town very nearly won at Upton Park.

My pal Mike spoke for many of us when he voiced his fears in a phone conversation a few days earlier: 'I can just see it. David James in some silly woolly hat, with the sun streaming into his eyes as the players chase the ball into the frozen corner of the pitch and ball comes over, James flaps, they score and we lose 1–0.'

Thanks to the 1 p.m. kick-off time, changed to suit the BBC's cameras, Denis, Matt, Fraser and myself leave Denis's West Hampstead flat at 9 a.m. on a Sunday morning. Big Joe has obtained a West Ham-style injury – he slipped on some ice and broke his leg while venturing out on Boxing Day morning to pick up a paper. What do four sad men discuss while driving a hired VW Golf to Macclesfield? Football trivia of course.

First there's current affairs: West Ham may sign Trabant (or is it Labant?) from Sparta Prague because he goes forever, while Matt says that he read Glenn now thinks he's made it as a manager as he can successfully lie about injuries. Then it's the transfer exodus. 'What do we get for Di Canio, we got a stand for Ferdinand,' is one comment. 'We get a jacuzzi if we sell Joe Cole,' interjects Matt.

Denis, an avid Celtic as well as Hammers fan, sparks off a contest to name 11 players who have played for both clubs. We get to Paolo Di Canio, Frank McAvennie, Stuart Slater, Marc Rieper, and Eyal Berkovic before descending into the mists of Celtic folklore and the useless information supposed to fire our imaginations that Tommy McQueen came from Aberdeen, Sandy Clark from Hearts and Neil Orr from, erm, we can't quite remember. Then Denis suggests we count the number of ex-West Ham players who will be in the World Cup and we can name Foe, Song, Wanchope, Suker, Ferdinand and maybe Lampard. Then Denis asks what's the most obscure place any of us has seen a football match. Matt wins easily, with his proud boast of having been to Yate Town to see Bristol Rovers Reserves play West Ham Reserves

The groundhopping aspect of the trip appeals to us all. None of us is ever likely to visit Macclesfield again and, even better, our fellow season ticket holder Nigel, a man who has almost completed the set of visiting all the Premiership and Football League grounds, can't go. As a political correspondent for a national newspaper, he has been assigned to Bombay to report on Tony Blair's visit. 'He was actually hoping that nuclear war breaks out between India and Pakistan, so the trip would be cancelled,' jokes Matt. We consider holding up a 'Nigel Part-Timer' banner for the live TV cameras just to irritate him further.

Throughout the journey, Matt's Macclesfield-supporting mate is texting messages about the state of the pitch, which we find even sadder than our own ruminations. Still, there can't be much else to do up there. Half an hour before kick-off Nigel rings up from Bombay to wish us luck. Never mind the threat of nuclear proliferation, the war against terrorism or Tony Blair's views on the new Euro, his heart is at Macclesfield.

'Maybe someone will whisper the result in Tony Blair's ear and it will be like the moment when George Bush heard about the World Trade Centre,' suggests Matt.

At last we leave the M6 and emerge in a land of middle-class Cheshire villages and pleasantly undulating countryside. You can actually see fields from certain parts of the ground. We travel along the Silk Road and park in the sort of cul-de-sac Bob and Thelma from *Whatever Happened To The Likely Lads* would have lived in. The sky is clear, the recent snow has thawed and it's ideal football conditions.

The trip is a salient reminder that many clubs outside the Premiership are close to bankruptcy. The £265,000 television money Macclesfield will receive from the live TV coverage – a month's wages to some top Premiership players – will make a huge difference to the club. Forget those Ferraris in the players' car park. The younger Macclesfield players earn £250 a week, while their record signing, Danny Adams, cost just £15,000 and was previously working as a postman while playing for Altrincham.

The ground is reminiscent of Southern League grounds from my youth – the Chelmsford City of Cheshire. There's one tiny stand to our left and the newer all-seater stand to our right, complete with executive boxes. The West Ham fans are on an open terrace and it's strange to be standing again. Jostling for position behind crash barriers, avoiding the big bloke in front of you, deciding whether the net impedes your view, all these are new experiences once more. The mood of nostalgia results in a greatest hits rendition of chants from the past.

When the sides emerge David James is greeted with chants of 'Dodgy barnet!' and 'Are you Seaman in disguise?'. The Hammers custodian has lost the peroxide Afro look and has now gone for the Egyptian Pharaoh image, his blond plaits now greased back in Rameses style.

The game kicks off before 5,706 fans and Macclesfield immediately set about the three times Cup winners. Kevin Keen is now acting as a midfield general and can still fire in low skimming crosses. Striker Ricky Lambert, who looks like an agricultural labourer who's been up since 6 a.m., causes Repka and Dailly much discomfort with his physical play down the channels. Keen is cheered by the Hammers fans as he takes a corner.

'Are you watching Altrincham?' chant the home fans, to general laughter from the Hammers contingent.

'Oh I drink ten pints, I beat my wife, 'cos I'm a northern bastard!' respond the Irons fans, in a somewhat dubious conversion to feminism, followed by: 'What's it like to see a crowd?'

Macclesfield have the better of the first half, forcing a series of corners and two saves from James. West Ham look predictable going forward. Moncur plays a high ball into the area. 'Moncur they play like that every week, that's meat and fucking drink to them!' bawls the gentleman behind us.

A seemingly good goal for Macclesfield is disallowed for offside and a free-kick is deflected onto the bar. We're close enough to hear Christian Dailly hollering Celtic insults at Sebastien Schemmel for neglecting his defensive duties – at least the defence now talk to each other. On 45 minutes there's an almighty scramble in the Hammers' goalmouth, before the danger is averted; Schemmel breaks down the right, crosses low and Jermain Defoe expertly turns a half-chance into a goal.

'We're shit and we're beating you!' chant the West Ham end.

The second half is less worrying, with Macclesfield demoralised at being a goal down against the play. The West Ham fans continue to plunder a mental jukebox of terrace chants from ten years ago, taunting Macclesfield keeper Walker's goal-kicks with cries of 'Whooooooh! You're shit! Aaaaaaaargh!'. 'There's only one Trevor Brooking!' is followed by the 'Hokey Cokey' and 'Twist and Shout'.

Interestingly, in the light of Di Canio's likely defection, the terrace responds to taunts of 'Where is Di Canio?' with a new song, 'Who needs Di Canio, We've got Jermain Defoe!'

Defoe seizes on a moment's hesitation by the home defence and chips a fine goal into the corner of Walker's net. Cue another chorus of 'Who needs Di Canio, We've got Jermain Defoe!' Clearly we are not Altrincham in disguise today. The goal leads to taunts of 'Two-nil in your cup final!'.

There's even time for Moncur to get sent off. Lasting a whole 90 minutes was always going to be difficult for the most combustible veteran substitute in the Premiership. After a lunge at Chris Byrne, he picks up the player by the shirt and an almighty mêlée follows. Moncs is given two yellow cards and trudges off, Dailly and Town's Adams are booked, but Byrne, who has head-butted Moncur, somehow escapes punishment.

The author at his field of dreams (which fade and die)
PICTURE: DAVID KAMPFNER

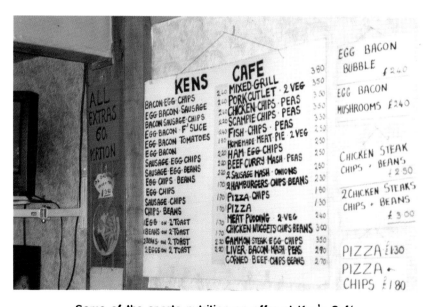

Some of the sports nutrition on offer at Ken's Café

The dreaded greengrocer's apostrophe strikes the programme stall at Upton Park tube station

The next generation of fans sample pre-match isotonic burgers
PICTURE: DAVID KAMPFNER

Waitress service in Ken's Café ('Number 63! I'm not telling you again!')
PICTURE: DAVID KAMPFNER

Feminism never quite reached this dry cleaners on Green Street . . .

Dan and Pete strike dodgy away match ticket deal inside Ken's Café
PICTURE: DAVID KAMPFNER

The new Dr Martens Stand — it's great,
only where's the mock tudor finish?

So that's why Verdi called Paolo's aria 'La Donne e Mobile'
PICTURE: DAVID KAMPFNER

A rare shot of Nigel, Dan, Matt and Fraser smiling at a West Ham match

The author leaves Upton Park a happy man after West Ham have beaten Sunderland 3-0
PICTURE: DAVID KAMPFNER

Glenn Roeder: 'I much prefer to come along the rounds quietly and unseen'

He goes above the Tottenham match day announcer! He's West Ham hit man Jeremy Nicholas with helpers Natasha and Russell

Nicola with baby Nell, sampling West Ham's own label chardonnay inside the West Ham Quality Hotel

The author enjoys the open spaces in the East Stand watching West Ham Reserves

HAMBURGER 1 50
HOT DOG'S 1 50
CHEESEBURGER 1 80
DOUBLE BURGER 2 00
DOUBLE DOG'S 2 00
DOUBLE CHEESEBURGER 2 30
CANS DRINKS 60

Ken's Café's fine takeaway service
PICTURE: DAVID KAMPFNER

Las Vegas look out: a neon-lit Ken's Café

From Cole to Moore: West Ham supporters are
still some of the most loyal in the land
PICTURE: DAVID KAMPFNER

THREE-NIL IN YOUR CUP FINAL!

Roeder brings on Hayden Foxe to stiffen the midfield. When he wins a free-kick on the edge of the Macclesfield box, he is acknowledged with a chant of 'Same old Hayden – taking the piss!'.

Even with ten men, there's time to score a third. Keen hesitates on the edge of the box and Joe Cole races in to neatly sidestep a defender and score a cool first goal of the season. Three-nil in your cup final and let's hear the draw for next round.

After the game Denis manages to catch referee Jeff Winter and his linesmen warming down on the pitch and asks about why Moncur was sent off and the ref explains about the shirt-pulling offence constituting a second booking. Now you wouldn't be able to do that at a Premiership ground. The Macclesfield mascot, Roary the Lion, walks past us and into the near deserted club shop.

We share a pint in the nearby Flowerpot with Matt's Macclesfield-supporting mate and, after Nigel neglects world politics to phone from Bombay again and check on the score, we drive back home, enlivening the jams by selecting the worst ever player we've seen in the Premiership. (Entries include Dowie, Raducioiu, Dumitrescu, Diawara and Suker.)

At the services a copy of the *Sunday Mirror* contains a piece by transfer-listed Trevor Sinclair headlined 'Good luck Paolo, I hope I will be the next to leave'. Conveniently forgetting that no one forced him to sign his current, very rewarding contract and that the club paid his wages for six months while he was injured last season, Sinclair is complaining that the club's £10 million valuation of him is deterring buyers. 'I am not going to back down. I still want to leave. I want to move to a bigger club – one that will give me European football and help my England situation. Unfortunately the club have made it virtually impossible for me to do so . . . I believe the fee they are asking is unfair. I would love to see them lower it.'

Sinclair has just scored the goal of the month on ITV's *The Premiership* and has been playing well enough at West Ham to make his England début. If he stays, the club could even stand a chance of gaining a UEFA Cup place. But no, we should sell one of our main assets at a knock-down price so that we can facilitate his dream move. Sinclair should talk to Kevin Keen or Macclesfield's former postman Danny Adams and realise just what a privileged position he's in.

Maybe we should get rid of them all and find a side who want to play for us. If Di Canio and Sinclair don't want to play for us then let them go. Kanouté too if he wants to leave. Roeder has signed James, Schemmel, Repka, Trabant and Hutchison, five players who could form the basis of the new era. Let's surround his men with youngsters who are committed to the club.

On Five Live we hear that there's been a pitch invasion at Cardiff and Aston Villa are 2–0 up against Man United as we reach London. Could we be on our way to Cardiff? Maybe the club, if not the for the final. By the time I've reached home at around nine-thirty, United have won 3–2 and a glance at Ceefax reveals that we've drawn Chelsea or Norwich away in the next round. And we all know where the likely victors can stick their blue flag.

TOP TEN DODGY WEST HAM BARNETS

1. DAVID JAMES: From peroxide tea-cosy to hot-dog with mustard squiggles to Simba from *The Lion King* all in one season.

2. ALAN TAYLOR: The 1975 FA Cup-winner's straggly blond locks were enough to give rats' tails a bad name. A wispy blond Paul Calf-style moustache also has to be taken into consideration.

3. FRANK McAVENNIE: Like a reject from a 1980s edition of *Neighbours*, the original mullet-headed Scottish striker had a peroxide barnet with long bits at the back. Very Jason Donovan.

4. JULIAN DICKS: Before he went for a shaved head, Julian shaved his hair at the sides and was an early advocate of the Forrest Gump look.

5. SVETOSLAV TODOROV: A pudding basin cut by a short-sighted Bulgarian barber was bad enough – but wearing an Alice band too was enough to see him sent to Portsmouth.

6. BILLY BONDS: A huge beard and unkempt mass of hair made for his legendary Captain Pugwash chic look in the 1970s. Any press mention of him was always prefaced by the word 'swashbuckling'.

7. PHIL PARKES: Septic elbows came and went but Phil's shaggy-dog look remained unchanged for millennia. Is probably now earning a living in Hall and Oates.

8. JOHN LYALL: Yes, for years we had an ageing teddy boy in charge. How many other managers sported a quiff in the 1980s?

9. JAVIER MARGAS: Once thought that dying his hair claret and blue was a good way of winning the fans over. Made Freddie Ljungberg look stylish.

10. JOE COLE: A peroxide sub-Gazza crop was followed by a shaved head topped with a J-shaped squiggle of red hair in the summer of 2002.

20. SHOULD I STAY OR SHOULD I GO?

West Ham 1 Leicester City 0 – 12 January 2002

Six days after the FA Cup tie at Macclesfield, Paolo Di Canio is playing against Leicester at Upton Park. The press say that this will be his last game for the Hammers and that he will sign for Manchester United on Monday.

Given the bizarre nature of the longest-running transfer saga in football history (26 December to 12 January so far) there's an air of unreality around the ground, although the crowd has been swelled to 34,698 thanks to the 'kids for a quid' marketing scheme – finally an example of progressive marketing at West Ham, even if Karren Brady was doing the same thing nearly ten years earlier at Birmingham.

Di Canio is cheered, but his aria is sung with less enthusiasm than usual, the fans' affection tinged with exasperation that he's leaving and resentment of Man United buying him as a squad player just because they're a striker short. As a game it's dire stuff. Leicester are now under the management of Dave Bassett and predictably they fire the ball at the lumbering hulk of Brian Deane whenever possible. Deane is trying to intimidate the back four and at one point Tomas Repka goes berserk at the referee when he fails to spot a blatant elbow from Deane in the Czech centre-back's face. Encouragingly, Joe Cole matches Dennis Wise for tackling while John Moncur, in the side for Carrick and playing his last game before a three-game suspension, achieves the rare feat of going in so hard on Robbie Savage that Leicester's hairy hard man appears to jump out of a tackle. And if Savage thinks someone's a nutter then we're surely talking *League of Gentleman* scale recidivist tendencies. Maybe Moncs has just been eating too much of that 'special stuff' from Royston Valley's butcher Harry Bliss.

As for Paolo, he's playing reasonably well, but his body language suggests that this will indeed be his final game. He's not even remonstrating with the referee by waving his arms around in the manner of a demented semaphore signaller with a hornet's nest down his shorts, as is normal with PDC. He

115

doesn't greet a misplaced pass or a failure of a teammate to read his intentions with a look that suggests they have just decapitated his grandmother. There's no holding of his head or beating the turf when a chance goes wide. He just gets on with the game.

For half an hour we struggle against a mediocre Leicester side. 'Schemmel looks like he should be an extra in *Henry VIII*,' declares Gavin after 15 minutes, and for several minutes I consider the pleasing prospect of Schemmel gnawing joints of bloody roast meat and throwing them from the banqueting table to John Moncur below.

Moncur goes close with a fine volley which is saved by Walker, then after 35 minutes comes the moment the whole ground has been waiting for. At which point two burks at the end of row F decide they have to leave their seats and sample West Ham's splendid in-house catering. We can just about see two backs in front of us as Cole's shot is blocked, Sebastien Schemmel heads the ball back across goal and Di Canio scores a rare poacher's goal with a finely controlled volley. Let's hope the exiting gentlemen enjoyed their meat pie, after all, what's so important about Di Canio's last goal?

PDC goes crazy, racing to the corner flag and then jumping at it and snapping it, before making a series of arm wielding gestures at the lower tier of the Dr Martens Stand. You can see all the tension of recent weeks suddenly released. A few minutes later a steward discreetly replaces the broken corner flag. Maybe the Di Canio flag-breaking goalscoring routine will one day replace Frank Lampard Senior's mad jog around the flag as celebrated at Elland Road in the 1980 FA Cup semi-final replay.

At half-time there isn't much to talk about save the goal. Our main entertainment is the 'Valentine's Night Dinner and Dance' at the West Ham Quality Hotel advertised in the programme. For £150 a couple you can enjoy a hotel room for the night with candlelit four-course meal in the 'sumptuous Premier Suite', followed by a disco and of course, a 'gift for ladies'. Female emancipation has apparently passed the club by; and does anyone still go to dinner-dances? The phrase evokes memories of late-night washing-up after freemasons and their wives had danced drunkenly to 'Y Viva Espana' at the Hutton Masonic Hall, where I had a part-time job in my sixth-form days. The world of *Hammer* has been a strange place ever since the 1970s, when as a child I spent long nights pondering the meaning of 'axiom' and 'custodian' and my dad detected various masonic references in its cryptic editorials.

The second half is another struggle, but before the game Roeder has told the players the importance of not being bullied out of the game. Eventually a half-fit lumbering Kanouté is replaced by Cole. Repka and Dailly battle steadily while Moncur is the pick of the midfielders, using his infamous stepover to surprising effect and even forgetting to get booked. Nigel Winterburn has a storming game, winning crowd-raising tackles just as the game descends into torpor and racing into overlapping positions on the left with the zeal of an 18-year-old. What's the matter, Nige? You're supposed to either get injured, play terribly, move into TV or take the Hayden Foxe out of us like all the other Arsenal rejects we've signed (cf. Radford, Robson, Wright, Suker, Diawara et al.).

On Friday West Ham completed the signing of the man the fans are referring to as Trabant – actually Vladimir Labant – a Czech left-back from Sparta Prague who's played in the Champions League this season. The effect has been to rejuvenate Winterburn and at last inject some competition for places into the side.

But it's Di Canio's day. He even gets to help mend the net after the linesman points out a hole in it. Dan imagines him telling the ref: 'These are my goals, we must make them perfect!' Di Canio overelaborates and infuriates at times but he's still capable of making everyone else on the pitch look stupid. He's denied a goal when Cole shows his immaturity by snatching a shot instead of passing it to the unmarked maestro.

The best present Paolo can leave us is three points, which will take us up to 28 points from 22 games, with only four wins needed from the remaining 16 matches to ensure safety. After years of watching West Ham fade and die we're all safety-first merchants. After the appalling collapse in form during the second half of last season, and with the imminent departures of Di Canio and Sinclair, anything could yet happen.

Bizarrely, the Irons defend deep for the last 15 minutes and invite Leicester to hurl long balls into the area. We must win this one. Even keeper Ian Walker races up for a corner and manages his side's only shot on target. After four minutes of injury time we hold on for a very nervous victory.

Paolo walks towards each stand, clapping the fans. His lingering farewell suggests he's halfway up the M6. Jeremy Nicholas has never been good at keeping a secret. 'It breaks my heart to think he might be leaving but let's hear it once more for PAOLO DI CANIO!!!!' he exhorts, playing the aria from *Rigoletto*. The tearful skipper trudges off the pitch and is given a manly, restrained English pat by Glenn Roeder. He's given a thoroughly professional performance under huge pressure. I leave the East Stand feeling like I've been hit by a John Moncur late challenge. Night hangs heavy over East Ham High Street. Is this really the end?

At which point – at least in my dreams – Di Canio tells United to stuff their three potential trophies and their European Champions League and declares that nothing can match the romantic ambience of a night with his missus in Ken's Café, that sharing tiramisu with Posh and Becks can't compete with a barbie round at Hayden Foxe's place, and that a Roeder roasting is far more terrifying than the Fergie hairdryer treatment.

117

21. I DON'T WANT TO GO TO CHELSEA

Chelsea 5 West Ham 1 – 20 January 2002
Chelsea 1 West Ham 1 – 26 January 2002

Only Paolo doesn't go. PDC's farewell is proving as convoluted as Rick's attempts to get two air tickets out of Casablanca airport for Mr and Mrs Victor Laszlo. After the Leicester game Di Canio lays the blame for his projected departure on the board. The whole saga is starting to make Proust's *Remembrance of Things Past* seem like something that he knocked up during a mini-break.

Perhaps Paolo just wants to be loved. He appears mortified that the club has not rejected all bids outright, and remarks that because it was simply a case of the money not being good enough then: 'I am for sale' (which rather ignores the old but true cliché that every player, even David Beckham, has his price).

After his tearful exit at the end of the Leicester game, Paolo told the press: 'I have not asked for a move. But if the board decide they want to sell me then I will be professional about it. If the club want to sell me there is nothing I can do about it. But I will play with passion and pride whatever happens. I am a professional and I will always give 100 per cent.' After which he feels compelled to add the fact that even when he plays with his two-year-old daughter he plays to win – which must lead to some fearful tantrums in the Di Canio household, with the toddler being pretty upset as well.

Does Di Canio want to leave or do the club want him out? Some supporters believe his agent is simply trying to negotiate a new contract for his client, others that United are deliberately trying to destabilise him. Another faction believes that it is the board that wants Di Canio out of the club; others that Roeder's 'I know nothing' line is a clever PR-spin, and he has decided to offload PDC for the right price.

What most fans want is simply to be treated with respect. Ever since the infamous West Ham Bond scheme the board has feared another fan backlash and the club's lack of transparency is again in evidence. If Roeder wanted to sell Di Canio for football reasons we should be told. Most fans would respect the manager's decision if he felt such a move was genuinely good for the long-term future of the team.

It's possible that Roeder feels that Di Canio's pivotal role in the team holds back others or that Kanouté would benefit from a more conventional strike partner. He might feel that Di Canio is a disruptive influence, criticising his teammates and calling them 'shit' after the Blackburn débâcle. Then there are the rumours about Di Canio not turning up for away games – vehemently denied by the player – and the fact that at over 33, it might be best to cash in on a player past his best.

A little honesty is all that is wanted, although Roeder insists: 'There has been an official offer and it was rejected very quickly. Now the ball is in United's court. There has been no increased offer since. At the moment Paolo is a West Ham player and you could see by the way he played against Leicester that means a lot to him.'

Roeder's 'farewell' tribute to Di Canio at the end of the Leicester match was certainly effusive. He spoke of Di Canio's 'God-given' skill and the valuable advice he passes on to Joe Cole and Jermain Defoe, but said that if you told him he was a genius he wouldn't want to know about that: 'He wants people to recognise him as a good, dedicated professional who works hard and trains properly, and who looks after himself.'

By the following Wednesday the fact that nothing has been heard from United is actually a news item on Teletext. 'It looks increasingly likely that Di Canio will play at Chelsea on Sunday' we learn. Great. So before every Di Canio appearance we have to wait to see if United have upped their bid before we can be certain he'll play. It seems that Jarndyce v Jarndyce will be settled before any move is completed.

By Thursday Di Canio has changed tack again, announcing on Teletext: 'I'm extremely flattered to hear that one of the great clubs in the world is interested in me. Everyone at the club, the players, management, and fans should be proud that one of their players has caught the eye of Sir Alex Ferguson.'

On Friday comes the encouraging news that Manchester United have persuaded Uruguayan striker Diego Forlan to reject advances from Midddlesbrough and sign for them, casting doubt on the whole Di Canio deal.

So the league game at Chelsea on Sunday, 20 January, may or may not be Di Canio's final appearance (again). For such a melodramatic player, making more farewell appearances than Frank Sinatra seems somehow appropriate.

It's a grey winter's day on the Fulham Road. A Christian with a megaphone ignores the drizzle to tell the chuckling Blues fans: 'Don't be a sinner be a winner. Ken Bates isn't the salvation of man, Jesus Christ is!' Mind you, even the Good Lord himself might have given up on the sinning Chelsea Four, Jody

Morris, Frank Lampard, John Terry and Eidur Gudjohnsen, who were fined two weeks' wages by the club for boozing and offending grieving Americans in a Heathrow Hotel the day after the 11 September attacks. Now Morris and Terry face further charges of affray after a nightclub incident earlier this month when the pair were out wetting Jody Morris's baby's head two days before a match.

Football fans fit uneasily into the plush surroundings of Fulham Road. A Chelsea fan with 'OLD MAN' on the back of his shirt stands outside the Britannia pub, pint in hand, while a blonde Hammers fan has 'NUTTY TART' on the back of her replica shirt as she queues for a hot-dog outside Café Brazil.

Like Patrick McGoohan, we are definitely in the Village. The bus stop now reads 'Chelsea Village', opposite the Village stores. The Stamford Gate leads to the plush Chelsea Village Hotel while the Shed Bar is now more bistro than boozer. There are smoked salmon bagels on sale and fish and chips cost £4.50. Even the programme is now an upmarket £3. It must have been strange for the Chelsea fans to suddenly find all this gentrification; a bit like discovering that Ken's Café is now into world cuisine and arabica coffee.

'I've paid £35 for a seat in the rain!' exclaims the disbelieving fan behind me. Today I am Pete No-Mates, as everyone else has opted to watch the match on ITV digital in the pub. My seat is in the very front row of the East Stand and here the roof proves useless against the downpour. Watching West Ham in the rain invariably results in humiliating defeat. Three years ago Big Joe and myself were saturated at Charlton watching Julian Dicks being terribly exposed by a rampaging Danny Mills and a 2–1 lead turn into a 4–2 defeat in the final five minutes of the game. Then there was the 6–0 defeat at Oldham in the Littlewoods Cup semi-final on an open terrace in a Lancastrian deluge where the bogs were flowing with rivers of mud and urine.

'Fuck off, Lampard, you fat piece of shit!'

Stamford Bridge has become an intimidating cauldron of sound now its redevelopment is finished. As the game kicks off Frank Lampard is subjected to some traditional Cockney banter from the wit behind me and chants of 'Big fat Frankie Lampard!'. It's all a little unfair of course, but then so are football fans. Frank's dad was a great player for the club and as Lampard himself has said in today's papers, he helped us pay for our new stand. The board must have known that when they removed Redknapp and Frank Lampard Senior it was likely that Lampard Junior would follow. We'd still love to beat him and his new side though.

Most of the first half looks like being a reasonably solid defensive performance. Kanouté and the returning Carrick both look less than match fit, Di Canio works hard but frequently chooses the wrong option. At least the defence looks relatively solid. James rescues a hesitant Repka when he saves from Hasselbaink and then tips a free-kick from the same player on to the bar. As the first half enters injury time I fear that now is the inevitable West Ham-concede-soft-goal-before-half-time moment. And it is. James makes a fine save from a woefully unmarked Gudjohnsen but Hasselbaink drives home the rebound.

The game is effectively over after 51 minutes when Carrick's feeble crossfield ball is easily intercepted and Terry plays a great ball through to Gudjohnsen. Repka is uncertain whether to mark or play for offside, as Gudjohnsen expertly controls the ball and fires it into the corner of the net for an exquisitely taken goal. Like Elvis Costello, I don't want to go to Chelsea. Nine minutes later a routine through ball from Zola sees the sheer strength of Hasselbaink hold off Repka, James makes another fine save but unluckily the ball rebounds straight to the Chelsea striker for a tap-in.

Can it get worse? Of course it can. After 60 minutes the anonymous Sinclair is taken off for stitches in a leg wound and replaced by Courtois. Still, even in defeat there is usually something to laugh about. As Hayden Foxe warms up with the other subs the away fans chant 'He's here, he's there, he's pissing everywhere! Hayden Foxe!'.

Chelsea warm up Jody Morris and as he runs down the touchline the bloke behind me hollers 'Oi Morris, you think you're hard, come over here!' – clearly a man so disgusted by violent nightclub incidents that he wants to give anyone allegedly connected with them a good kicking.

It seems West Ham are in for a Blackburn-style thrashing after 70 minutes when Jody Morris wraps his legs round Di Canio in a niggly tackle. The strain of a transfer saga more mysterious than anything seen on *The X-Files* shows as Di Canio reacts and stamps at Morris. It's petulant rather than violent but with the referee standing at the scene it's a red card. At least there's no ref-pushing. He walks off meekly removing his armband. 'Where is Di Canio?' ask the Chelsea fans in the Matthew Harding Stand. Roeder finally replaces the mediocre Kanouté, whose personal stereo seems to have been playing Nick Drake songs all afternoon, with Jermain Defoe.

Chelsea are mesmerising and on this form, with Hasselbaink and Gudjohnsen looking the best partnership in the Premiership, it's mystifying why this team isn't at the top of the league. After 87 minutes Cole gives the ball away in midfield, and Gudjohnsen bamboozles Dailly with an electric shuffle and another fine goal. James kicks the ball away in disgust, at least showing that he is one player hurt by such a defeat.

In today's Sunday papers there has been considerable outrage about the US treatment of terrorist suspects captured in Afghanistan and held at Camp X-Ray in Cuba. Prisoners arrive wearing blacked-out goggles, ear muffs and surgical masks. Such sensory deprivation doesn't seem such a bad idea at this moment. Fat blokes in the Chelsea end taunt the Hammers contingent with 'We've got Frank Lampard!' and one of them mystifyingly pulls up his jumper and pats his burgeoning belly.

'You're gonna win fuck all!' respond the West Ham fans, earning a riposte from the home crowd of 'You've never won fuck all!'. This in turn leads to 'We won the fucking World Cup!'. Even if it was in 1966.

Then, amazingly, the Irons pull one back. Jermain Defoe runs on to a Schemmel through-ball and neatly sidesteps Lampard and Terry to score a quality goal. 'We're gonna win 5–4!' chant the Hammers fans. Two minutes later the limp Hammers defence is dragged halfway to Fulham Broadway station as sub Forssell fires across the prostrate James.

Oh well, it's been quite a successful day really. Di Canio will be suspended if he joins Man United, Sinclair is injured if Liverpool pursue their interest and Chelsea will be thoroughly complacent before the FA Cup tie between the clubs next Saturday when we will inevitably thrash them.

In the post-match interviews Glenn Roeder points out that, bizarrely, West Ham have the best defensive record in the Premiership at home (just seven goals conceded) and the worst defensive record away (a whopping 32 goals let in). 'We're not a physically big side and the other teams know that. But that record would suggest that we are mentally as well as physically frail.' He talks of 'a mental block' and this fan knows how he feels.

Paolo Di Canio is contrite and admits he has played badly and reacted stupidly. He jokes: 'Now I'm banned for three matches maybe Manchester United will not buy me for £1.' On this performance Paolo's being optimistic; Glenn Roeder's side has moved into negative equity.

West Ham's Sunday roasting causes Glenn Roeder to see a psychiatrist. Dr David Houlston is recruited to try to boost positive thinking in the squad. Glenn says: 'I believe the problem has got to be inside the players' heads and comes up when we play away. Dr Houlston has spoken to the players for the first time and has been trying to instil positive thoughts.'

What the psychiatrist said when he encountered Paolo we can only speculate, although I'm reminded of the famous line from *Fawlty Towers* when the visiting psychiatrist says of Basil: 'There's enough material there for an entire conference.'

As for being West Ham supporters – the problem is definitely inside our heads. Still, a psychological boost arrives with the knowledge that West Ham fans have twice as many seats for the FA Cup tie at Stamford Bridge the following Saturday and last night Hayden Foxe's wet Christmas antics were used as a question on *They Think It's All Over*.

We have taken over the Chelsea supporters' home end, the lower tier of the Matthew Harding Stand, and despite all the talk of the diminishing magic of the Cup (that morning's Middlesbrough versus Man United tie attracted a mere 17,624 fans) there's something inspiring in seeing such a huge number of West Ham supporters away from home singing that marvellous ode to the stoic acceptance of misfortune, ineptitude and even David Kelly, 'I'm Forever Blowing Bubbles'.

It's another filthy day. Rain lashes the pitch as if God was Hayden Foxe after a bladder full of lager. Even King Lear would have stayed at home this afternoon. The touchline is heavily sanded and there are gaps in the Chelsea seats, the attendance of 33,443 being nearly 7,000 down on last week's league encounter.

With Sinclair injured, Roeder has surprised everyone by playing a five-man defence with the forgotten Ragy Soma in as a third centre-back. The last game in which he played was the 7–1 thrashing at Blackburn, but at least Roeder is still proving a manager capable of innovation. Oh, and Di Canio makes another final, yes absolutely final, appearance in the claret and blue colours. The deadline for new players to be eligible for the Champions League is next Thursday, 31 January, and Glenn Roeder says that he hopes the saga will be resolved one way or another by then.

It's immediately apparent that the Irons are playing with far more pride than last week. Chelsea create early chances with James saving well from a Hasselbaink header but Schemmel is surging down the right to get in testing crosses, Don Hutchison has a header and a long-range drive saved by Cudicini, and Winterburn slices wide of a gaping goal. Repka, redeeming himself after last Sunday's abject performance, makes a crucial saving tackle from Forssell.

Guardian reader Graeme Le Saux whips in some fine left-foot crosses for Chelsea and while taking a corner diffuses the taunts of 'Le Saux takes it up the arse!' by laughing and offering his backside to one of his detractors. He wins applause all around the Hammers end.

At the back Soma has performed some neat interceptions considering his long absence but still looks terrified of the lethal Jimmy Floyd Hasselbaink. After 21 minutes he does his 'rabbit caught in the glare of headlights' impersonation and backs off Hasselbaink, who surely can't score from an oblique angle on the corner of the box. Jimmy Floyd dutifully curls a screamer into the top left-hand corner of James's net.

'Small club in Fulham, you're just a small club in Fulham!' chant the Hammers fans at their gloating Chelsea counterparts.

At least West Ham respond with some spirit; a neat pass inside from Di Canio finds Kanouté who scoops the ball wide. Just before the first half ends the PA causes considerable mirth by announcing that a Chelsea fan has become the father of a baby girl called Maisy Sherbert. 'Maybe that's their code message for a security alert,' suggests Nigel.

Early in the second half Frank Lampard, still being barracked by the Irons fans, slices an excellent volley just wide, while the turning point of the game is when James makes a superb low save from Zola's placed shot. Repka makes a couple of storming tackles that must surely inspire his teammates.

However, it still looks like we're going out of the Cup but at least the alert Nigel notes that the advert for the Chelsea Village Hotel on the scoreboard has misspelt 'luxury accomodation' (sic).

Roeder then makes some crucial substitutions, replacing Winterburn with Labant, Hutchison with Lomas and Soma with Defoe. Labant immediately demonstrates that he has a fine left foot with a dangerous free-kick being bundled behind for a corner. Lomas too has an instant effect. Earlier in the week there was newspaper outrage over the controversial TV drama *Bloody Sunday*; having witnessed West Ham's own bloody capitulation on the previous Sabbath, you sense that the fiery Ulsterman is in no mood to see anyone else lay down and die. He tackles fiercely and wins balls he has no right to, and through his workmanlike endeavour fires up the dilettantes around him.

Defoe injects pace alongside Kanouté and the often peripheral Di Canio – unable to dominate games in the fashion of two years ago – makes better progress on the left. Cole has a fine shot punched away by Cudicini and when Di Canio is brought down by Ferrer, Labant fires in another free-kick from the right. Carrick shoots, Cole helps it on, and Kanouté turns on the loose ball and fires it home from the edge of the six-yard box.

Cue pandemonium. The life of a football fan is mapped out in images and this is one of those enduring pictures that make a season; 7,000 fans in an explosion of joyous celebration and Fredi Kanouté, after a Brazilian-style baby celebration with Cole and Carrick to mark the birth of his son, forsakes his Walkman and leaps into a sea of outstretched arms. At that moment he even looks like he wants to play for us.

Before the end there's time for James to make another good save from Zola and for Fredi to head narrowly wide after beating Cudicini to a loose ball. The final whistle sounds and the West Ham fans celebrate as if it's a victory. Under the lights at Upton Park we must stand a chance of beating them. James throws his gloves into the crowd and there's a final, obligatory chant referring to Chelsea fans, blue flags and orifice politics.

22. TALES OF A RIGHT-WING STRIKER

'Theatrics, sulking, gesturing, turf beating, ball wrestling, self-substitution, referee pushing, shorts tailoring and dodgy hair colouring . . .' These were just some of the qualities cited when the fanzine *On A Mission* awarded Paolo Di Canio a spoof 'certificate of madness' after his performance in one of the greatest games ever seen at Upton Park, a 5–4 home win against Bradford towards the end of the 1999–2000 season.

He might not be having his greatest season, but there's still a profound sense of depression that he seems destined to leave for Manchester United. Di Canio was the greatest player seen at West Ham since certainly Trevor Brooking and very probably Bobby Moore. There was a time in the early 1990s when going to games at Upton Park was almost a duty. But for the past three years, going to matches has been enjoyable once more because with Di Canio on the pitch absolutely anything might happen. For £1.5 million – the price much reduced because of his notorious push on referee Paul Alcock while he was playing for Sheffield Wednesday – Di Canio has to be Harry Redknapp's greatest ever signing.

That performance against Bradford was typical of his deranged genius. With substitute Stephen Bywater suffering from début nerves, West Ham were 4–2 down at home. Paolo had already had two penalty appeals turned down and when the referee dismissed a third blatant penalty, you feared Di Canio would do an Alcock on him. Only this time he walked over to the bench, making changeover gestures with his hands, and demanded to Harry Redknapp that he be taken off. There then followed the amazing spectacle of a Premiership manager pleading with his star striker to stay on the pitch.

As Paolo was to reveal in his autobiography (the imaginatively titled *Paolo Di Canio: My Autobiography*, published by CollinsWillow), it wasn't that he was paranoid, but at that moment 'I felt a rage well up inside me. I felt the anger of a million injustices, a million wrongs that went unpunished, a million vendettas that went unserved.'

When West Ham were finally awarded a penalty, the normal penalty taker

127

WEST HAM

Frank Lampard went to take the spot-kick only for Paolo to wrestle with him for the ball, rather like two kids at nursery. All around me the Upper East Stand fans were laughing hysterically at this bizarre incident, which was more in keeping with Sunday league football than the Premiership. Lampard just saw the look in Di Canio's eyes and gave him the ball. Di Canio scored, of course, then laid on the equaliser for Lampard, and a legendary comeback was completed when Joe Cole scored to make it 5–4.

There have been numerous other sublime moments: the Italian maestro scoring *Match of the Day's* goal of the season for West Ham against Wimbledon, a sumptuous volley with both feet off the ground; the winner he calmly toe-poked past Barthez at Old Trafford in the FA Cup last season, before running to the cameras and telling them 'I can play away!'; a FIFA fair play plaudit for catching the ball when seemingly certain to score and stopping play to allow the injured Everton goalkeeper Gerrard to receive treatment; juggling the ball over the head of Tony Adams to volley a marvellous winner against Arsenal; a meandering dribble across the area and a shot into the top corner at Charlton; the ability to back-heel the ball in mid-air; twisting away from four defenders against Spurs at Upton Park . . . As the Human League might say, these are the things that dreams are made of.

With Paolo's likely departure my thoughts turned towards an interview I did with him just after the publication of his autobiography. We met at the Hammers' Chadwell Heath training ground, with my brief being to discuss his views on London for a listings magazine. It was immediately evident how well he fitted into English football; mistiming a volley he exclaimed ''kin 'ell!' in perfect Anglo-Saxon and after he was charged complained about the new speed camera fitted outside his house.

This being West Ham, we had to conduct the interview while standing up in the reception area at Chadwell Heath, but despite the unprofessional environment, with agents and players shuffling around us, Paolo revealed a very different aspect to the fiery on-pitch striker and was clearly a convert to London life. For example, he's an even bigger fan of Chigwell than Sharon and Tracey from *Birds of a Feather*.

'I live in Chigwell which is a fantastic place for my family. We have a big garden and a beautiful view, but I like to go all round London, to Chelsea and Covent Garden, Trafalgar Square and the National Gallery,' he enthused in his animated, garrulous style, his near-perfect English still permeated by a strong Italian accent. In person Paolo was smaller than you'd imagine, with lively, dancing brown eyes and a clear zest for his adopted city.

Unlike past Hammers stars, who've tended to prefer Hollywood nightclub in Romford to high culture, Di Canio wanted to discuss his love of art.

'At the National Gallery you see the history of painting from all cultures. Now with all this technology we have we don't see the same colours or the same situation. They were phenomenal people. But I like modern art too, such as *Apocalypse* at the RA and I like the Tate Modern; that area will be one of the best in London soon.'

Superstar or not, he is as enamoured of the capital as most other tourists but he also saw similarities between his native Quarticciolo area of Rome and the East End: 'They are very similar, both working-class areas. Life is like a rock where everyone knows each other. We stick close to each other and you grow up fast, at 12 you look like 16, it's very tough. There is romance in the West End, but I think there is also romance in working-class people trying to give their children good principles. I was lucky, my father and three brothers taught me to go in a good way. They taught me you have to work hard or stay in this society.'

Like his friend, the ex-Chelsea manager Gianluca Vialli, Di Canio claimed to enjoy the relative anonymity of London: 'They are used to seeing famous people like Madonna. I am happy if people recognise me because we all have a little bit of vanity, but you can walk, they don't try to keep you for 20 minutes, not like in Italy where you can't go out, especially in the south, because there they have so much passion they don't leave you with your food.'

One of his most amazing admissions was that he has even sampled London by tube. For his first five months at West Ham he was unsure of the rush-hour traffic and so used the underground.

'Not many people recognised me because people on the tube they read, or they're asleep after finishing their jobs,' explained Paolo. 'I was lucky because every time I took the train from Chigwell nobody was on it. After five or six stations then everyone got on. I met many foreign people. Many times I recognised Italian people not from their language but the style of what they wear.'

And forget about ref-pushing, in keeping with his new post-FIFA fair play award 'gentleman of soccer' image, Di Canio revealed: 'Of course, if I saw old people I gave up my seat to them, because I am an athlete and I can stand.'

Di Canio's political views are as, erm, unusual as some of his on-field antics. I managed to slip in a question about the section in his autobiography where he says that he owns numerous biographies of Benito Mussolini and feels the former Fascist leader was a 'deeply misunderstood individual' – which probably makes him quite left-wing in Essex. At one point Paolo compares Mussolini to Scotland's William Wallace. Presumably, if Di Canio ever becomes a manager he'll make the training run on time . . .

Di Canio, who clearly relished discussing politics, emphasised that this did not mean he is a Nazi or racist. To be fair, Paolo, this view is not unusual in Italy, although at times I did feel a little like a passenger stuck on a journey from Chigwell to Upton Park with a right-wing taxi driver.

'I never said I was a fan of Mussolini, but for the media it is more easy to make the polemic,' he explained, at which point I'm wondering how many Premiership players could say 'polemic' even in their first language.

'I said that after Mussolini no one political man was a patriot or a nationalist, because nationalism is not equal to being a Nazi. English people are very proud of their nationalism too; my nationalism means you are proud because you are Italian. But I have a big respect for English people, German or foreign people if they come to Italy if they come with good intentions. I want to help them, not to leave them living under bridges like homeless people. If foreign people come to Italy they have to be the same as Italian people . . .'

Yes, Paolo, now moving on . . . But Paolo on politics – rather like a Chigwell cabbie on the demise of the Tories since Mrs Thatcher stood down – was not someone who could be easily silenced.

'In Italy if the right or left win the election they don't think in three or four years' time we will give people a better society, where they pay less tax or have more confidence in management, they think they're gonna have a financial crack. They don't think tomorrow we can work for the people, they think tomorrow we start the publicity for the next election. They have no vision. With Mussolini I'm sure we would have had a better situation, but not in a wrong way, not with a union with the Nazis because I am not a fascist. Then was a different time, nobody wants war, now we want peace . . .

'I have my ideas about the political system, but black or white or yellow people, gay people, men or women, they can come in my house and be my friend because I am not xenophobic. I want peace and a good life for everyone.'

So has he ever considered a career in politics? 'In politics you have to be little bit snake,' he said, making a wriggling gesture with his hand, 'If I have to say something I will say it even to my boss.' As Glenn Roeder surely now knows.

A more likely post-football career may centre around his love of good food. In his autobiography Di Canio lists his recipe for tiramisu and mentions that he would like to open an Italian deli in London (customers are advised not to question the quality of his pesto) serving food from Umbria and Tuscany. Hmm. At this point I asked him one of the most penetrating questions of his career; had he ever dined at Ken's Café?

'I am man with an open mind in life, but maybe not the food!' he grinned. 'Not the chips. My daughter likes to have French fries but this is not good for me to eat because I am a professional footballer.'

Di Canio emphasised that he planned to stay in London after he retired and became quite lyrical as he described his ideal night out after a game.

'London is one of the top ten cities in the world,' he declared. 'What I like most is the view when I drive in from Chigwell and come out of the tunnel and see the Tower of London and Tower Bridge. My wife and I like to go out after a game, especially if we win, to San Lorenzo, our favourite Italian restaurant in the West End. Betta and I see the river, Big Ben and Buckingham Palace and every time we drive the car we have the same feeling. We feel we are lucky to live here and see this every week. Then we come back after dinner and there is a romantic atmosphere. This is a good moment for us.'

And to think that he might swap all that for the Arndale Centre in Manchester . . .

23. SAINTS AND SINNERS

Southampton 2 West Ham 0 - 30 January 2002

It seemed a good idea to go to Southampton. After all, Cameron Diaz has worn a dress in West Ham colours to the Golden Globe Awards, so it must be a sign. The train fare is only £14.45 from London with a network card and Gavin has his real ale guide with him. He knows a good away trip when he spots one; this is after all a man who once travelled to Southampton for a 1–0 defeat in the Zenith Data Systems Cup, and admits it with something close to pride.

It's going to be a late night, as the last train leaves at 10.50 p.m. Gavin begins his perpetual quest for a football special in the travel centre. 'There's no train between 9.50 and 10.50? I think it's a bit much, we'll miss the tube, are you sure there isn't a football special?' pleads Gavin to an unmoved customer services officer. 'Not unless West Ham have laid one on, we haven't heard of anything,' comes the response.

So we take a taxi to the Waterloo Arms in Shirley, a comfortable, roomy pub, free of football crowds, and enjoy a pint of Hotbacks Best Bitter, followed by the light and pleasurable GFB. 'This is one of my all-time favourite beers,' confides Gavin. 'In London you can only get it in a tied house in Colliers Wood.'

Sadly the football intervenes, and another cab takes us through the docks to Southampton's new ground of St Mary's. It's an impressive stadium compared to the old raggedy Dell and inside we are served at any catering outlet within three minutes as opposed to the millennia it takes to get some boiling water with brown mud in it at Upton Park. We take our seats and even if the stadium is the same on every side of the ground, the views are excellent and the playing surface good.

As usual there's an amazing turnout by West Ham fans for a midweek fixture in Southampton, and with noisy choruses of 'Bubbles' and 'Glenn Roeder's claret and blue army!' (even if it doesn't quite scan) the team can't complain of a lack of support.

131

WEST HAM

The first 15 minutes are messy, then West Ham start to create chances. Di Canio crosses for Kanouté to head over. Cole screws another good chance wide and a clever back-heel by the in-demand Di Canio releases Joe again, who takes the ball a fraction too wide before firing at the keeper.

'Paolo Di Canio, he's such a wankio!' chant the comic talents among the Saints fans.

The Hammers away crew, seeing Matt Le Tissier warming up, respond with 'We've got Di Canio, you've got Pinocchio!'.

A Hutchison rocket is tipped away by Paul Jones with no one to net the rebound and we're looking likely to go in at half-time unlucky not to be winning. Southampton haven't created a worthwhile chance until, after 45 minutes, they gain a free-kick on the left. When it's fired in, David James – so magnificent and resolute in recent weeks – punches the ball straight on to the stomach of Kevin Davies and it bounces slowly over the line. It's the first calamity for James of his Hammers career.

We have played reasonably well. Dailly has been calmly efficient, playing the ball out well, Lomas has added bite to midfield, but now we concede a comedy goal before half-time.

The Wimbledon-style set-piece mugging continues after the break. Hutchison has another shot saved after a good build up, but then Repka concedes a free-kick in a dangerous position just outside the box. The Frenchman Fabrice Fernandes blasts a stupendous shot into the roof of the net. Two set-pieces, two goals.

Our game then falls into disarray. Glenn Roeder rushes forward into the technical area then paces back to his bench like a man doing indoor bungee jumping. Joe Cole over-indulges and refuses to play the simple ball while some fans turn on Di Canio as he fades from the game. 'Get him off!' shouts the geezer behind me as Di Canio plays another wayward ball. Even substitute Defoe can't find a chance. The game fades into oblivion. We book a taxi to meet us by the flagpoles outside, and with Gav determined to make a dash for the 9.50 p.m. train to London, I break my cardinal football law, and leave before the final whistle.

The taxi isn't there, but a phone call later we discover that it is in 'the main road' wherever that is. Eventually we find the main road, not aided by a directionally challenged taxi controller, and collar a cab from the right firm but waiting for someone else. After a long delay behind a police road block, the morose driver ferries us to the station. We arrive at the station at ten past ten to find that the 9.50 p.m. has not been held for the numerous fans requiring it. 'It did leave three minutes late,' says the railway company official, as if this was some kind of huge concession.

'I think it's a bit much, we'll miss the tube, are you sure there isn't a football special?' asks Gavin again, hoping that some kind of kinetic power will usher a train into the platform.

132

'Football specials, they haven't existed since the 1970s,' chortles the inspector. 'You're lucky to get any trains, didn't you read about yesterday's strikes?'

We find a nearby pub, stuffed with similarly stranded West Ham fans and wait for the 10.50 p.m. train to London. The other results make bleak reading. West Ham are now only three points clear of Bolton, who have slipped into the third from bottom relegation spot. Could this, our tenth season in the Premiership, be the season we finally go down?

Inside the new Dell, Roeder is complaining of two goals conceded from unnecessary free-kicks and that 'in open play we weren't really troubled by Southampton'. Meanwhile, the Di Canio saga may be over. Manchester United's attempted sale of Dwight Yorke to Middlesbrough is off because of the player's huge wage demands, thus scuppering United's Di Canio bid as the board was insisting Ferguson sold Yorke before he bought Di Canio.

'I'd have thought the move is history now, I'm pleased he's still with us and he did some clever things here,' insists Roeder.

Only elsewhere Paolo is still feeling decidedly unloved and is telling the eager hacks: 'I know that West Ham desperately want to sell me, they desperately want me to leave the club. I never asked to leave but they want to sell me to bring money into the club maybe to buy other players. The situation is clear. I do not want to leave. I signed a contract a few years ago and have always said I want to stay. It is absolute rubbish to say I want to join Manchester United. This is not my problem and I can relax.'

Which rather ignores the role of his agent in the whole furore and the question of who has or has not been planting stories in the press. Are the club trying to unload Di Canio? If so, is it Terry Brown or Glenn Roeder? It's all as convoluted as trying to find a train back to London.

There follows a long day's journey into post-football night. The last train from Southampton to Waterloo stops at every godforsaken hamlet between Hampshire and London. Fleet, Basingstoke, Woking . . . these are the dark regions of the long-distance football supporter's soul.

After midweek games in strange destinations there must be many migratory souls returning at anti-social hours through forgotten outposts of civilisation. At ten minutes past one the train finally ambles into London. We dash across Waterloo Bridge to suddenly encounter a deluge falling on the Strand and opt for taxis to south and north London respectively. At 2 a.m., £12.60 lighter in the pocket after paying the fare, I fumble for the key and open my front door. West Ham don't deserve us.

24. WALKING IN AN UGLY WONDERLAND

Like recovering alcoholic Tony Adams, West Ham fans have to take one day at a time. It just takes one casual aside, one tactless remark or even a chance photograph in a football programme to return us to the abyss and remind us that addiction has both highs and horrors. And there it was in the Southampton programme – a picture of Iain Dowie.

It was surely calculated to make all Hammers fans hyperventilate and then grab hold of a wrist and mutter 'calm, calm, calm' in the manner of Michael Palin in *GBH*. Even more extraordinary, it was a picture of a young Dowie with flowing blond hair, looking eager and almost mobile, back in his Southampton days. He has, of course, played for both the Saints and West Ham, but even so, did they have to remind us?

Dowie first turned up at West Ham in March 1991 when he was signed from Luton for £480,000. He was a Northern Ireland international, of course, but then so is just about any footballer born in Northern Ireland. To be fair, he did score four times in 12 games in the second division, but even so manager Billy Bonds sold him to Southampton that summer, obviously feeling the lumbering Ulsterman was not quite up to first-division standard. He was replaced by Mike Small, the world champion offside runner.

It was in September 1995 that West Ham gaffer Harry Redknapp re-signed Dowie from Crystal Palace. At the time he was most famous for being the subject of numerous jokes on Baddiel and Skinner's *Fantasy Football*, based upon the fact that he is not the most handsome footballer in the world. In fact when Dowie played at Palace, the West Ham fans at Selhurst Park noisily chanted 'Dowie is an ugly cunt!', but still he chose to join us. When I first took Nicola to watch West Ham her initial question was: 'Who's that player who looks like Frankenstein?'

Southampton boss Alan Ball had warned Redknapp that signing Dowie would get him the sack. But it didn't and, indeed, for that season Dowie proved to be an inspired signing at just £500,000. True, he still didn't look remotely skilful, but he was a big difficult lump to mark, and through sheer effort and perseverance he scored eight league goals at the end of the 1995–96 season.

For a while West Ham fans were walking in an ugly wonderland. There could be no more surreal sight than the entire Bobby Moore Stand indulging in ironic chants of 'Dowie!' to the tune of whatever that aria Charlton fans sing is. Or chanting 'We've got Dowie, you ain't!' and 'We all agree Dowie is better than Bergkamp!' when 4–0 down against Arsenal at Highbury. Iain Dowie had travelled the path from barracked journeyman to cult hero. At least I think the fans were calling him a cult.

Only then came the mother of all goal droughts. His last league goals were on 23 March 1996 against Manchester City, which in Premiership terms was the Jurassic era, when lumbering giants like Dowie roamed amid statuesque flat back fours. In fact Steven Spielberg could have saved millions in special effects for *Jurassic Park* simply by filming the clash between Dowie and Steve Bould. He did manage to score two goals in a Coca-Cola Cup tie against Nottingham Forest on 23 October 1996, but apart from that, nothing, nil, bugger all. A fanzine printed 'I was there when Dowie scored' T-shirts, only they were destined never to be sold. Dowie didn't score a league goal for the Hammers from March 1996 until his departure from the club in January 1998. For a while Redknapp tried to pair Dowie, who possessed all the speed of a steamroller, with the sublimely fast Portugeezer Hugo Porfirio – Porfirio's permanent expression of bemusement and sometimes downright amazement at his strike partner is still vivid.

Perhaps it is unfair to accuse Dowie of suffering from a goal drought. Let's not forget the one time Dowie did score, a towering header that gave the keeper no chance when West Ham played Stockport in the Coca-Cola Cup. Unfortunately it was past Ludek Miklosko, as Dowie, in a form of footballing dyslexia, appeared to have forgotten which way his side were kicking. There was not a Stockport attacker within approximately 68 million miles of him. But for some reason he rose like Nat Lofthouse to thunder one of the most powerful headers ever seen past the floundering Ludo.

Looking more and more like the Frank Spencer of football, he then broke his ankle trying to score at the other end as we lost 2–1. Perhaps this was why 'Two Bob' Florin Raducioiu preferred to shop at Harvey Nicks rather than play at Stockport – he had a terrrible presentiment of what Dowie was about to do.

Of course, it was possible to make out a strong case for the merits of the journeyman's journeyman. While at Crystal Palace it was said that although he only possessed a tenth of Chris Armstrong's natural ability, he worked ten times as hard. He scored more goals for Northern Ireland than George Best, tackled harder than Matt Le Tissier and headed the ball better than Trevor Brooking. Dowie had a sense of humour too, declaring that 'We've now got two good-looking blokes up front' when West Ham signed film star-like Portuguese youngster Dani.

None of which could disguise the fact that Dowie was essentially useless. He had the ball control of a cement mixer and the speed of one of those two-storey-high trucks you see in South American copper mines. He was a qualified rocket engineer and would often shoot with the power of a rocket – but unfortunately with the same trajectory. His head appeared to be a cross between a sponge and an old threepenny bit, the ball being either harmlessly cushioned or pinging off it at any possible angle throughout 360 degrees.

Yet in a strange kind of way you couldn't help but love the hapless striker because he gave everything. In most matches he worked his neck bolts off. In 1996 we couldn't all be Spice Boys and finish like Robbie Fowler.

And somehow Dowie looked familiar. Those balls bouncing off his shins, the lack of pace, the misplaced passes . . . he was me, you see. It was just like my own efforts on the pitch. And thanks to Iain we could all fantasise that work rate might be enough. Dowie gave hope to every Sunday morning five-a-sider that Harry Redknapp might one day decide we can do a job in the Premiership.

Finally Dowie left West Ham to sign for QPR in the greatest masterstroke of Harry Redknapp's career. Even Arthur Daley's conscience might have been troubled by such a deal. For a mere £2 million West Ham signed Trevor Sinclair and sent Dowie and Keith Rowland to Loftus Road. Sinclair inspired some of West Ham's best ever seasons while QPR, despite Dowie scoring twice in 30 appearances, were eventually relegated to the second division. Many Irons fans still wake up at night with cold foreheads and ripped sheets following traumatic dreams that the deal has been revoked for contravening the Trades Description Act.

West Ham might have just lost to Southampton at St Mary's, but tonight we had Paolo Di Canio and Fredi Kanouté up front. Back in 1996 it was Iain Dowie. As Fatboy Slim might put it, we've come a long way, baby.

TOP TEN LEGENDARY WEST HAM CENTRE-FORWARDS

JOHN RADFORD: Knackered ex-Gunner who played some 3,000 games for the Hammers (or so it seemed) without scoring. When sold to Blackburn, he immediately scored on his début.

DAVID KELLY: Bought to replace Tony Cottee, he was expert at getting caught offside and falling over.

MIKE SMALL: Started reasonably well, then boasted of playing for England, and proceeded to perform like the least mobile target man in history. Formed a legendary offside partnership with Kelly.

MIKE NEWELL: One of Harry's loan signings, only instead of the bloke who was once quite good for title-winning Blackburn we seemed to get the Mike Newell who directed *Four Weddings And A Funeral* instead.

ALAN DICKENS: John Lyall converted the mild-mannered midfielder to a centre-forward with astonishing success. Dickens was so prolific – three goals in 1985–86 – that the fans immediately forgot about the departed Frank McAvennie.

PAUL HILTON: West Ham beat Bury 10–0 in the League Cup and so we signed their centre-half. And then converted him into an emergency centre-forward, with unspectacular results.

ALEX BUNBURY: Well, he was an international – albeit a Canadian one. Billy Bonds signed him on loan and thrust him into the second division, where he played a couple of games, was generally useless, and is now remembered solely for having a silly name.

ADE COKER: In the early '70s Ade scored at Crystal Palace and was hailed as the great hope among the emerging crop of young black players. So he immediately faded into obscurity.

TOMMY TAYLOR: Once converted to an emergency centre-forward by John Lyall for three games in the late '70s. Immensely successful with a strike rate of nil. A master of close control and springing the offside trap.

LES SEALEY: The late goalkeeper once came on as a substitute at Arsenal and was forced to play up front as all the other Hammers substitutes had been used. Immediately inspired a chant of 'We all agree, Sealey is better than Bergkamp!'.

25. A FISH NAMED PAOLO

West Ham 2 Blackburn 0 - 2 February 2002

Finally, it appears that Paolo is staying with West Ham. The deadline for signings being eligible for the European Champions League passes and with that, it seems that Manchester United have lost interest.

In the same week, some of the tabloids are suggesting that Fabio Capello will be the new Manchester United manager. Could this be the real reason Di Canio didn't move? In Paolo's autobiography he reveals how he ended his career with Milan by telling their then manager, the very same Fabio Capello: 'You're crazy, you're sick in the head. You go fuck off . . . I'm not going to hang around here and look at your ugly penis face any longer!' Their reunion would have been, erm, interesting, as indeed would the prospect of what might have happened if Di Canio had ever addressed Sir Alex Ferguson in such terms.

Paolo celebrates his continuing career with the Hammers by utilising the Eminem manual of diplomacy and making an extraordinary attack on the club in the *Daily Mail*, in an interview given to the man who ghosted his autobiography, Gabriele Marcotti. Perhaps this is all part of his bargaining for a new contract at the end of next season, but as negotiations go, it's about as subtle as his genital-oriented insults once aimed at Fabio Capello.

While reiterating that 'This is my second home, my shirt is like my second skin', Di Canio insists that the move did not break down because of his demands for a loyalty payment, an extra year's contract at United or the failure of United to sell Dwight Yorke. Had he wanted a move: 'I could have been a Manchester United player by Christmas. If I want a move I know how to get a move.' But he is still bitter at the way the transfer saga was handled, saying: 'The supporters must be treated with more respect, the club should have the honesty to tell them I was up for sale. Instead, they put all the burden on Glenn Roeder.'

He then lambasts the board, in terms that are likely to infuriate the traditionally conservative men who run the club: 'Roeder is the scapegoat for

139

everything. I don't think most of our fans even know what Paul Aldridge [the managing director] and Terry Brown [the chairman] look like. They should be showing their faces to the fans.'

Di Canio then goes on to assert that 'Glenn Roeder was given the job but not given the tools to succeed' and accuses the board of being asset strippers – 'It's obvious the club intends to sell the best players and replace them with cheaper, mediocre versions.'

He says that he worries that young stars like Carrick, Cole and Defoe will be sold because Roeder does not yet have the clout that Harry Redknapp had, and, most worryingly, compares the club to Sheffield Wednesday: 'Even Blackburn, a club which is no bigger than us, spent £15 million on two players alone. What worries me is that I've seen this before at Sheffield Wednesday and look where they are now. We can't continue unearthing talented young players or getting bargain players on the cheap, like they did with me.'

These are worries that many fans might articulate in the Boleyn pub, but is it helpful to reveal them in public at this moment? You start to wonder if Di Canio is believing too much of his own publicity or if he is simply raging at the fact that, at 33, he might be expendable. He criticises the media for twisting his words, but then uses it himself to lash his employers. The surest way of not having your words twisted is to say nothing to the press. It seems that Roeder simply felt the player might want to move to Old Trafford and, if that was so, then £3.5 million was a decent price for a player of Di Canio's age.

Glenn Roeder is, as ever, tactful, but basically seems to be telling Paolo to stop sulking. Significantly, he contradicts one of Di Canio's main claims. On the eve of the Blackburn game he emphasises: 'I never wanted Paolo to go and neither was I put under pressure to sell him. When I took this job I didn't have to sell anybody and that still applies. I want to draw a line under this now.' He says that the Di Canio saga has become a distraction but now he wants to get on with trying to win games. He also seems to be challenging him to produce his best form: 'Paolo is an integral part of this team and I want to see him at his very best for what remains of the season.'

Perhaps much of the problem lies in Di Canio's complicated psyche and his feelings of insecurity. He feels West Ham owe him a debt of loyalty but perhaps he should also remember that it was West Ham who rescued his career after the infamous referee shoving incident. Very few managers would start negotiating a new contract when a high-earning 33-year-old still has a season and a half of his current contract left.

The Blackburn game comes as a welcome distraction. As the game kicks off it's reassuring to know that at least Dan didn't bet on West Ham to win the league. On the morning of the game Big Joe informs me that West Ham are now officially 1,250 to 1 to win the Championship.

There is going to be no repeat of that 7–1 débâcle today. Despite his midweek outburst, Di Canio immediately looks more happy and involved and is a major influence on the game with his dribbles and flicks. Steve Lomas has another fine game in midfield, the anchor behind all the Fancy Dans, and West Ham look lively and sharp. After 17 minutes Kanouté plays a through ball past Blackburn's non-existent offside trap to Trevor Sinclair. Tricky Trev glides round the Tellytubby-like Taylor and smacks an emphatic shot into the corner. It's another fine goal from the man who is certainly not playing like a malcontent, despite his transfer request.

Blackburn's Duff presents a danger on the left with some fine dribbles and crosses, while Andy Cole threatens with his speed, but Christian Dailly, newly discovered football genius, shackles him effectively for most of the game.

A key moment comes early in the second half when Duff again beats Schemmel to plant a glorious cross into the box, which Matt Jansen flicks at and David James brilliantly tips onto the post. Or maybe he was just put off by the keeper's yellow tea-cosy hairstyle.

Kanouté pokes a good chance wide, but just as we're worrying that he's knackered after staying up with his newborn baby, he knocks one in. On 56 minutes Di Canio plays a quick-fire exchange of passes with Fredi and sends the Frenchman clear to poke the ball past Friedel. The celebrations are bizarre. Di Canio has a one-man conversation with the Bobby Moore Stand, elaborately kissing his badge and gesticulating and shouting in a manner that would have him certified if he was in Leicester Square after dark.

Paolo's ebullient mood continues as for the first time in weeks he seems to be really enjoying himself. The crowd chant his aria with real passion again. After Cole is brought down another bizarre incident occurs as Cole, Defoe and co. wrestle over the ball. As he runs over to take the resulting corner Di Canio playfully mimes a series of punches as if he is enjoying the young pups scrapping and anticipating cuffing them again in training soon.

As the final whistle blows on a 2–0 home victory, Di Canio continues his one-man mission to show the government why care in the community is not working. He rushes to the Bobby Moore Stand again, kisses and punches his badge, pats his backside and then appears to be playing charades as he goes into an elaborate writing mime. He could be asking for a new contract, then again maybe he's just referring to a three-syllable title of a film. Is this man an aria short of an opera? He is talking to himself, clutching his badge, kissing it, gesticulating again and generally performing a one-man piece of performance art worthy of a place at the Edinburgh Fringe. The Reduced Shakespeare Company could never compete with this. If Paolo was selling *The Big Issue* you'd pay your money and scarper. As entertainment it certainly beats all those mime artists in Covent Garden.

After the match Roeder says that he is 'absolutely delighted' that Di Canio is staying and the man himself surprises everyone by revealing that the real reason he didn't sign for Manchester United was not contract haggles, loyalty payments, or United's failure to sell Dwight Yorke, but a fish named Paolo. He reveals: 'The man who comes to my house and feeds my piranha fish said he would kill them if I left West Ham to join Manchester United. So I told him I would not go. And I begged him don't kill them, they are like my children. And now the fish are happy.'

Perhaps Paolo felt outdone by Eric Cantona's seagulls following the trawler. He goes on to explain: 'Yes, I have a lot of piranhas. I don't give them names though. Only one – the biggest and the fattest. My daughter Ludovica named him Paolo Di Canio because he wants to eat up everything. He is all over the tank getting at the other piranhas.'

It was left to the *Evening Standard* to trace the man who sold Paolo his piranhas, one Keith Thomas of The Stow Aquarium in Walthamstow. Hammers fan Thomas revealed that Paolo always made him coffee when he visited, loved talking about West Ham and now has ten red-bellied piranhas (no relation to Monty Python's Doug and Dinsdale Piranha).

Thomas said: 'Paolo actually wanted 11 to make up a whole team, but I could only get him ten so I told him the other one had been sent off.' As for the on/off transfer saga, Thomas revealed: 'I knew that he didn't want to leave Upton Park. He was getting more and more unhappy about it. I was desperate for him to stay so I took drastic action. I knew Paolo was Italian so I talked about the piranhas and made him an offer he couldn't refuse.'

Hence Paolo continues to sleep with the fishes, the sharks have been outwitted, and for once Fergie has failed to reel in his man.

26. NIGHTMARE ON GREEN STREET

West Ham 2 Chelsea 3 - 6 February 2002

Only West Ham could turn an FA Cup fourth-round replay at home to Chelsea into an anti-climax. The club's crass decision to charge top prices for our third game with Chelsea in 17 days, which is also being televised live on Sky, results in an attendance of 27,272, some 8,000 below the expected sell-out crowd. It doesn't even make commercial sense. Surely there can be little difference between a full house paying slightly lower rates and a crowd that is 8,000 down. Reduce the prices and you create a well of goodwill; squeeze the fans and take advantage of their loyalty and you just create yet more cynicism. And who knows what difference an extra 8,000 West Ham fans in the ground might make to West Ham's progress?

You wonder if the board really understand football supporters. It seems that little has changed since the days of 1991 when they attempted to foist the hated Bond Scheme on fans, asking them to pay £1,000 for the right to buy a season ticket in order to fund redevelopments required by the Taylor Report. That turned into a débâcle and resulted in relegation and a drop of 10,000 on home gates. Charlton, for example, reward their supporters by laying on free coaches to an away game once a season. But then they're run by fans.

Tonight my seat has cost £42 plus a £1.50 booking fee, £2.50 for a programme and £4.40 for a tube pass. Several of my fellow season ticket holders have turned into West Ham refuseniks. Tonight there are just myself, Fraser, Matt and Matt's brother in row F beside a bank of unoccupied seats.

But at least Jeremy Nicholas does his best to build up the atmosphere. 'Will anyone not willing to cheer their hearts out for West Ham please go home now!' he pleads, before naming the sides and introducing a new monicker for 'Vlad "The Impaler" Labant!' (with a nickname like that, let's hope Frank McAvennie doesn't mistakenly introduce him to any page three models).

Paolo Di Canio has started his three-match suspension and has flown back to Italy to spend more time with his dentist. Michael Carrick is having an

143

operation on his troublesome groin and will be out for six weeks, while Fredi Kanouté is unfit again. Lomas and Defoe come in, along with Paul Kitson, who has several days' growth of beard and appears to be auditioning for a part in a spaghetti western.

It turns out to be a cracking cup-tie. The crowd raise themselves with several choruses of 'Stick your blue flag . . .' Within a minute Terry goes close for Chelsea before Trevor Sinclair sweeps downfield on an inspired run to shoot across the face of Cudicini's goal. West Ham appear to be up for it. Schemmel may well win my vote for player of the year for his tireless surges down the wing; Kitson is doing well for someone who hasn't played for weeks and Sinclair looks to have the beating of Ferrer.

After 37 minutes West Ham take the lead. A Lomas cross is nodded down by Kitson and from wide on the right, both feet off the ground, Defoe cheekily volleys the ball towards goal, where it strikes Terry's leg and deflects past the floundering Cudicini. No other striker would have even tried it. The strike is instinctive and the technique superb. It's reminiscent of the young Michael Owen for its audacity. This boy can score from anywhere.

Kitson almost makes it two when he ghosts behind Le Saux, takes Sinclair's pass down well, but fires too tamely at goal, allowing Cudicini to save.

Then come those five dreadful minutes when all Irons fans live in terror of the legendary half-time wobble effect. The players have been repeatedly warned not to give away free-kicks around the edge of the box. Repka duly handles the ball to prevent Petit going clear and is booked. It is debatable whether Petit would have got a shot in with Christian Dailly waiting to cover, but even if he had, anything would have been preferable to facing a Hasselbaink free-kick. Referee Poll stands over the ball as James lines up the wall, then obligingly moves out of the way as Hasselbaink arrows the ball into the top corner. James, otherwise brilliant, is still by his near post apparently reading *Dodgy Hair-Colouring Weekly*.

The game is even more frantic after half-time. On 50 minutes Schemmel surges down the right again, does well to win the ball back from Desailly and play it to Hutchison whose first-time shot from the right is pushed out by Cudicini into the path of Defoe, who has again reacted before anyone else. Hammers are in the lead and the ground erupts. Preston, Preston, you are next. It's looking good, at one point the impish Defoe, apparently in a cul-de-sac, wriggles past three defenders on the edge of the box, beats World Cup winner Desailly and fires low across the Chelsea goal.

Don Hutchison is playing well too, attempting to slow the play down and doing some fine defensive work, including a great saving tackle in the West Ham box. Only on 65 minutes he does the unthinkable. Attempting to send a cushioned back header to James he merely plops the ball into the path of Forrsell. Time slows down, a collective gasp of horror grips the Upper East Stand. Forrsell pokes the ball apologetically over the line. Hutchison looks like a man who has just bought 100,000 shares in Enron the day before the company went bankrupt.

'Hutchison, you farrrking wanker!' echoes a cry in the night. What was he doing? Was it a mental aberration? Whatever, it's tough on a man who has been one of our better players.

Hutch visibly loses confidence, making more unforced errors, but then almost redeems himself when he has a header tipped over by Cudicini. If he had placed it anywhere else but around the keeper's head he would surely have scored. James makes a fine block from Hasselbaink, then there's a bizarre Sunday league scramble in the West Ham goalmouth before the ball is cleared. The substitutions say everything about the respective strength of the squads. They bring on Zola, we bring on Todorov.

'Do we have to pay extra if it goes into extra-time?' I ask the others.

'Yep, they just deduct it straight from your credit card,' says Fraser. 'Half an hour plus pens, that'll be £21.' We begin to have fearful visions of Todorov and Foxe missing vital penalties.

Then on 85 minutes sub Labant plays in a great left-foot free-kick which Dailly meets with a firm header. The ball strikes the post, bobbles on the line and is fumbled clear. It would have been Christian's first goal for the club and we'd have been into the next round.

James makes a great close-range save from Stanic. We move into injury time and no one can say that West Ham do not deserve a draw at least. Only Hutchison's horrible header has cost us the win.

Chelsea force a late corner which Lomas heads behind. Le Saux fires in another corner. There are 92 minutes gone. Three Chelsea players stand together on the edge of the area then run in all directions. Terry races into the box to beat Repka to the ball and head against the post and the ball bounces into the net above a powerless Schemmel.

Total silence in the stand. Pandemonium in the Chelsea end. Fraser wipes his eye and looks blankly ahead. Matt and his brother have the look of Martin Sheen at the end of *Apocalypse Now*; these are men who have seen too much. A few seconds later and the final whistle blows. Frank Lampard joins the celebrating Chelsea players in front of their fans.

'Oh well, it's only going to be 23 years before we win something again,' I mumble. With brilliant timing, Jeremy Nicholas plays the Stereophonics' version of the maudlin 'Handbags and Gladrags'.

On Sky, Glenn Roeder has the dazed look of Conrad's Mr Kurtz and it would be no surprise if he simply intoned 'The horror! The horror!' at the cameras.

He composes himself and speaks: 'I've spoken to the lads, there was no need to shout and scream. The three horrible goals we conceded disguised the performance. I thought the performance was good. All the goals were sloppy from our point of view. The first free-kick was unnecessary, the second spoke for itself and the winner 30 seconds from the end, Terry's had a free header which is very disappointing to say the least.'

Outside the Bobby Moore Stand a sea of blank, disbelieving faces are in motion, shuffling automaton-like towards Upton Park tube. A legion of stunned, disbelieving humanity suffering from post-traumatic cup syndrome. 'Fucking hell! . . . another dead season! . . . every fucking year! . . . it was worse than Tottenham . . . they didn't score their second, Hutchison did . . . it was awful . . . if only Dailly's header had gone in . . . our header hits the post and bounces out, their header hits the post and goes in . . .'

There is no God. We have all become existentialists now. We are responsible for our own actions. And we have dedicated our lives to a team that may never win anything ever again.

On Green Street a fan simply bellows 'Choker!' followed by a primeval cry of 'AAAAAAARGH!'. For some reason a police van is behind us trying to crawl through a crowd of 27,000 people. An irate crowd shout abuse. In front of me the angriest man in the world, neck veins bulging, punches the windows and hollers, 'You think this is fucking clever! You fucking wankers!'

Matt, Fraser and myself head to the Prince of Wales and seek some amelioration of our state through lager and IPA. 'The Cup's been devalued since it went to Cardiff. We're saving ourselves for Wembley,' suggests Fraser. And at least we're saving the money on the Preston tickets.

Matt cheers us up by announcing that not only did we turn down the chance to sign Andres D'Alessandro an Argentinian super kid now valued at £16 million, Harry once gave Ukrainian star Shevchenko a trial in a match at Barnet. In fact we could conceivably have had Chilean superstar Salas (once on offer at £2 million) and Shevchenko up front together. Which makes us all feel a lot worse.

Fraser reveals that at a premiere in the West End last night he was almost hit by a bus in Shaftesbury Avenue. 'You'd have died thinking we could still get through. Mind you, your estate would never have got a ticket refund out of the club,' says Matt.

Matt and myself take the district line westwards. There are people on the train returning home late from work, some who have simply been for a night out. What could they know of our suffering? As Conrad wrote in *Heart of Darkness*: 'They trespassed upon my thoughts. They were intruders whose knowledge of life was to me an irritating pretence.'

'I'd have settled for the semi-finals even. That's almost success. I've had my expectations lowered . . .' mutters Matt.

'I could have taken a routine 0–2 home defeat,' I say. 'But we actually played well.'

'I know,' says Matt. 'It's like John Cleese said in *Clockwise*, "It's not the despair I can't take . . . it's the hope".'

27. ON THE ROEDER SOMEWHERE?

'Most of the time I'm pretty serious because that's me being natural,' says West Ham gaffer Glenn Roeder. 'I don't like false people. I do have a dry sense of humour, but not laughing and giggling all the time. We're paid professionals and I can't see how you can concentrate 100 per cent on the training ground if everything becomes a joke and a laugh.

'Surely it's not asking too much of highly paid professional sportsmen to concentrate from ten thirty to twelve thirty or one o'clock most days? I like to hear the banter before training. I like to hear the boys laughing and screaming and shouting, but once ten thirty comes this is our workplace, boys, let's concentrate and let's try to come off the training ground every day thinking even if I've only learned one thing at least I've learnt something.'

Serious person or not, just a week after the Chelsea defeat in the FA Cup, Glenn Roeder might be excused a wry chuckle, having just been given a three-year extension to his original one-year contract. When he was appointed last summer he was derided by the fans and was one of the early season favourites for the sack after that humiliating 7–1 defeat at Blackburn. But slowly Roeder has turned the club round, buying reasonably well, dealing with the on/off Di Canio transfer saga and Hayden Foxe 'pisser-gate' incident with dignity, and trying to instil a new professionalism into the club.

In person Roeder combines his trademark undertaker's suit with a Billy Bragg-ish accent and a quiet self-belief that is reminiscent of his former employer Glenn Hoddle. There is none of the Cockney geezer banter of ex-gaffer Harry Redknapp. You can tell Roeder is a purposeful man by the speed he walks. I struggle to keep up as he glides briskly past reception and into the bowels of the new Dr Martens Stand.

As we enter a hospitality room, Roeder denies Sky an interview because they don't have an appointment, telling press officer Peter Stewart, 'Nah, they're cheeky!' then joking with Stewart about doing lines for being late. He summons up some coffee from one of the hotel staff as Paul Goddard pops his head round the door to joke: 'Is this your office now?' An outsider gets the impression of a happy and businesslike working environment.

WEST HAM

Roeder talks in slow, measured sentences, but beneath this there is controlled passion. Brought up in Poplar (or 'Popular' as he calls it) and Hornchurch he was a West Ham fan as a boy, standing either in the Chicken Run or on a beer box by the players' tunnel. 'You knew Bobby Moore was leading the players out because he'd throw the ball up, you'd just see the ball first and then Bobby and the players. It's always been unique and special at Upton Park, the banter, the tightness to the pitch. I was eight or nine then, but after that I didn't get the chance to see West Ham much because I was playing football myself and it took over my life.

'One of the games that sticks in my mind was standing in the Chicken Run and watching us lose 6–1 at home to Manchester United, as they won the Championship. Charles scored first for West Ham, then Charlton, Law and Best took over. It was a rotten day but now when you look back and understand things more you realise what a brilliant team that Man United side was.'

That serious side of Roeder's nature is evident when I mention the fact that Paolo Di Canio refused to move to Man United because the man who feeds his piranhas had threatened to starve them if he left, and ask if he himself has any unusual pets. GR is apparently the only person in the country not to have read this in the newspaper accounts of the Blackburn game.

'I didn't know he had piranhas. I do have ten fish, four goldfish and four coy carp in a garden pond, which I find very relaxing, just looking in and watching them . . .' At this point I'm imagining what might happen should Paolo have a disagreement with the Hammers boss, envisaging coy carp being set upon by piranhas in the mother of all West Ham fish wars.

'You could say it's corny, but my hobby is my wife Faith and my three children,' continues Glenn. 'Without their support the job would be a lot tougher than it is. You have to be in the pole position to realise it is a tough job. It's very rewarding when you win, there's not a better feeling than preparing a team all week and winning; you get a feeling of glowing satisfaction on a Saturday evening. You prepare them all week and they've done the job. But you can get pretty fed up when you don't get the result.

'On Sunday mornings I go to Chadwell Heath for an hour to check on everyone, thereafter I spend Sunday with my wife, daughter and two boys. It's nice to shut the front door and be with my family. That's about the only hobby I've got or am interested in.'

Roeder might not be aware of Paolo's piranhas, but a lot of commentators did predict he would have trouble handling him. Yet he seems to have won Di Canio's respect and handled the whole Man United transfer saga with some tact and skill.

'Paolo Di Canio has not been a problem to handle,' he emphasises. 'It's a question of mutual respect. If you treat people correctly, and if they're decent people, you hope they respond and show you respect too. I think I have a good working relationship with Paolo. I would say that I understand him as much if not more than any other manager he's ever worked with. He's been here three years now, which is longer than he's stayed at any one club.

'He is a very professional person but what has at times upset him greatly is that his personal standards are so high and when he sees others not coming up to the same standards, he gets disappointed with them. I've seen that in other gifted players that I've played with. Sometimes they can't understand why everyone is not as talented as they are and that frustrates them.'

Despite the FA Cup defeat by Chelsea it's been a good week for the West Ham boss. Normally stars make transfer requests after cup defeats, but astonishingly Trevor Sinclair has withdrawn his. In addition, it has emerged that Roeder was only on a one-year contract; a sign that the board saw his appointment as a huge gamble. But now the board has acknowledged his good work by offering him a three-year extension to his contract.

Sinclair's decision has clearly delighted him, and he's not slow to claim credit for Trev's change of mind. 'I think it's testimony to what we're trying to do that Trevor Sinclair has come off the transfer list. He's 28 and I'm saying to Trevor, "Why not stay and be part of what I would hope would be a successful rebuilding programme, be one of the key players over the next couple of years and take some credit for that yourself, take some satisfaction from that."

'OK, I understand he wants European football season in, season out, which all footballers should want, but a club that he would like to join hasn't come forward. So I've said, "Why don't you stay with us, Trevor, and take some satisfaction over the next couple of years and be a part of what we hope will take the club forward. I know you've been here a long while, I know you've seen players sold which upset you – but hopefully this is a new start for all of us and I want you to stay and be part of that and if we do move the club forward."'

As for his new contract, Roeder acknowledges, with engaging honesty, that he was not the fans' choice.

'Terry Brown and the board of directors had to show an amazing amount of courage to give me the opportunity in the first place. It would have been far easier to appoint a manager with years of experience in the Premier League and there were some of those out of work who made themselves available, and there were several younger managers of my age with experience at Premiership level who have done well too. So it would have been a lot easier to go down what appeared to be a safer road.

'But I'd like to think that now they've worked closely with me for seven months and know absolutely where I'm coming from and what we're trying to achieve – they only partly knew me as a coach here before. There is an excellent working relationship with the MD Paul Aldridge, we probably talk a dozen times a day. They've seen me work at close quarters and they feel safer and more confident that in their eyes I've shown enough to trust the club with over the next three years because it really is going to be a tough few years ahead.'

Did he ever doubt himself after those humiliating defeats at Everton and Blackburn?

'No, I didn't have doubts!' he laughs. 'It made me realise there was a lot more work to do on the training ground. And we do work hard there. We try to structure the practices in a way that challenges the players' brains. They shouldn't become bored with what we do with them every day because we do like to vary what we do, get some pattern of play into the team. At times we've done that well. We've tried to stick to our 4–4–2. When we've had our best eleven out we've had some good performances. The down was Blackburn, the high was winning at Old Trafford. We certainly upset them that day because they then went unbeaten for nine games.'

That faith in coaching has certainly proved beneficial to West Ham's most improved player, defender Christian Dailly, and Roeder is clearly pleased that I've mentioned him.

'Christian Dailly came to the club and it didn't go as well for him as he would have wanted. First impressions are important in football. So it was a case of having to work with him on the training ground. He's a very nice man, he's an excellent player to coach, he listens. I would say that we have been able to get more out of him than he's ever got out of himself before, anywhere in his career,' declares Roeder with some pride. 'I would say that overall Christian's been in the form of his life! We've got every ounce out of him and he's got every ounce out of himself, we just need to keep him going to the end of the season in that vein of form.'

Roeder's approach has been vindicated in the Scot's performances and Dailly is in my running for player of the season. 'I think he's started to win a lot of the supporters over,' continues Roeder. 'I was so disappointed for all of us, and particularly him, that had he scored against Chelsea we'd have held on and won the game 3–2. That would have been a brilliant personal achievement for him, but it came off the inside of the post. We've had to work with the coaches to improve what we've got because we have to, we can't just discard players and buy someone else. We have to work with what we've inherited.'

What did upset Roeder was the criticism that came from Harry Redknapp after the Blackburn débâcle. When asked about this he inhales sharply and pauses before saying: 'I thought, to be honest, I was an easy target and I thought it was sad and a shame that some people who had been in the job and knew how tough it was could have a swipe. I wouldn't stick my fingers up to 'em and I certainly wouldn't have a go back. I wouldn't want to go down to their level because that's a cheap way going through the media. There's only one way to deal with people like that and that's by hopefully being successful and getting the results that they obviously don't want you to get. But it's sad, I look at them as pretty sad people.'

ON THE ROEDER SOMEWHERE?

He is careful not to mention Redknapp by name, but the sense of outrage is clear. The whole episode was shoddy, and diminished Harry's reputation in the eyes of even those supporters like me who had defended his undoubted success in establishing West Ham as a Premiership side on virtually no money and building up a superb youth policy.

Roeder believes that he has 11 good players and his long-term plan is to strengthen the squad. Will that mean sales of Defoe, Carrick and Cole?

'The good thing is that the directors have said to me you don't have to sell any player you don't want to sell to raise funds. We do not want to have to go down that road of selling any of those young players that we produced ourselves. The downside is there aren't any funds already there to spend. Without doubt you have to have a squad in the Premiership, you can't get through the season with just 11 good players. We have got 12 good players who I'd call real quality players, but if you scratch the surface we haven't got strength in depth.

'I'd like to be able to change that overnight and I've got confidence in my own ability to select players who are good enough to wear our shirt. I like to feel with all the signings I've made people can see where I'm coming from and they've all done well. But to do it more quickly you'd have to throw more cash at the job and the board have been crystal clear, they've shown me the facts, we're not in a position to do that.'

You wonder if he ever becomes frustrated at the club's perpetual lack of cash. His answer is typically diplomatic: 'It's human nature to want to be able to run before you learn to walk and I'm no different. I'd like to be able to get on with restructuring the squad, but I've got to show patience by being as selective as I can with the players that I bring in over the next two more seasons. Hopefully we'll come through this period and end up with a stronger squad.'

Roeder emphasises he is now having to target his signings carefully: 'I have probably spent close to £15–£16 million which is a little bit more than the Frank Lampard money, my deficit in the transfer market is £4–5 million, with maybe a little money left over from Rio. We have probably seven, eight, nine players that I would want to build a squad around. It's no good selling any of that group of players because it is self-defeating. You take one step forward, two back. So when I'm dealing in the market it's easier to make a mistake buying players for less than a million.

'Buying Alan Shearer for £15 million is not a gamble. It's not finding a player. Buying Sebastien Schemmel at £450,000 is a big risk, because at £450,000 he shouldn't come up to the level that we want. But he has been one of our best players this season. His value now is probably two million plus. Vladimir Labant was £900,000 from Sparta Prague, the Manchester United of the Czech Republic. We feel we're going to get value for money.'

We talk some more about the other subtler changes that Roeder has made around Upton Park, such as making training more private by banning the public from watching, except at school half-terms. When he talks of banning agents from Chadwell Heath it again appears to be an unspoken criticism of Harry Redknapp.

'Agents can't just walk in when they want to anymore. Now if an agent wants to come in and see me he has to make an appointment. At Spurs or Arsenal agents can't just walk in and sit in the canteen. We had a situation where players were sitting next to complete strangers day in, day out. Players have got to feel comfortable talking to each other without worrying who's listening.

'The other change was we took on fitness coach John McCarthy, but that's undercooking him, he's a sports scientist. Fitness is not just running, it's working in the gym with players on specific weight programmes. Cole, Defoe, Carrick are young players who need to build up their upper body strength. We've now formed good habits. Players don't have to be told to go in there, they know their programme and in they go and do them. I'll wander through the gym and there are always players in there making their bodies look beautiful.'

Roeder seems unaware of the undertones of that remark, as I imagine our beautiful squad being drooled over on Old Compton Street. Mind you, all those good habits in the gym couldn't prevent the infamous Hayden Foxe 'pisser-gate' incident at the players' Christmas party . . .

In the manner of a pained and disappointed housemaster, Roeder pauses, purses his lips and addresses the subject.

'It was one player,' he says. 'One player let the side down and scored a big own goal. The strange thing is that when I found out who it was, I was surprised because he's never been a minute's problem while he's been at the club. He's a decent chap, hard working in training . . . He regretted it and was obviously disciplined in a way he accepted. Hopefully it will never happen again, full stop.'

Harry Redknapp appears to have irritated Roeder again after this incident. He continues: 'It's all very well people afterwards – again managers they should know better – saying that "I've had this problem in the past, so I banned Christmas parties". But that's not telling the full truth. Yes, they did ban Christmas parties, but are they that naïve to think that the players never went out? Of course they went out. The manager concerned might have banned Christmas parties at the club, but they still went out, I saw that with my own eyes.

'What disappoints me most about that episode was that for a couple of days before going out, and the morning after training of the day they went out, I sat all of them down and reminded them of their responsibilities. It was reading the riot act really, so it was really imprinted on their minds that there mustn't be trouble and everyone remembered, bar one. You educate by keeping talking, keep reminding them until they all remember. But it was one player . . . over 60 per cent were already at home in bed when the incident occurred. But one player let the team down.'

So was he a good pro himself?

'I'm one of those people who says he who has never committed a sin start throwing the first stones. But I'd say be shrewd, be sensible, be clever, use common sense. It would have been nice to stay on at school and achieve great academic results. But I wanted to play football and left at 15, so from my perspective of not having an academic career at school, I think the biggest quality you can be given in life is to be given common sense. Know what's right and wrong and you'll get through your life no problems. We all know what's right and wrong, when we're thinking "hold on, this is wrong, don't do it" . . .'

We move on to discuss his managerial influences. His friend Glenn Hoddle was obviously a mentor during their England days together (although hopefully Roeder will never grow a mullet and make a single with him), but perhaps the biggest influence on his thinking was playing for Terry Venables at QPR.

'We still keep in touch and I think Terry is pretty proud that the likes of John Gregory, myself and several other players have gone into management. He's left a bit of himself on all of us. Terry is an excellent coach and a good man manager, it's just a shame that other things didn't help him. It's a shame he's not still managing at the very top. I think his talent is wasted on that *Premiership* programme every Saturday night, because he's got so much more to offer.'

Another huge influence on Roeder's style was Arthur Cox at Newcastle. 'Arthur was great at getting the best out of players through what we'd now call sport psychology. He just knew what turned a player on and off. Take Chris Waddle and Peter Beardsley. Waddle played better after a good telling-off, it fired him up. Peter Beardsley always played better if you put your arm round him and gave him a cuddle and told him how good he was. Waddle would have taken his foot off the pedal if you'd put your arm around him, while rollicking Peter would not have been good for his confidence.'

So does Roeder ever give his players rollickings? 'One or two you can fire up with a rollicking, others fall apart. You've got to know your players. At this level you're dealing with very wealthy people. For me the days of slinging teacups at walls were rubbish. I could never have gone down that route, that wasn't me by nature. If I had a manager who ranted and raved I had no respect for them, because they're not being constructive in their criticism. If you rant and rave you just shout the first thing that comes into your head and it's water off a duck's back, it's nonsense.'

At the start of the season, like many supporters, I'd greeted his appointment with some foreboding. But meeting the man has left me more reassured than I'd have imagined. It's typical of Roeder's style that West Ham's reserve game against Arsenal kicked off ten minutes ago but he's still happy to talk.

Unusually, in Premiership football, he is a manager who thinks long term and stresses the value of patience, particularly with injuries and the careful nurturing of youngsters like Jermain Defoe. Gone are the days of strapping the likes of Stewart Robson together and hoping their cycle shorts would hold all the bits together.

'We're going to need our fair share of luck too in keeping the right players fit,' adds Roeder. 'We've just lost Michael Carrick for six weeks, which is desperate news for us. Young Michael is without doubt going to play for England many, many times. He's been capped as a teenager and he's not going to just get one cap, he'll get many. But he needed the groin operation and he's too valuable a player to ask to soldier on and not be quite as good as he can be. I've always believed that patience in the long run will pay off and it was the right thing to do for a player that is so valuable to us. Have the operation, bite the bullet and hopefully he'll be back for the Man United game.'

There are no other extravagant predictions. When I ask about his grand four-year plan for West Ham and mention UEFA Cup qualification his answer says much about the man himself: 'Only a fool would try and predict football results and put pressure on the players. I much prefer to try and come along the rounds quietly and unseen.'

28. DOWN TO THE BARE BONES

Bolton 1 West Ham 0 - 9 February 2002
West Ham 1 Middlesbrough 0 - 23 February 2002

It's any old Irons at Bolton. West Ham are without six first teamers, the suspended Di Canio and Repka, the flu-ridden Sinclair and the injured Hutchison, Carrick and Winterburn. We are, as Harry Redknapp habitually declared, 'down to the bare bones'. The perpetually half-injured Fred Kanouté returns, and in comes Richard Garcia, the Aussie youngster who impressed during last season's loan at Orient, making his first full start. Hayden Foxe, Scott Minto and Vladimir Labant also start as, without Repka, Roeder tries to seal his leaky defence with a 3–5–2 formation.

At least the pain of defeat in the Cup by Chelsea has been ameliorated slightly by the astonishing news that Trevor Sinclair has withdrawn his transfer request. Aren't players supposed to leave rather than stay after Cup defeats? Sinclair tells the press: 'I am enjoying it more than ever, and a lot goes down to the players I play with; if they didn't support me it would be different. The coaching staff are good and I am enjoying it – I couldn't be happier.' He also adds that he doesn't want to be seen behaving 'like a spoiled brat'. Footballer in humility and sensible decision shock. It's equivalent to a £10 million signing and hopefully ends all talk of a player exodus at Upton Park. Trevor has at last realised that he is in the international frame, playing well, scoring goals and working for a decent, honest manager.

Meanwhile Paolo Di Canio, perhaps feeling miffed at not having made the back pages for a couple of days, announces that he will be leaving – not for Man United but at the end of his contract in the summer of 2003 as he wants to return to Italy to be closer to his extended family after the death of his aunt.

Back at the Reebok, Bolton have not won for 12 Premiership games, a statistic which always sends the dread chill of fear into the hearts of Hammers fans. Winless runs, goal famines, hundredth league goals, whatever ailment plagues your side it can be cured by the simple measure of playing West Ham.

Why, we even rejuvenate careers; almost single-handedly we restored Nick Barmby to the England side after he scored a hat trick in a 4–0 home defeat by Everton a couple of years ago.

The Irons start confidently with Defoe missing a good chance early on. But gradually a nervous Bolton take hold of the game through the superbly named Stig Tofting – surely a man destined to play Compo in any remake of *Last of the Summer Wine*. Nicknamed 'The Lawnmower', the veteran is, as they say, an abrasive midfielder, who cost just £250,000 and looks as if he's been recruited from Vinnie Jones's old building site. His tattooed muscles and sheer energy galvanise Bolton, who score after 37 minutes when the Hammers defence fails to clear Tofting's long throw and Gardner drills the ball home through the crowded area.

In the second half David 'Simba' James could comfortably watch a video of *The Lion King* in his goal without undue disturbance. Cole dominates midfield despite numerous clumpings. Labant, Kanouté and Schemmel have decent shots, and Dailly and Garcia go close with headers. In injury time Kitson has a header saved by Jaaskelainen and the final whistle blows to roars of delight from the Bolton fans. The players have tried hard and West Ham have had twice as many shots and corners as Bolton.

After a fortnight's international break in which Joe Cole and David James make appearances in England's draw against Holland and Steve Lomas scores in Northern Ireland's defeat in Poland, West Ham play their last game of February against Middlesbrough at Upton Park.

Inside Ken's Café we watch seasons collide. Bright winter sunshine gives way to rain and then fleeting snow. It's another 'kids for a quid' game today and several youngsters are being introduced to the benefits of Ken's Café's sports nutrition and isotonic tea. Part-timer Mike has brought along his son Scott to see West Hampstead (at least that's what he keeps calling them) while an old school pal and exiled Hammer living in Cornwall, Steve Flory, has come with another Scott, the six-year-old foster son of another old school friend, Alison, who as I've said once described Upton Park as 'like walking into a room full of really angry men'. Although quite what the adoption agency would make of exposing a youngster to the class A drug that is West Ham United at such an age is a matter of some concern.

Young Scott's introduction to football culture is swift. Walking down Tudor Street we come across four lurching, very drunken Boro fans carrying a blue bag of Hammers scarves and hats which they have apparently nicked off some hapless street trader. As they leave a trail of claret and blue scarves behind them, one of them accosts young Scott, already in a replica shirt, and places a scarf around his neck and a Hammers' baseball hat on his head. 'There you go, son, aye he's all kitted out now!' slurs the amiable Boro beer monster. In the two minutes' walk from Ken's Scott has already witnessed drunkenness and theft – and the game hasn't even kicked off yet.

DOWN TO THE BARE BONES

West Ham are still without the suspended Di Canio, Schemmel and Sinclair, while Carrick is still injured. Glenn Roeder has opted for a five-man defence again, with Ian Pearce making a welcome return from nearly two years of injury problems to partner Repka and Dailly in central defence, and Winterburn and Lomas on the flanks as wing-backs. But far more important than the team news is the dodgy barnet selection. Joe Cole has opted for a peroxide crew cut while David James, our stylistically challenged and apparently colour blind custodian, has replaced the Simba look with a bizarre series of blond squiggles – the much-admired mustard on a hot-dog look.

The new system creates problems and Middlesbrough have the better of the first half with Boksic and Whelan both missing good chances. Pearce looks rusty, having only played 70 minutes of a reserve game in his latest comeback, but sticks to his task. The rest of the side look muted and lack width. In the absence of Schemmel, you realise how much of West Ham's attacks are channelled through the underrated right-back.

Young Scott proudly shows me his three Kit-Kats and seems intent on eating them at once. He fidgets and spends much of the half looking behind him at the other kids in replica shirts. 'When are they going to score a goal?' he asks hopefully. Ah, if only goals arrived on schedule. I can only tell him that we'll score again, don't know where, don't know when, but I know we'll score again some sunny day.

The main excitement for the kids is the odd chant of 'Judas!' directed at former Hammer Paul Ince. Most of the youngsters would not even have been born when he infamously posed in a Man United shirt while still a West Ham player.

To compound our injury crisis, on 42 minutes Don Hutchison is stretchered off with a nasty-looking leg injury. Substitute Vladimir Labant immediately endears himself to the Hammers faithful by clattering into Paul Ince and receiving a booking.

In the second half West Ham improve a little, with Cole at last dominant in midfield and Ehiogu booked for bringing down Labant on the left. Aided by the tireless Nigel Winterburn, Labant gets in some good crosses but also spends much of the half falling over. He rushes to the touchline and complains anxiously about his footwear. It seems likes he's borrowed the legendary 'Goddard's Boots', the magic footwear that enables the wearer to fall over in nearly all goalmouth situations. Or maybe he's playing in white Astroturf trainers as that was all he could afford to buy in Slovakia.

Ince is having a good game in midfield, however, judging his defensive tackles well and on 66 minutes David James makes a brilliant save to keep his fierce shot out. Ince is then booked for a foul on Vladimir Labant and shouts abuse at the linesman in front of the Chicken Run, which goes down about as well as George Bush at a Pretzel-makers convention. (Bizarrely, the US President has just nearly choked on a Pretzel.) Actually, the hacks among us conclude that Ince's defence, that the Man United shirt-wearing incident was in fact a press cock-up, has a ring of authenticity to it, even if we do still 'ate Paul Ince.

The chant of 'Stand up if you 'ate Paul Ince!' wafts around the ground. There must be several thousand youngsters thinking that the entire Bobby Moore Stand are the bastard sons of Dr Hannibal Lecter. The kids certainly have a lot of work to do on their swearing. Two youngsters behind me are directing cries of 'Minstrel!' and 'Pilchard!' at Paul Ince and co.

At least Jeremy Nicholas, a man who'd get excited by a barn door opening, has remained awake and gleans great enjoyment from interrupting the game to announce 'Today's attendance is 35,420 – the biggest crowd at Upton Park this century!' He fails to add that they are attending the most tedious game of this or any other millennium.

Just when it's looking as if thousands of juveniles will be permanently mentally scarred by the experience – or, even worse, become Man United supporters – the breakthrough arrives. Labant plays a fine early ball down the left for Defoe to chase, Boro keeper Schwarzer races out to boot the ball down the pitch and back to Labant. Managing to stay upright for once, the Slovakian midfielder plays an instantaneous, precise long ball across the pitch to Fred Kanouté, lurking on the edge of the Boro area. Fred, who was described by fanzine *Over Land and Sea* as being 'so laid-back he could play in a deckchair on wheels', suddenly remembers that he is in fact a slumbering genius and controls the ball on his right before volleying home with his left as Schwarzer scrambles back across his goal. It's a great finish and the ground erupts in relief. Even young Scott looks moderately impressed.

There are only 14 minutes left but that's still enough for West Ham to defend deep and create the usual sensation of blind panic among the home supporters and for Ugo Ehiogu to be booked for the second time after bringing down poor Vladimir Labant again. The new signing has what they term an eventful game, being repeatedly kicked, falling over, getting booked and making a goal. Ince goes postal, haranguing the referee, pointing at Labant, pointing towards the tunnel and generally performing the role of pantomime villain to perfection. 'Stand up if you 'ate Paul Ince!' echoes around Upton Park once more.

The final whistle sounds and in an uncharacteristic display of emotion Glenn Roeder unfolds his arms and punches the air. It's been an ugly victory but a vital one. We now have 34 points, nine more than Blackburn who are third from bottom, and can look towards a top-half finish rather than a relegation struggle.

Jeremy Nicholas reads out the day's other results, does a cod Scouse accent for the Merseyside derby, and then declares: 'We go above Sunderland, we go above Middlesbrough, when you turn to page 324 of Ceefax tonight we'll be on the first page – we're in the top half of the table!' Well, at least we will be until tomorrow afternoon, when Charlton play, but that doesn't worry the ebullient announcer, fast becoming the Dr Pangloss of Upton Park. There won't be a light ale or tub of jellied eels left untouched in Chez Nicholas tonight.

Only in the aftermath of an important victory comes more bad news. Don Hutchison, our second most expensive signing ever, has damaged his cruciate ligament and will be out until Christmas, while the luckless Steve Lomas, having just recovered from a broken toe after long-term injury, has now suffered ankle damage at the end of the game that will keep him out for a further four weeks. At this rate Trevor Brooking might have to be pressed into action. Harry Redknapp must be turning in his Director of Football's deluxe padded seat at Portsmouth. There are more bare bones at Upton Park than in all my collected videos of *Time Team*, *Meet the Ancestors* and *Secrets of the Dead*.

29. A BUNCH OF STIFFS

West Ham Reserves 2 Tottenham Reserves 1 –
26 February 2002

Suppose they gave a match and nobody came. It's time to enter the twilight zone of reserve-team football, where tumbleweed blows across the pitch and has-beens and wannabe stars collide within empty stadiums. The reserve game is frequented by the footballing twitcher; the sort of anorak with metaphorical binoculars who will delight in viewing a rare outing from a blue Titi Camara or a lesser spotted Gary Charles.

West Ham Reserves are playing Tottenham Reserves at Upton Park in the snappily titled FA Barclaycard Premier Reserve League South on a cold, clear night in late February. By reserve standards it's a relatively healthy crowd. Some 500 or so fans are huddled together in the Lower East Stand; the only part of the ground that is open. Normally reserve games are played at Dagenham and Redbridge, but today's local derby has seen the club switch venues. In the Upper East Stand sit the dignitaries, agents on the trawl, fifty-something men still sporting greying footballers' haircuts, and the likes of West Ham's assistant manager Paul Goddard and director Trevor Brooking.

The programme is one sheet of A4 white paper containing the teams and a match report by Roger Cross. Bizarrely, Sergei Rebrov, an £11 million signing who was playing in the European Champions League two seasons ago but has since been ignored by manager Glenn Hoddle, is playing for Tottenham Reserves. Alongside him are young hopefuls with first-team experience such as Alton Thelwell, Anthony Gardner, Stephen Clemence, and Matthew Etherington, plus the experienced former Wimbledon and Liverpool Norwegian international Oyvind Leonhardsen.

For West Ham, Steve Potts – my fellow season ticket holder Nigel's favourite player – is at the back, a one-club veteran of 399 Hammers appearances up to the start of this season. Pottsy is a player who in recent years has been undervalued, coming into the side during our habitual injury

161

crises, but however well he played always ended up being dropped whenever a big-name signing returned. Tonight he is as calmly efficient as ever, making unfussy interceptions and passes and nursing his fellow centre-back Izzy Iriekpen, who has just returned from long-term injury, through the game.

The rest of the side is made up of squad players like Raggy Soma and Laurent Courtois, promising youngsters like Glen Johnson, Shaun Byrne, Grant McCann and Omer Riza and flop big-money striker Titi Camara.

The crowd are an unlikely mix of schoolchildren and parents, families of the players and old men. As we enter the game a man with a quite splendid beer gut, naked flesh exposed above his trousers, is selling copies of *Thames Ironworks* fanzine beneath the old Chicken Run. By the stairs punters are handed a free one-page programme with the teams on the front and the fixtures and a match report by manager Roger Cross on the back.

After six minutes Spurs gain a corner and Rebrov loses Byrne on the far post to place an easy header past David Forde, the new keeper from Barry Town. That's not good enough for the old geezer behind me. When Rebrov sends another chance wide he growls: 'That's why you're not in the first team Rebrov!'

Interestingly, poor old Titi Camara is barracked even in the reserves. There are groans when he miscontrols the ball and shouts of 'You're fuckin' useless Camara!' which he must be able to hear in the deserted stadium. Just what happened to Titi Camara? The 30-year-old striker was bought from Liverpool last season by ex-gaffer Harry Redknapp for £2 million and may have partially contributed towards Harry's demise. Camara is a full international with Guinea and has had a good career, playing for St Etienne, Lens and Marseilles in France and signing for Gerald Houllier's Liverpool in 1999. Yes, he was once rated by Gerald Houllier, the man who won the treble for Liverpool.

During his first season at Anfield he scored nine goals in 33 matches, including some blistering 30-yard shots and the winning goal against West Ham at Anfield. Then he fell out with Houllier, moved to West Ham, played six games in which he fluffed chances, looked slow and out of form, got injured and disappeared into a time vortex in the Chadwell Heath area. Tonight he looks overweight and unhappy, having travelled the path from Anfield hero to West Ham reject. Did he lose his desire and settle for easy money? As mere fans we'll probably never know. Roeder has only played Titi in the first team once all season; a five-minute stint as a sub during the win at Old Trafford when he came on and looked awful, and Camara is now one of the expensive signings on good money that he plans to unload. Although naming a West Ham striker called Titi may well become a pub quiz question.

After Rebrov's goal West Ham reserves fight their way back into the game and Grant McCann hits the bar with a shot that bounces on the line, Geoff Hurst style, but no goal is given. After 27 minutes West Ham equalise, and ironically enough the scorer is Camara, who at last shows a glimpse of the class he must once have had. He turns inside one defender, then another and slots the ball into the corner of the Spurs net for a finely taken goal. 'We've seen Titi Camara score in a West Ham shirt!' exclaims my companion, elated at joining this exclusive club.

For the Hammers England Under-19 international Glen Johnson looks a future first teamer, displaying an easy mastery of the ball on the right side of defence. But nothing is certain in football, for in front of him is Adam Newton, the right-back who looked a future star when in the Youth Cup winning side, but has so far made just two appearances as a sub in the first team and a fleeting Intertoto appearance for the Hammers two seasons ago. He plays reasonably well but no longer stands out as he once did, and a couple of weeks after this match is shipped out to Leyton Orient on loan.

At half-time the press and dignitaries have free coffee and snacks in the Sir Geoff Hurst Lounge in the Upper East Stand. The food is an immense improvement on what is offered to the punters downstairs; tea or real coffee with silver trays of samosas, quiche, chips and chicken are on offer around the room. Interestingly the Sir Geoff Hurst Lounge is pitted with pictures of former stars ranging from Sir Geoff and Bobby Moore to the likes of John Hartson and Eyal Berkovic (no, not that infamous picture of Hartson trying to kick off Berkovic's head in training) and, for some strange reason, Samassi Abou. Now Abou might have scored five goals for the Hammers and have inspired some legendary booing whenever he scored ('ABOOOOOOOOOO!!!'), but even Mrs Abou (Betty Abou?) would hardly claim that he is a Hammers legend. They'll be putting up pictures of Ralph Milne next.

Reserve games are undoubtedly a good means of spotting famous names. Trevor Brooking is sipping a coffee nearby and at the previous home reserve game against Arsenal, Arsene Wenger was in the Sir Geoff Hurst Lounge for half-time refreshment – although sadly he stuck to his principles on sports science and healthy nutrition for athletes and eschewed all the chips on offer. Club chairman Terry Brown is there with his wife and a fellow journalist says hello to vice-chairman Martin Cearns. He is a huge contrast to the public perception of a football director, personified by the likes of Warren Clarke in *The Manageress* and the character of Frank in *Footballers' Wives*. Martin Cearns is famously reticent with the press. In person he comes across as an affable middle-aged bank manager – perhaps because he is an affable middle-aged bank manager, more Sergeant Wilson than Captain Mainwaring, the type of man you'd be happy to meet over a suburban hedge in the stockbroker belt. My mind goes back to the necessary fans' protest over the Hammers Bond scheme of 1991 and how such open revolt must have horrified this shy man. In the personality of Cearns you can see why the club has always gone for stability and the more dignified end of the managerial market in the likes of Ron Greenwood, John Lyall and Glenn Roeder.

Cearns is quietly spoken and jokes that he stopped taking *The Observer* because it was too left-wing and then stopped taking *The Sunday Times* because it was too right-wing. On football matters he is something of a West Ham anorak. He goes to all the reserve games and tells us that he also attends the Under-17 and Under-19 games at Chadwell Heath on Saturdays. Engagingly, Cearns is self-deprecating about his football knowledge asking if we saw ex-Hammer Jimmy Bullard star for Peterborough against Newcastle in the FA Cup, and admitting that when Bullard was at Upton Park he thought him absolutely useless, yet now he is one of Peterborough's best players.

Us fans routinely criticise the board, often with good reason, but it has to be said that they do have the commitment to turn up at all sorts of West Ham games, which is at least one reason to be optimistic about the club's future.

In the second half Omer Riza (does he play Omer and away?) looks lively up front. He is brought down just outside the area with a professional foul, provoking cries of 'Off! Off! Off!' from the Chicken Run. The second team are just as bad at free-kicks as the first; the ball is scrambled clear. Riza plays a great ball out to Newton on the wing who balloons the cross behind, perhaps illustrating why he has not made the first team. Titi Camara reverts to form by spooning a chance wide, and one fan hollers: 'You're a useless waste of space Camara!' Some kids taunt the Spurs keeper Gavin Kelly with cries of 'Whoooah . . . you're shit! . . . aaaaargh!', while at the other end David Forde shows his promise by making a fine reaction save to keep the scores level.

It looks like being a draw until three minutes from the end when West Ham are awarded a free-kick on the left of the Spurs' area. Grant McCann bends the ball around the wall and into the net just inside the near post and hares away on a victory run to the Chicken Run as if he has just scored the winner in the World Cup final. Who says that goals in the reserves don't mean anything? And if you need proof that reserve football is a strange footballing parallel universe, a West Ham side has won a game in the last few minutes instead of losing it. A few more years at Chadwell Heath and we'll soon knock that habit out of the youngsters.

30. WELCOME TO THE
HOTEL DOCTOR MARTENS

Aston Villa 2 West Ham 1 – 2 March 2002

Who needs mini-breaks in Paris when you can take your loved one to Upton Park? Housed within the club's new Dr Martens Stand is the West Ham United Quality Hotel, where for 85 quid a night you can sleep in a room with a pitchside view. The Quality in the title might sound like the club are trying a bit too hard, but the move makes economic sense. The rooms are executive boxes on match days and would otherwise be empty all week. Whether Carol from Ken's Café would be in charge of the catering or not ('Number 68!! Full English breakfast, I'm not telling you again!!') was clearly a matter that had to be investigated.

As the Eagles almost sang: 'Welcome to the hotel Doctor Martens . . .' Come to think of it, several of the lines from 'Hotel California' seem particularly apt for West Ham fans, such as, 'we are all just prisoners here of our own device' and of course the final warning that, 'you may check out any time you like, but you can never leave'.

Just before we left home West Ham had lost 2–1 to an injury-time goal at Aston Villa. The journey to the hotel is little better. Sometimes getting to Upton Park can take longer than the Eurostar to Paris. Having dispatched our older daughter, three-and-a-half-year-old Lola, to her friend Corinna's house for a sleepover, Nicola, myself and our youngest child, one-year-old Nell, head towards Upton Park. Unfortunately on a very busy Saturday afternoon the District Line is closed between Bromley-by-Bow and Plaistow. We carry the buggy up numerous stairs and put an irascible Nell onto a replacement bus service which contrives to make the journey between Bromley-by-Bow and Plaistow seem like an interminable tour of every gasometer and rusting canalside warehouse in East London. Eventually we arrive at Plaistow and feed Nell, then move the buggy up and down more stairs and finally arrive at

165

Upton Park where, as the sign says, we 'alight here for West Ham United Football Club'. (Is this some kind of appeal for self-immolation by frustrated fans?)

Finally we arrive in the reception of the Dr Martens Stand, complete with a mosaic of the club crest on the floor. Our first impression of the hotel comes from Louise, a friendly and engaging Irish receptionist, who sorts out our room swipe card and is apologetic for the fact that our requested cot has been nabbed by the wedding party also staying at the hotel. Yes, they do wedding receptions and even marriages at Upton Park, although Nicola immediately states she has no intention of ending our living-together-in-a-Frank McAvennie/Jenny Blyth-style-love-nest status by even contemplating an on-pitch marriage.

After ascertaining that Sunday papers are not delivered to the rooms as the local shops don't open early enough, although there are plenty of *Newham Recorders* at reception, we travel up a *Space 1999*-style lift and into a world of corridors with endless claret and blue signs. Only when we get to our room we discover a holdall and someone else's clothes on the bed. We explain our predicament to a passing member of staff, who passes us on to a manager. You can tell how good staff are by how they deal with problems, and everyone we meet is helpful and courteous. We are given coffee in the vice-president's suite while the room situation is sorted out, and then sent up to the third floor. Every room/executive boss has the holder's name outside and we are a few doors down from David James's room, in a box normally held by 'The Romford Group', whatever that might be.

Finally we enter our room, complete with claret and blue duvet cover and team photograph on the wall. Behind the claret and blue curtains are sliding glass doors providing a vista of the pitch and a glimpse into the nearby commentary box of Jeremy Nicholas. We are not worthy indeed. We're close to the Bobby Moore Stand and almost exactly opposite my normal seat in the East Stand. Interestingly, the goals have been folded down, making the place look a little like a disused Subbuteo pitch.

West Ham have certainly got their brand-to-brand combat in first. The club badge is everywhere, on the chair and crockery and everything in the smart en-suite bathroom. It's a bit like a blissful remake of *The Prisoner* for sad Hammers fans. After being mysteriously abducted you suddenly awake to find yourself in a mini-village where the only paper is the *Newham Recorder*, the only colours are claret and blue, the team photo is on every wall and the West Ham crest is on all chairs, cups, water bottles, sugar bowls, towels, shampoo and shower gel.

One major design flaw is the locked glass doors. A call to reception reveals that the club is not allowed to open the doors for safety reasons, lest, recalling the last-minute events against Charlton, Liverpool, Chelsea and Villa, you climb out into the stand and hurl yourself downwards to oblivion.

WELCOME TO THE HOTEL DOCTOR MARTENS

Consequently there is no way of ventilating the room. As Nell has eczema and needs to sleep in a ventilated room at night and Her Indoors works at Friends of the Earth and is so green that she can't sleep without a tempest coming through an opened window, this goes down as well as an underhit Don Hutchison backheader.

But at least Nell enjoys crawling over the claret and blue duvet, there's a fine selection of real teas in a box on the dressing table and a TV for *The Premiership* lowlights of defeat at Aston Villa. As Kenneth's Bistro is closed we decide to eat in the hotel. Dinner is served in the Ironworks Bar opposite reception. Cables hang from the walls, there are no pictures as yet and it has an unfinished air. Saturday evening TV blares from four monitors around the bar. It's somewhat soulless, as we seem to be the only guests present, the only other denizens being various staff members knocking off their shifts. Still, the barmaid is decidedly friendly and when we mention that Nicola can't have dairy products because of the effect they might have on Nell's eczema, she proves to know all about allergies, having had some 30 of them herself since she was a child. We order a bottle of West Ham's own label Chardonnay, which revitalises Nicola. 'This is very *Footballers' Wives*. I thought it was a new East End drink called char-doh-nay,' she says.

As Nell plays happily on the laminated floor, we opt for quiche, scampi, vegetable stroganoff and cheese and biscuits. It's fine as a good bar meal, but it has to be said that at £20 a head (you have to pay for three courses regardless of whether you want them or not) it's overpriced.

We explore some more on the way back to our room. In the vice-president's suite it appears that a meeting of Sunshine Dessert types has been in progress for a flip board reads 'Plan, Prepare, Practise, Present' and 'If you fail to prepare, prepare to fail'. Great, super.

In the White Horse Suite the wedding reception is under way with a disco blaring out the Nolans' 'You Make Me Feel Like Dancing'. Not since the days of the late great Bill Remfry can Upton Park have heard so much bad music in one sitting.

Our own big night in is disrupted by baby Nell's eczema attacks. For the first year of her life she has suffered from atopic eczema, having to sleep in a gloved suit and having to wear socks on her hands in the daytime lest her nails scratch into her red and dry skin. She's currently on antibiotics after her scratches became infected, strangers think that I've been beating her up, and we normally get about as much sleep as Glenn Roeder after a 7–1 defeat at Blackburn. Nell lies between us all night, with one person holding each arm to prevent her scratching herself as I try not to dream of John Radford.

Despite the room overlooking the Upton Park pitch, I survive the night without too many dangerous flashbacks of Steve Whitton or Kevin Keen – bar the odd nightmare that I have just scored the winning goal for West Ham in the FA Cup final, only to discover that I've played in an earlier round while

167

on loan to some third division no-hopers, leading to the whole side being disqualified.

On Sunday morning we wake up to unusual silence. There's no traffic noise and the Boleyn Ground without fans feels almost rural. It's down to the White Horse Suite, where the hotel does an excellent breakfast, either fried or healthy with fine peeled oranges, lots of juices and fruits, and you don't even have to take a number like in Ken's. The wedding party hoover up real coffee, sausages and scrambled eggs as the groom thanks various guests for coming. Nicola really seems to be getting into the footballing ambience, although betrays her posh origins as she asks: 'What are those polo sticks on the carpet for. Or are they croquet sticks?' while looking at a pair of hammers on the club badge. Still, the picture of the famed white horse clearing the horses on the pitch at Wembley goes down well.

We depart into a clear and sunny morning and head back towards north London to pick up Lola. What price Casablanca, Bogart and Bacall when you have the West Ham Hotel? Nicola can no longer claim that I haven't involved her in my grand West Ham project. We stand at the bus stop on Green Street, desperate for a ticket to Stratford. 'If you hadn't stayed in the West Ham hotel, you'd have regretted it, maybe not today, maybe not tomorrow, but soon and for the rest of your life,' I tell her.

'Chardonnay, I'm booking this ticket on the Silverlink from Stratford to Highbury and Islington in the name of Mr and Mrs Victor Laszlo,' I say stoically as a packed bus judders into view, before mumbling, 'I guess we'll always have George Parris.'

31. JOIN THE PROFESSIONALS

West Ham 1 Everton 0 – 6 March 2002

Five successive defeats away from home mean that West Ham are still over-reliant on their form at Fortress Upton Park. The Wednesday night match against Everton becomes another must-win game; three points will have us on 37 and edging towards the magical figure of 40 points for survival, while it would leave Everton on 30, just one above Blackburn in the relegation places.

After Saturday's defeat to a 92nd-minute goal at Villa, Glenn Roeder has publicly criticised his side, pointing out that when Arsenal were winning at Newcastle, late in the game Kanu was in the Newcastle penalty area but then went to the corner flag to waste some precious time. 'We on the other hand are still trying extravagant things in advanced areas. We're not learning and it has to change.'

Paolo Di Canio returned from his three-game suspension and a visit to his dentist in Italy to play Villa. He scored a coolly taken penalty and brought a fine save from Schmeichel, even if he and Sinclair appeared to be playing in the same position at times. His perpetual contract row also rumbled on. The capricious forward went back on his earlier announcement that he was going to retire at the end of his West Ham contract, and said that if West Ham did not offer him a new deal he would be open to offers to play for a season elsewhere in England. He admitted that after West Ham's managing director Paul Aldridge failed to respond to his demands for a new contract: 'I was angry for two or three days, but now it is not a problem. I know that West Ham have no intention to keep me here at the end of next season but I have made my decision and I want to stay here until then . . . Perhaps West Ham will change their mind but if not then I'm sure there are a lot of clubs who already want to sign me.'

Sensibly, Glenn Roeder, presumably now used to regular back-page headlines in the *Standard* concerning Di Canio, fielded the latest story by pointing out that 'it's not the time to be talking about contracts . . . 18 months is a long time in football' and also that when contractual negotiations are entered 'players can take their eye off the ball'.

It's Big Joe's return from injury, having broken his leg auditioning for the Winter Olympics and falling over on the ice on Boxing Day while buying a paper for the racing. He never got his paper, and all his horses lost anyway. Even worse, he drives an automatic and was therefore still able to work through his injury.

We drive to the game from Joe's Islington office. In Barnsbury we disagree about the merits of Christian Dailly while Joe feels that Hutchison won't be missed because he was a useless lump anyway. By the time we're in Hackney he's voicing the fears of all middle-aged West Ham fans. A trip to Villa with the in-laws hasn't improved his state of mind.

'I keep worrying that we'll end up the Coventry City of the Premiership, always staying up but never threatening to do anything . . . I'm going to be an old man and never have seen West Ham win anything. When I was a kid you thought that West Ham would always be there or thereabouts every few years. Even up to the '81 League Cup final and when we finished third in '86.'

It turns out that Joe missed the Cup finals of both 1975 and 1980, but did see us lose the 1976 Cup-Winners' Cup final and the 1981 League Cup final. At least I've seen us win the FA Cup twice, even if the last time was 22 years ago. We then start reflecting that if only it hadn't been for Manny Omoynimni playing while ineligible we'd surely have beaten Leicester in the semis and got to the 2000 Worthington Cup final. Which is always fatal.

Almost the entire team are in Ken's Café before the game, Dirty Den and partner Clare, Dan, Gavin, Joe and myself. Our favourite intimidating matriarch Carol is on fine form as kick-off approaches. 'You're not touting are you?' she shouts at Dan, adding: 'My dear boy has to wait to see who can't go before he gets in.' She then playfully refuses to let the agitated Denis leave and points at Clare – 'You're not going until she's finished her chips!'

It's more entertaining than much of the game. Kanouté has recovered from his cold but we're still without Carrick, Lomas, Hutchison, Moncur and Foxe. Ian Pearce partners Repka and Dailly in a five-man defence with Labant and Schemmel as wing-backs. Roeder again shows his talent for tactical improvisation by surprising everyone and playing Trevor Sinclair as a central midfield player behind Joe Cole.

After a mediocre first 20 minutes, when Everton's Blomqvist threatens the home defence and shoots just wide when well placed. Schemmel has a shot deflected over and Ian Pearce manages to dribble the ball across the Everton area and out to Di Canio who tries an audacious chip which lands on the roof of the net. Perhaps he should have blasted it instead, as he had a clear shot on goal, but then who dares question his improvisations? With Paolo if you shackle the artist within then you destroy the player.

Everton look mediocre, with the freshly signed journeyman Lee Carsley their big hope. At least David Unsworth manages a joke with the Chicken Run while taking a throw-in. 'I wonder if he knows where Birmingham is yet?' asks Joe. It was the geographically challenged Unsworth who famously left West Ham to sign for Aston Villa apparently thinking that Birmingham was near his native Liverpool.

Up front Kevin Campbell is well marshalled by the newly shorn Tomas Repka, who has a fine, decisive game at the back. Things improve a little in the second half. Sinclair is doing well in the unfamiliar role of central midfield, playing the ball simply out to the wings while the peroxide Joe Cole, looking like Billy Idol's younger brother, shows commendable maturity by starting to take responsibility in midfield. Uncharacteristically Di Canio balloons his second volley of the evening way over the top and we reflect again that, while still committed and influential, he's not quite the player he was. 'I'd take anything, I mean when did we last score from deflection,' says Matt.

The curse of Matt, who shouted 'Don't cross it you twat!' just as Schemmel crossed it for Kanouté to score against Arsenal, works as well as ever. In the 59th minute Cole cuts inside two Everton defenders on the left and shoots. It takes a massive deflection off Trevor Sinclair and goes past Simenson into the net. Sinclair runs to the East Terrace pointing to his chest and claiming it as his goal.

Di Canio then has a good claim for a penalty turned down after being caught by the arm and boot of Stubbs. Then Paolo races out of his own half on the left, plays a one-two with Sinclair and fires over a great ball to Kanouté who shoots into the side netting. It's the best move of an average match. There's more entertainment when an Everton player goes down injured and West Ham put the ball into touch. Some sections of the crowd boo, but Di Canio, who won the FIFA Fair Play Award for 2001 for catching the ball at Everton when in a goalscoring position as their keeper had sustained an injury, waggles his hands and engages in an impromptu discussion of the merits of fair play with the Bobby Moore Stand.

'There will be three minutes' stoppage time played,' announces Jeremy Nicholas, which is a great improvement on the old system of trying to keep half an eye on a board that might appear from the dugouts. Extra time proves to be hilarious. After Roeder criticised them for not taking the ball into the corners at Villa we now do nothing but play keep-ball in the corner beneath us. The apparently mild-mannered boss must have terrified them, for we now resemble Revie-era Leeds. Di Canio, Labant, Cole and Sinclair juggle the ball, flick it up, pass it to and fro and wait for the frustrated Pistone to clatter Paolo from behind. We win two corners but make no attempt to play the ball into the middle. It's a bit like watching the Harlem Globetrotters.

'At last, we've found a set-piece we can do, rather than just hoof the ball at their keeper we hang onto it. With all our ball players and back-heelers we can do this forever,' I enthuse.

'They're going to start doing it earlier and earlier every game,' chuckles Dan. 'Next week we'll be doing it 20 minutes from the end.'

The shock of West Ham being professional ends with the final whistle and Di Canio walking round the ground talking to himself, gesturing and generally resembling a *Big Issue* seller. My parents once took me to a wrestling match in the 1960s and I reflect that with all his theatrical abilities Di Canio would surely have had a great career as the Mick McManus of his generation.

Jeremy Nicholas announces that we go above Fulham, Southampton and Middlesbrough to tenth. We're in the top half of the table again! Our next opponents, Manchester United, will be quaking.

32. MANCHESTER, SO MUCH
TO ANSWER FOR . . .

West Ham 3 Manchester United 5 - 16 March 2002

Games between West Ham and Manchester United at Upton Park have always been special: Bobby Ferguson saving a George Best penalty in a 3–0 win for West Ham in the 1970s; Kenny Brown scoring a bizarre winner for the already relegated West Ham and depriving United of their first title in nearly three decades; Ludek Miklosko playing brilliantly to deprive Andy Cole and United of the title; Beckham's first away game after his sending-off in the 1998 World Cup; Paolo scoring twice and then shooting instead of passing to Frank Lampard which would have made it 3–3, as we lose 4–2 at home in season 1999–2000.

Today Paolo Di Canio will be playing against the club he would have signed for were he not a piranha fish lover. That bizarre transfer mystery becomes even more like an outtake from *The X-Files* as Di Canio insists on the club website that 'Whatever the rumours I could have gone but I didn't want to. I didn't push because I love it here.'

Rows of police vans and officers in riot gear line the road behind the East Stand – presumably ready to give the away fans a safe escort home to Surrey. Upton Park contains 35,281 fans and even Jeremy Nicholas doesn't feel the need to hype up the game as for once he reads out the West Ham side without inserting any nicknames. Trevor Sinclair has gone down with food poisoning, so Labant and Lomas play on the flanks with Michael Carrick returning and earning from Glenn Roeder the accolade that 'privately he knows how good he is but there isn't an ounce of arrogance about him'. And Roeder's clear-out has started. Svetoslav Todorov has been sold to Harry Redknapp's Portsmouth for £750,000 in midweek.

Paolo begins the game like a piranha deprived of fish food, having a fierce shot blocked and then shooting just wide of Barthez's far post. On eight minutes

173

the impossible happens, Di Canio links up cleverly to find space for Labant and the Slovakian's quick high cross is met by Steve Lomas, who thumps a header into the top corner of Barthez's goal from the edge of the area. It's as if the Northern Ireland skipper has suddenly eaten three shredded wheat and been transformed into Nat Lofthouse. Lomas removes his shirt after scoring, reveals a white torso and ginger chest hair to the Chicken Run and causes several spectators to be treated for shock.

It's a great goal, although our contingent immediately exchange clichés about wounded beasts being most dangerous when provoked. Sadly we're right, as United equalise nine minutes later with a world-class goal. Despite the easy options available, Joe Cole attempts to play what Terry Venables later describes as a 'Hollywood ball'. Paul Scholes intercepts, instantly controls the ball, and from the halfway line plays it to Beckham breaking behind Labant on the left. As Dailly comes across to cover, Beckham chips the ball first-time from the edge of the area and it arcs over David James for a sublime goal.

Three minutes later though, the Hammers counter attack with a move that would have been worthy of United at their best. Schemmel makes a typically forceful run down the right and his cross is thumped into the bottom corner by Fredi Kanouté, who pauses to do his Gallic disbelieving goal shrug routine. So now we just need to hold on to the lead – although this season we could probably provide enough discarded leads to keep Geri Halliwell in adopted dogs for perpetuity.

We only suffer the agony of hope for two minutes. Repka gives away another wasteful free-kick for shirt-tugging. It's crossed in once but the referee orders it to be taken again. This time it's a quick one and, with the West Ham defenders apparently pausing to read a FIFA tactical manual, unmarked Nicky Butt scores with an acrobatic scissor-kick. Phew, 4 goals in 22 minutes, which is very similar to what happened at Charlton. Today's match looks like it could end at five all.

The rest of the first half produces more lovely football, with the elegant Carrick and United's ginger geezer Paul Scholes, miffed at having been dropped by United for their previous match against Bayern Munich, both excelling, but no more goals.

The second half begins with Fabien Barthez jogging into his goal in front of the Bobby Moore Stand and being greeted by thousands of fans waving one arm in the air. Rain now lashes the ground and Sir Alex Ferguson is off the bench and getting a soaking. But United seem inspired by having twice come from behind; as is Glenn Roeder, who is so sodden that at this rate he might have to reveal whether he has more than one Fila jacket. Scholes is still drifting inside to support the tough-tackling Butt and Keane and Carrick and Cole are outnumbered. For once Roeder seems to be caught out tactically, failing to put Lomas on Scholes to nullify the midfield inequality.

United don't just step up three gears; it's more like Jon Pertwee's car Bessie in *Doctor Who*, which suddenly breaks all known land speed records through the diligent application of Timelord technology when he's been sufficiently goaded by the Master. West Ham concede a horrible goal. Solksjaer is surrounded by both Winterburn and Repka on the dead-ball line but is, almost criminally, allowed to get a cross in. Lomas and Cole are ambling back with all the speed of half-time programme sellers returning for a cup of tea, and have allowed Scholes to run into the area and tap the ball past the disconsolate James. The West Ham keeper looks so mad he could change his hairstyle.

Cole does a lovely double back-heel to flick the ball away from Keane, but it's not doing any damage in areas that matter, while Di Canio has faded after a good start. Then Carrick heads the ball over the United defence towards Kanouté who is strolling back in the manner of a man listening to some particularly mellow ambient music on his Walkman, clearly expecting an offside decision; only the flag is never raised and Kanouté has missed a chance of going one on one with the keeper.

The relentless black and white (yes, it's yet another new kit from United) surge continues. Beckham sweeps in another first-time cross, Repka dives to head clear but the ball unluckily rebounds into Van Nistelrooy, who pokes the ball towards James. The ball again rebounds off James, straight to Solksjaer who hits it at Schemmel, the ball rebounds yet again straight to the United man and pinball wizard Solksjaer pokes it into the net.

At last our home form is now matching our away form. The United fans break into a chorus of 'We Shall Not Be Moved'. It seems like the fifth is inevitable, as Scholes finds Keane whose cross whizzes across goal just beyond the boot of Van Nistelrooy.

But is it really all over? Roeder has at last brought on Defoe with 16 minutes to go, which is surely too late. But the tiny striker, who has scored five times as a substitute already this season, more than any other Premiership player, does it once again. Joe Cole shows the positive side of his game and partially redeems himself for the error that led to United's first goal. The peroxide kid tenaciously dispossesses Butt and plays the ball wide to Kanouté on the left. Showing his deceptive pace, the big Frenchman takes on Johnsen for speed, races to the dead-ball line and angles the ball back for Defoe to outpace the ageing Blanc and finish with cool precision.

The Upton Park crowd start to make some serious noise, sensing a thrilling 4–4 draw. It nearly happens when a free-kick is awarded for a foul on Defoe. Labant's cross is headed on by Defoe at the far post, Lomas does an overhead kick, the ball falls to Dailly who has a shot blocked and it rebounds into the path of Kanouté, who clearly has his shirt held by Ronnie Johnsen as is confirmed by the later TV replays.

The game is reaching an unforgettable climax as the Hammers press for an epic equaliser – at which point Gavin, as maverick a spectator as Paolo Di

Canio is a footballer, walks out, citing a need to be home early. What a moment to choose his first early departure of the season. 'Don't worry Gav, it's not a very good game, it's only 4–3 . . .' Nigel tells him.

Gav does miss a goal, but it's at the wrong end. One minute from time the tireless Scholes makes another run into West Ham's penalty area and Repka attempts to make a sliding tackle but takes the man first and then the ball. It's Repka's first season in the Premiership and he is clearly a good player, but his concentration needs to improve. It's not the maligned Dailly who has made mistakes in this game; it's the shaven-headed Repka who has conceded the free-kick for the second goal, allowed the cross for the vital third and conceded a penalty. Beckham strolls up and thumps the ball into James's net before running to the United fans.

'Only five games in the Premiership have had eight goals and West Ham have now been involved in three of them,' points out Statto Dan, always ready to ameliorate defeat with a statistic or three.

It's been superb entertainment, but the tube journey home from East Ham offers cause for reflection that West Ham have scored three very good goals against the best side in the country, yet conceded five dodgy goals at home. My mobile rings with a text message from my Man United-supporting friend Nick, reading 'just the five'. As Roeder says after the game: 'When you analyse the game we contributed to all the goals ourselves and when you make a mistake Man United don't let you off the hook.'

So much for the best home defensive record in the Premiership. The morning papers have revealed that according to researchers at Northumbria University, testosterone is the key to home advantage in football. They have discovered that levels of the sex hormone surged by more than 50 per cent in players before home matches. This is linked to the primal urge to defend home territory, where testosterone boosts aggression. Which could be why Paolo keeps referring to himself as a 'big balls' player.

But now United have walloped the Hammers 5–3, rather ruining the scientists' theory. Or maybe not. Before the game, we spotted six Japanese kids sitting outside the away end with a sign saying they were looking for tickets. Now since most United fans now come from Surrey or the Far East, playing in London is probably as close as United ever get to playing at home. Becks, Scholesy and co.'s testosterone levels must have soared at Upton Park surrounded by so many Cockney Reds and that's why they had dismissed the Hammers with their sexy football. Hopefully the lads can work on topping up their testosterone levels with some extra ball work and tuition from Paolo at Chadwell Heath before the visit of strugglers Ipswich.

33. EASTER RISING

West Ham 3 Ipswich 1 – 30 March 2002
Fulham 0 West Ham 1 – 1 April 2002

West Ham players do exceptionally well in the midweek internationals. Joe Cole comes on as a substitute for England against Italy and promptly makes a goal for Robbie Fowler with some tenacious tackling back – only to then dribble the ball in his own half and needlessly give it away as Italy's Montella surges forward to equalise with a long-range shot into the top corner. Even worse, in the last minute David James rushes from his line to bring down Maccarone and give away the penalty that wins the game for the Italians. The *Daily Mirror's* back-page headlines have clearly been written by a Spurs fan, as they read 'Sven's Hammer House of Horror' and 'You Big Jessie, James'.

Oh, and Steve Lomas is sent off as Northern Ireland can only draw 0–0 with Liechtenstein, while Grant McCann plays in the same match and picks up an injury that will keep him out for five weeks. Finally, Christian Dailly is in the heart of Scotland's defence as they are thrashed 5–0 by a scintillating French side. Blimey. We're bringing the international sides down to our level.

At least West Ham might have got something right in the boardroom though. It's announced that ITV Digital is going into administration having paid a ridiculous £315 million to broadcast Football League matches. Many clubs have already spent the anticipated TV money and may now go bust as ITV still owes them £178 million. The collapse of ITV Digital will surely result in Sky bidding less for Premiership TV rights when the contracts are renegotiated and the days of endless TV money being recycled straight into players' salaries may be ending (West Ham's wages are 70 per cent of turnover). Even Rio Ferdinand's new club Leeds are rumoured to be having to sell off at least one player in the summer.

Glenn Roeder warns: 'This is going to cause a massive financial shakedown throughout the game. We are going into a period now when we'll be looking at a lot of clubs who have very little transfer cash in the kitty . . . There seems

177

to be a new mood of realism – clubs realising they can no longer spend money they haven't got.'

Few West Ham fans would recognise chairman Terry Brown and after the Rio and Frank sales even fewer would praise him. But his words in the Chairman's Annual Statement of November 2001 seem remarkably prescient: 'The growth of digital subscription television may be slowing and television viewing figures are at best steady . . . Rapidly rising revenues which do not lead to rapidly rising profits should be a warning to us all. Borrowing excessively against future revenue streams or selling share stakes . . . and ploughing these capital receipts into revenue expenditure cannot be justified.' And maybe when all the other Premiership clubs go bust West Ham will win the league.

Two weeks after defeat at home to Manchester United, and hardly buoyed by international performances, West Ham begin the crucial Easter weekend programme with a home match against the Tractor Boys of struggling Ipswich. Interestingly, both David James and Joe Cole have had their blond hairstyles cropped for the day, perhaps as some form of penance.

Roeder has given the players a long talk before the game, explaining: 'I consider this to be the most important month of the season. I have to keep the players motivated, keep their eye on the ball.'

Ipswich have a couple of early chances but slowly the Hammers take control. On 36 minutes Di Canio swings over a cross, Ipswich keeper Serini does a Count Dracula, and Steve Lomas heads home his second goal in successive games.

'Thank goodness he hasn't taken his shirt off,' I mutter, still having flashbacks of his naked white torso as displayed against Manchester United.

Schemmel is having another rampaging game on the right, and through sheer doggedness wins the ball back to square it to Cole in the area, whose first-time poke at goal produces a brilliant save from Serini. Dailly and Repka are looking solid enough, with the bouncing Czech not so much heading as physically assaulting the ball whenever it comes near him. Upon giving away another dangerous free-kick he shouts abuse at the referee and is lucky to escape a booking. 'What's the point in him arguing with the ref when he don't speak English? He's like a pet Labrador, he only knows two words, sit and dinner,' says an exasperated Dan.

'Roeder looks very funereal today,' remarks Gavin. On the last morning of March, GR has discarded his Fila jacket and is back to his black suit and white shirt and tie. As is the trend with forward-looking young coaches, he periodically takes notes during the match – orders for flowers, messages of condolence, that sort of thing.

Cole is playing sensibly on the left, sometimes switching to the right, while the unshowy Michael Carrick is holding it all together with his calm, unhurried distribution. For all his obvious skill, Fredi Kanouté is having one of his ambling games, as if someone has swiped the ambient tape from his

Walkman and inserted discordant techno. When he falls over in a heap while claiming a penalty we worry that his batteries might have fallen out.

Soon after the restart Paolo jinks down the left, swirls a tantalising cross over Serini and Fredi blasts over the bar from three yards. Schemmel has two shots saved and then Sinclair joins in. Might Fredi's miss be the turning point of the match? Possibly so, for after Fredi stumbles when presented with another good chance, Ipswich score the scrappiest of equalisers when they should have been several goals down. Repka miscues and causes the entire West Ham defence to do a Corporal Jones. James blocks Miller's header but then Marcus Bent calmly finds the corner of the net. The Ipswich section erupts, scenting another precious point towards survival.

But not with Di Canio in this mood. Some of his promptings have failed to come off but this time he cuts inside and fires a swerving shot at Serini. The keeper parries but the alert Di Canio runs in to acrobatically volley the ball home. It's a corking goal. PDC goes bonkers, whipping his shirt off, hurling it lasso style around his head and throwing it to the heavens. Revealing his muscled torso and a series of tattoos he then holds a mini-rally standing bare-chested on a hoarding in front of the Bobby Moore Stand, imparting his thoughts on the European Monetary Union, the decline of the Roman Empire, and his ideal recipe for tiramisu. His acolyte Trevor Sinclair dutifully returns Paolo's shirt after the great man has finished his Corialanus-style strut.

You're not singing anymore. Kanouté finally gives way to Defoe and, sure enough, he scores another late goal against a tiring defence. Di Canio finds the prodigy and three Ipswich defenders seem mesmerised as Defoe deftly pokes the ball into the corner of Serini's goal. Roeder pats every West Ham player as they leave the pitch.

Not even the news that Newcastle manager Bobby Robson is to report the Hammers for an alleged illegal approach to Newcastle player Olivier Bernard ('No charge to answer,' says Roeder) can dampen the fact that West Ham have reached 40 points, the likely total for safety, with seven games to go. It's a triumph for Roeder, the man who the press insisted would get West Ham relegated. As that chant against Blackburn went, back in 1995: 'I said we are staying up, I said we are staying up!'

A trip to Fulham on Easter Monday is a somewhat more genteel experience than a promenade down Green Street. Outside Putney Bridge tube station there's even a secondhand bookshop, just in case you want to thumb through a black-spined Penguin while ambling to the game past the tree-lined riverside as you make your way through Bishop's Park. Outside the Eight Bells pub is my old journalist chum Michael Magenis and his daughter Lily. The last time I saw Fulham with Michael was when they lost 4–1 at home to Cardiff on the way to promotion from division three. That was considered to be a huge success in those pre-Al Fayed days.

WEST HAM

Michael's lending me his sister's season ticket in the Hammersmith End and is despairing of his side's six defeats in seven games. It's good to know that other fans moan even more than West Ham ones. He announces that Fulham's tactics are 'an increasingly disinterested-looking goalie, two wing-backs who can't cross, two centre-backs, a captain on the sub's bench, two defensive midfielders, two wandering out of position midfielders, and any number of forwards who can't score'.

We walk past the front of the Stevenage Road Stand, a listed building, and it makes you feel like you've returned to an era of fans in cloth caps. In the close season only the façade will remain, with the entire stadium being redeveloped with Al Fayed's millions.

'They didn't have any fat fans then,' says Michael as he reveals the narrow turnstiles with a proprietorial air. 'And look at those slits in the wall for the ticket office, you just went up in your cap and slipped your ten bob note in,' he adds, pointing to a series of black grilles the size of fire grates.

Inside the Hammersmith End it's a bizarre experience to be standing again and able to choose your own spot with enough room to sit on the concrete and read your programme. The crowd are a mixture of old codgers who look like they grew up with Johnny Haynes and younger fans in replica shirts, some with lip studs and goatees, who look as if they have eaten a fair amount of the club sponsor Pizza Hut's offerings. Behind the goal someone has a drum and its periodic thumps mark several choruses of 'Tigana's black and white army!'.

Inside the ground the sense of being in a time warp continues, as the club DJ is 'Diddy' David Hamilton, a man I haven't heard since inadvertently catching my mum listening to Radio 2 in the early 1970s. An old radiogram, a copy of Elton John's 'Don't Shoot Me I'm Only The Piano Player' in the lounge, banana and custard on Mondays, wondering if one day I too would have really cool sideburns like Trevor Brooking . . . Diddy David's sonorous voice evokes numerous memories of an Essex childhood. It would be no surprise if Ed 'Stewpot' Stewart were to emerge from the bowels of the Cottage and play 'Puff the Magic Dragon'.

After the teams emerge from the famous old Cottage (no Joe Orton references, please) Hamilton asks the crowd to turn off their mobile phones and introduces a minute's silence for the Queen Mother, who died on Saturday night. It's perfectly observed, which again makes me think that with such deference we may be in the 1920s, and is followed by 'God Save The Queen'. Hammers skipper Paolo Di Canio will surely be pleased to hear such patriotic strains in his adopted country. Mind you, the dear old Queen Mum might not have been too amused at the next chant from the Hammersmith End celebrating Fulham chairman Mohammed Al Fayed, the man whose son Dodi died in the Paris car crash with the Princess of Wales – 'Al Fayed, whhhhoooah, he wants to be a Brit, and QPR are shit!'.

The game kicks off, with Labant in for the rested Nigel Winterburn, and Fulham have a great early chance when Saha plays in Barry Hayles, who shoots straight at David James's legs. 'He's fuckin' useless! . . . he just had to lift it over the keeper!' curse the Fulham fans around me.

'Where were you when you were shit?' chant the West Ham fans to my left.

'We've never been anything but shit!' shouts the engagingly cynical Fulham fan in front of me. Fulham are woefully lacking in confidence and the Hammers' defence copes comfortably with most of their attacks.

'Get stuck in Monica!' shouts another Cottager. It's something of a mystery who the player the fans keep referring to as Monica is, until I remember that Fulham have a player called Legwinski, who presumably takes to the field wearing presidential kneepads rather than shin-guards.

Fredi Kanouté is holding the ball up well for West Ham, but with Di Canio more or less in a five-man midfield the Hammers create few chances. Di Canio wins a free-kick on the edge of the box – to loud accusations of being a diver – which is typically wasted. Labant goes off with a back injury, causing Schemmel to move to left-back and substitute Ian Pearce to play at right-back. Pearce sensibly boots the ball back up the field whenever it's played near him and neither of the out-of-position full-backs are particularly troubled.

As the game meanders into midfield muddle, the West Ham fans break into a chorus of 'Stick your blue flag up your arse!'. This attack on mutual enemy Chelsea wins applause from the home fans who then sing their own version: 'The black and white you'll never pass, stick your blue flag up your arse!'

Cordial relations end there, as the fans then spend much of the game debating football history from 1975 and 1966.

The Hammers fans taunt the Hammersmith End with 'There's only one Alan Taylor!', a reference to the ex-Hammer who scored the winning FA Cup final goals against Fulham in 1975.

Fulham respond with cries of 'You're not famous anymore!' and 'You've never won fuck all!'.

The West Ham fans retaliate with 'We won the fucking World Cup!'.

The home fans laugh derisively and chant 'There's only one George Cohen!' referring to their own World Cup winner.

The first half seems destined to end goalless, when right on half-time Trevor Sinclair plays a one-two with Steve Lomas, then puts over a delicious cross which Fredi calmly heads home. Kanouté runs to the West Ham fans and does his mysterious one upraised finger on each hand goal celebration. It's the sort of goal you concede when you're struggling at the bottom and West Ham look almost apologetic for scoring against such a nice club.

Half-time is enlivened by a proposal from a Fulham fan asking for the hand in marriage of his girlfriend in the Hammersmith End. Cue a mass chant of 'You don't know what you're doing!'. A bizarre penalty routine follows on the pitch, where four Fulham fans and a solitary Hammer try to chip the ball into a rubber tyre suspended from the crossbar. Diddy David Hamilton does his best to be a poor man's Stuart Hall and somehow this shambolic entertainment fits in with the olde worlde charm of Fulham, the friendly club by the Thames. Next comes a half-hearted interview with old Fulham and Chelsea star John Dempsey and then the Cravenettes, shattering the belief of many an Irons fans that the Hammerettes were a unique concept dreamt up by Frank McAvennie after a crate of Bolly at Stringfellow's.

In the second half the home fans become increasingly frustrated. Dailly is enjoying a fine game at the back, not making a mistake all afternoon, while Repka's belligerent style is well suited to Fulham's misfiring attack. After 59 minutes Jean Tigana brings on £12 million striker Steve Marlet and Louis Boa Morte, and later ex-Chelsea player Jon Harley (which makes you think that soon Steve Harley and Cockney Rebel might come on to make us smile).

Maybe Roeder is bored, as in response to Tigana's substitutions he decides to take off Di Canio after 67 minutes and replace him with John Moncur. Di Canio had a great game against Ipswich, but although working hard has been affected by the general mediocrity today; and presumably at pushing 34 Roeder has decided to rest him after two games in three days. Glenn's decision goes down about as well as eating one of Paolo's piranhas. Di Canio throws off his captain's armband, brushes aside Roeder's pat on the shoulder, shouts that he wants crisps now (no sorry, that's my three-year-old daughter), grabs his coat and makes a long theatrical walk round the pitch to the changing-rooms. Derisive whistles greet his strop, perhaps caused by the fact that his big brother is in the stands watching him and Roeder has shown disrespect to his family.

Moncur does his job effectively and for once West Ham look professional away from home. Cole and Carrick show some neat touches and threaten to get several breakaway moves going, then Joey shoots over, while the closest Fulham come is when Jon Harley heads just past James's post. Goalkeeper Van der Saar joins the attack for two corners, but after a nervous three minutes of injury time the whistle blows and the Hammers have secured six points out of six over Easter. It has been a poor game, but after five successive away defeats three points wrapped up in a Harrods bag will do very nicely, thank you.

Roeder agrees, calling it 'a bit dogged'. He reveals that he'd asked his full-backs to stay back and play as a unit with the back four as: 'We have enough creative players in midfield to nick a goal or two.' As for the supposed rift with Di Canio he tells the cameras: 'They [the press] will make of it what they will. I don't have to comment.' He later adds that 'Paolo had a super game on Saturday, scoring one and playing well. He played well today for 66 minutes but I thought that at that stage I needed a more defensive midfield player.' He then adopts a Wengerian blind eye, adding: 'I didn't see what Paolo did, I was watching the game, but nothing was said to me afterwards.'

On Monday night the three points have not only ensured Premiership survival but have sent the Hammers soaring to eighth in the table (at least until Aston Villa play on Tuesday). Will Jeremy Nicholas's pulmonary valves be able to cope?

There's much talk in the press about nosebleeds, only by Thursday morning it's all overshadowed by Di Canio again, increasingly sounding as if he may be a piranha fish short of a full tank. It seems that Roeder has disrespected the greatest West Ham player in history by substituting him. Still, maybe GR has escaped lightly as when Fabio Capello benched Paolo in Italy, PDC famously called his boss an 'ugly penis face'.

'If West Ham do not want me around in the future then they have only got one thing to do – give me a free transfer by the end of the season,' rages Di Canio. 'I never let myself be taken for a ride, even by such respected managers as Giovani Trapattoni and Fabio Capello, I am not prepared to be treated like a kid who has just started his career.

'Glenn Roeder is still at the beginning of his managerial career and young managers have to learn in the same way young players have to learn. But he should appreciate he will not go far if he cannot find the courage to substitute the players who need to be substituted.'

Which is surely what Roeder did. Di Canio goes on to explain that he and Kanouté had been asked to double up on the wings every time West Ham lost the ball, but that Kanouté's 'contribution defensively wasn't as intense'. This rather ignores the fact that Kanouté was having an excellent game as a lone striker, keeping the Fulham defence busy with his considerable physical presence and scoring the winner.

Carrick and Cole were doing well in midfield while Lomas and Sinclair are better tacklers than Di Canio. Roeder's decision worked and West Ham won the match. Yet Paolo's sense of raging injustice turns the tactical switch into proof that everyone in the Village is out to get him. 'I have a funny feeling that maybe people at the club are trying to imply that I am getting tired easily. That I am not up to it. That is not true. It seems to me that to sacrifice yourself and your technical skills for the team doesn't pay off. If this is the case I would rather play the way I prefer, than the way I am asked.'

How long will Roeder tolerate such open questioning of his management? Just imagine if Paolo had gone to Old Trafford and Sir Alex Ferguson had tried to rotate him – the confrontation would have made Tyson versus Lennox seem good natured. PDC would attempt to insert Fergie's famous hairdryer alongside Chelsea's blue flag and would then probably receive a Glasgow kiss in return. Paolo has been a legend at Upton Park, but no player is above being substituted (apart, some would say, from the departed Frank Lampard during the Redknapp era). Perhaps someone should tell Paolo, great player that he is, that football is a team game.

The Di Canio furore erupts across the tabloids as PDC, sounding increasingly like a particularly difficult girlfriend who keeps using the commitment word, insists that West Ham must show they care. He claims that Roeder is now trying to ditch him because West Ham have reached safety.

'I like Glenn, he is a good manager and can become one of the best the club have had, but he hasn't spoken to me since Monday . . . I work on morals, respect, a sense of values and I love this club,' says Di Canio. 'Maybe he pulled me off [at which point ex-boss Harry Redknapp would have quipped "but the other players only got oranges at half-time!"] because he thought that with 43 points we were safe in the table. But he should have been big enough to do that a few games ago if he wanted.'

He then achieves the impossible – making Julian Dicks seem like a pillar of responsibility. The legendary former Hammers left-back, nicknamed The Terminator, frequently sent off and once nearly punched by Billy Bonds for underperforming in training, announces that West Ham should get rid of their volatile skipper.

'You can't let one player unsettle the camp and they should just get rid of him,' says the man who is now terminating with Canvey Island. 'It's not nice being substituted, but it's the manager's decision and if he can't accept it then maybe it's best for everyone if he left. If you have a problem you speak about it in the dressing-room. Paolo's done this a few times – caning the players and the manager. But you can't do it, especially as captain.'

At this point many Hammers fans will have been momentarily distracted by the prospect of Di Canio and Dicks in the same changing-room. How would Paolo react to the offer of a litre of non-diet Coke and Iron Maiden on the team's ghetto-blaster – it would surely be the closest thing to *Rollerball* we'd see this side of the twenty-second century.

Whereas some managers would sack Di Canio at once for calling them naïve, Roeder adopts a more paternal pose, refusing to comment or take seriously Di Canio's outburst until his tantrum is finished. It's either brilliant man management or weakness, depending on your viewpoint.

He says the obvious, that 'I couldn't very well take Kanouté off because he gives us a physical presence' and that 'I've seen no evidence Paolo is upset. He has been in for training every day and has been superb.' GR says that Di Canio will play against Charlton and that he is sure he will still be here next season as 'he has a contract for the next 12 months'.

Di Canio has had a good season, scoring nine goals so far, making many more, and topping the Opta index for West Ham players so far. But the most pointed remark that Roeder makes is about young Jermain Defoe, saying that after holding him back this season, next year if Defoe is scoring goals 'he will keep the shirt'. Perhaps this is a subtle message to Di Canio that he is no longer indispensable to West Ham.

TOP FIVE WEST HAM STROPS

PAOLO DI CANIO: Walked off in a huff after being subbed at Fulham and called Glenn Roeder a 'learner'. Asked to be substituted against Bradford because the ref turned down a penalty appeal, then wrestled with Frank Lampard for the ball when a penalty was finally awarded.

PAOLO FUTRE: Walked out of Highbury when he discovered that he was not going to be allowed to play for West Ham in his favourite number 10 shirt.

FLORIN RADUCIOIU: Rather than be a substitute at Stockport in a League Cup tie he decided to go shopping at Harvey Nick's instead.

HARRY REDKNAPP: When a West Ham player, Redknapp yelled 'You're always picking on me!' at Ron Greenwood and hurled a bottle of beer across the dressing-room, which shattered on the wall, narrowly missing physio Rob Jenkins. Jimmy Greaves was most upset as the bottle was full.

MARCO BOOGERS: Hardly played for the Hammers, sent off for nearly cutting Gary Neville in half at Old Trafford, then declared himself mentally unfit for football and was rumoured to be living in a caravan as he Boogered off back to Holland.

34. WE ARE SEVENTH IN THE LEAGUE, I SAID WE ARE SEVENTH IN THE LEAGUE!

West Ham 2 Charlton 0 - 6 April 2002

Despite his super sub sulk, Paolo Di Canio skippers the side against Charlton at Upton Park. Roeder, by now expert at dealing with PDC's emotional outbursts, says simply: 'It never entered my mind not to play him, I always pick the best team available.'

Paolo's agent is visiting for the weekend to hold discussions with the club. 'Presumably to insert that no substitution clause in his contract,' I suggest over a cup of tea in Ken's Café as the Upton Park intelligentsia digest the Di Canio saga. In fact if proprietress Carol was PDC's manager he'd have never dared query his substitution. She'd have just stood there in her blue apron, becoming increasingly red-faced as she hollered, 'Number 10! Number 10! Where's number 10? How many times do I have to call number 10? If you don't come off now your tagliatelli goes in the bin!'

'He's a nutter, that's why we love him,' says Joe. 'You never know what he's going to do so he's always value for money.'

A mutual friend reveals that one of the former contributors to *Fortune's Always Hiding*, now an important TV person, is meeting Paolo's agent after the game to discuss doing a TV special with him. We agree that he would be most suited to a move into acting.

'That game against Bradford, that was opera, it had everything . . . drama, pathos, love, hate, revenge,' enthuses Joe, referring to the 5–4 thriller of 1999–2000.

'And he's already got the stage limp perfected . . .' I add.

Upton Park is bathed in early April sunshine as Jeremy Nicholas introduces a new nickname with 'Sebastien "Archie" Schemmel' and then reads out a long tribute to the Queen Mother describing how she loved the East End and visited it during the war. Joe suggests that she might also have personally manned the anti–aircraft guns during the Blitz. There's some debate about whether the Queen Mum was a Hammers fan before another well-observed silence and then 'God Save The Queen'.

The Hammers start with confidence and verve. Paolo looks in the mood again and you almost wonder if Roeder insulting his honour each week might not be a good tactic for bringing out the best in him. Joe Cole is causing trouble on both flanks and Konchensky is soon booked for scything him down. Paolo weaves his way into the Charlton penalty area and is clattered to the ground by Richard Rufus. For once the referee points to the spot. 'Bet he misses it,' says Nigel, anticipating another poncy penalty. We needn't worry, though, as this time there is no delicate chip, just a routine stroking of the ball into the corner. 'West Ham's goal was scored after 23 minutes by Paolo Diiii Caniiiiiio!' gushes Jeremy Nicholas in cod Italian.

'Maybe Roeder should sub him now, just for a laugh . . .' I suggest.

Eleven minutes later the Irons score a superb second. It's a real team goal; Cole gains possession on the left, plays it inside to Kanouté who in turn finds Di Canio. PDC plays a perfectly weighted pass into the path of Sebastien Schemmel, who, right on the by-line, screws the ball back for Fredi Kanouté to fire into the top of the net. It's Fredi's second goal in successive games and an apt answer to the few fans who booed him during the Ipswich match. We all know that Fredi has ability and could be an awesome international star – if only he'd realise it himself.

'Well done, Archie! I've lost count of the number of times he's done that this season . . .' enthuses Nigel, quickly adopting the Frenchman's mystery nickname. 'I think it might be some reference to Archie Gemmill . . .' he suggests. Cue a Gallic look of puzzlement in Seb's Chigwell home: 'Archie, who eez zis Archie?'

West Ham try hard to concede the traditional soft goal before half-time: Johansson heads against the post and James produces a superb fingertip save to deny Konchensky and enhance his England chances.

In the second half the game slows down to become one of those ambling end-of-season mid-table affairs, although Charlton still manage to create the better chances as Kinsella wallops the bar. Then on 68 minutes Di Canio goes down after a challenge by Scott Parker and falls to the ground flailing his arm and pleading for treatment. Surrounded by a cluster of worried players Di Canio is stretchered off the pitch having damaged his knee, and is vigorously applauded. It looks like being a sad end to his season and maybe his Upton Park career.

'He's been subbed three games in a row,' says Matt. 'He'll be off now!' Still, at least there must be a clause in Paolo's contract allowing him to be substituted when injured, as he is promptly replaced by Jermain Defoe.

There's still time for Trevor Sinclair to hit the post and Charlton to be awarded a penalty. The ball hits the West Ham woodwork again and Nigel

Winterburn brings down Johansson who is chasing the rebound. Konchensky strides up to take the worst penalty ever seen at Upton Park – even more abysmal than Paolo's poncy penalty against Aston Vila – and balloons the ball way over David James's goal. Charlton have now missed their last four penalties and at this rate the whole side will soon be doing a collective pizza ad. Having hit the woodwork four times they are entitled to think they might have got at least a draw today. But who cares? If Tottenham and Villa continue to lose, then we are seventh in the league. A week ago we were worried about survival. Now someone asks why we haven't entered for the Intertoto Cup.

'We were banking on an automatic Champions League place,' suggests Joe. (In reality Roeder argues that with players such as James, Carrick, Cole, Sinclair and Kanouté possibly away on World Cup duty then it's not feasible to play more games in July.)

For the final few minutes of the game we contemplate our entry into Europe. 'I think we can still get into Europe in seventh place if the top four go in the Champions League, but if Arsenal or Chelsea win the FA Cup, then the Cup-Winners' UEFA Cup spot goes to the sides in fifth and sixth place in the league, plus Worthington Cup winners Blackburn,' I explain. 'Then if it's a leap year and a team is relegated for financial irregularities . . .'

'And at the end of the month five planets align . . .' adds Joe.

'Then we qualify for Europe by finishing seventh,' I confirm.

The whistle sounds and Jeremy Nicholas confirms that Villa and Spurs have lost. We go above Villa! We go above Spurs! West Ham are up to seventh and even Paolo must be considering allowing Glenn Roeder to discard his L-plates.

More good news comes on Monday with the news that Di Canio has only twisted his medial ligament and may return before the end of the season. And we could still qualify for Europe in seventh place as England is in the running for an extra UEFA Cup place through the Fair Play League, where all sides rated above eight marks out of ten go into a draw for an extra place. And if the conjunction of Mercury, Venus, Mars, Jupiter and Saturn in a dazzling cosmic necklace really happens, as the cosmologists promise it will on May 4, and this is added to the fact that a unique bronze age gold goblet from 1700 BC has just been unearthed in a field near Sandwich by a metal detecting enthusiast; then these might just be considered as omens from the gods that we are predestined for a European tour.

TOP TEN THOUGHTS OF CHAIRMAN PAOLO IN 2001–02

FISH FRENZY: 'The man who comes to my house and feeds my piranha fish said he would kill them if I left West Ham to feed Manchester United. So I told him I would not go. And I begged him don't kill them, they are like my children. And now the fish are happy.' (After failing to join Manchester United.)

YOU'RE SHIT, AAAARGH! 'We have to realise how shit we are.' (After 7–1 defeat at Blackburn.)

BALL PLAYER: 'I do play hard in away games. I scored at Liverpool on the opening day of the season – a "big balls" goal.' (After 5–0 defeat at Everton.)

L–PLATES: 'Glenn Roeder is still at the beginning of his managerial career and young managers have to learn in the same way young players have to learn. But he should appreciate he will not go far if he cannot find the courage to substitute the players who need to be substituted.' (After being subbed at Fulham.)

FULL THROTTLE: 'I never had the intention to strangle him. If you look at my face I have a very relaxed face and that is unusual for me in a game, so this proves that I had no bad intentions.' (After being photographed with his hands around Barry Hayles's neck.)

PRESS GANG: 'I can't accept this any more. I intend to take legal action because they [the press] are absolutely bad people.' (After press allegations that he tried to strangle Barry Hayles.)

PEA BRAINS: 'I feel sorry for reporters that invent and recreate old comments to sell their newspapers. They have no real value of life and must be very lonely people without any real friends. I think they must have brains the size of a pea. When the truth does come out they will be made to look foolish.' (After the *Sunday People* recycles old quotes to make it look like he can't wait to join Man United.)

INVISIBLE MEN: 'Roeder is the scapegoat for everything. I don't think most of our fans even know what Paul Aldridge [the managing director] and Terry Brown [the chairman] look like. They should be showing their faces to the fans.' (After defeat at Southampton.)

SOBER ANALYSIS: 'If you go out drinking all night after what happened you don't understand the enormity of the events. It's right to fine them two weeks' wages but they should have been left out for a month after doing that. It was terrible.' (On the Chelsea Four, caught drinking the day after 11 September.)

STARS AND STRIPES: 'I didn't wear the armband because I had any friends in America, I just feel like all the American people are friends and family to us. It's so sad what happened and I just want to live in a peaceful world – but we must not give in to the terrorists.' (On wearing a Stars and Stripes armband against Newcastle.)

35. OFF THE RECORD

Jeremy Nicholas sits overlooking the empty Boleyn stadium after the Charlton game, assessing the scores coming in on his television and attempting to convince me that West Ham really can qualify for the UEFA Cup by finishing seventh. His commentary box, in the wraparound corner of the Dr Martens Stand, is reached via the Bobby Moore Stand reception and a maze of half-finished corridors full of builders' dust. ('At least we have a decent view here; before, we were stuck behind a pillar.') He's accompanied by his helpers: Russell, a media studies student from Loughborough University in a Hammers replica shirt, and Natasha, who was working for *Bella* and has just got a job on *Cosmopolitan*.

Nicholas then gathers together his team for a ceremonial walk around the pitch. 'If we win we always walk round it in the same direction, if we lose we have to walk round the pitch in the opposite direction,' he explains. 'Although sometimes we forget which way we walked round the week before. Anyway, if we don't do it, it brings bad luck for evermore.'

Once the pitch has been lapped and I've resisted the temptation to fire a ball into the gaping nets, we proceed down the mouth of the players' tunnel, and stand beneath the new 'Welcome to the Academy' sign (not quite up to 'This Is Anfield' but it's a start), where Nicholas chats with club secretary Peter Barnes and gently ribs him, accusing him of being a Spurs supporter. In the tunnel Richard Rufus rushes past while Scott Parker is telling a posse of microphone-wielding journalists that he now realises how much West Ham meant to Charlton gaffer Alan Curbishley, after his reaction to defeat here.

The tunnel leads out into the reception of the Dr Martens Stand and as we join the departing crowds David Essex comes over to Jeremy to say hello. 'Note that he recognised me!' jokes a chuffed Nicholas after a couple of minutes' chat with the husky-voiced old charmer and Hammers regular.

Then we say goodbye to Natasha and Russell and move on to the Central pub in Barking Road, packed with celebrating fans. Nicholas recognises a steward and discusses bets with him, while a female fan then good-naturedly lambasts him for ignoring her request. As I queue at the bar a fan nudges his mate and mutters, 'That's that DJ bloke over there!' It's not a description Nicholas enjoys: 'I hate being called the DJ, I'm the match-day announcer.'

After pleading with him to get someone to re-record 'Bubbles' rather than be reminded of the endless beards and sideburns of yesteryear by the 1975 Cup final squad's version, I ask Nicholas about the difference between Redknapp and Roeder. Clearly he had grown a little tired of Harry Redknapp's over-protective attitude to his players.

'Harry didn't really like me saying anything during the game. He didn't like me building up the players. One time when Rio and Frank both got into the England squad I mentioned it and after the game Frank Lampard Senior came up to me and said: "We don't want you doing that because Trevor Sinclair hasn't made the squad and it doesn't make him feel very good." It's ridiculous because Trevor had never been in an England squad at that point. Can you imagine the announcer at Man United or Leeds not mentioning England call-ups in case it upsets another player? We hadn't had a player in the squad since Alvin Martin! Then Harry would always say don't get the fans going before the kick-off because it puts pressure on the players, which I thought was rubbish! Don't get the fans noisy, we don't want that!

'With Glenn I made a conscious decision not to ask him what he wanted, just wait and see if he complains and he never has. Now I get to do all sorts of outrageous things like announce the time added on. With Harry if I'd said we have three minutes' injury time added on and the other team had scored in those three minutes it would have been my fault, he'd have said I'd spurred the other team on by telling them there was three minutes left!'

Nicholas gets inspiration for players' nicknames from fanzines and websites. ('Although if Paul Ince was still here he'd probably demand that I call him The Governor.') With today's 'Archie' monicker attached to Sebastien Schemmel he explains this came from a website punning on Archie Gemmill. 'I did get a letter accusing me of dumbing down when I referred to "Tomas 'The Hit Man' Repka", only "dumbing down" was spelt with a double 'm'!'

He's quietly pleased with his 'We go above Southampton!' routine, which is particularly suited to a team that wins at home and then always drops a few places after losing away. 'There was one Christmas game though when I said: "We go above Man United!" and I hadn't used the latest table so then everyone wrote in to point out that I was using out-of-date tables!'

Other humorous moments have included the time he announced at an England Under-21 game against Bulgaria at Upton Park. 'It was live on Sky and I had to play the Bulgarian national anthem by clicking manually from five to 17 on the CD and praying I didn't get the German national anthem at 16 by mistake. And today when I played "God Save The Queen" as a tribute to the Queen Mum that's one click away from the German national anthem. If I'd played the German anthem by mistake I'd probably have been sacked.'

During a long media career, Nicholas has worked for the likes of GLR,

Channel 5, Sky and Talk Sport. He's been match-day announcer at Upton Park since 1998. Managing director Paul Aldridge had heard his pro-Hammers comments on his GLR show and asked him if he'd be interested in working on match days. He initially turned down the job because he wanted to remain watching games as a fan, but after dreaming for three nights that he was the West Ham announcer welcoming back Rio who had scored the winner in the 1998 World Cup final, he decided to take the job. I ask him if during this time he has ever had stick from opposition managers.

'I had Gordon Strachan pin me up against a wall once. We'd just won the Youth Cup final. We were 3–0 up from the first leg, it was live on Sky, and 23,000 fans had come to Upton Park because you could get in for a quid. The head of security said that the police had said the presentation wouldn't take place if any fans ran on the pitch. So five times during the second half I announced: "The presentation to the winners will take place live on the pitch after the game. If anyone runs on to the pitch the presentation will not take place." We were 9–0 up on aggregate and the fifth time I said: "The presentation to the winners – whoever they may be – will take place after the game."

'An hour after the game Strachan came to the directors' bar where I was having a drink. One of the directors had warned me he'd been looking for me. He pinned me up against the wall and said, "I've got 16-year-old boys in the dressing-room crying their eyes out because of what you said." I said, "I think it's probably because they've lost the cup final 9–0 on aggregate." He said, [adopts a thick Scottish accent] "You think you're being clever, taking the piss, you're not funny!" I thought to myself, OK you're quite scary, you're ginger-haired, you're Scottish, you're volatile, so I just said "You're absolutely right, Gordon, I don't know what came over me."'

Mind you, a ruck with Strachan hardly compares with being punched by Brian Clough. When Nicholas was a reporter with Radio Nottingham he covered Steve Hodge's move back to the City Ground.

'Brian had sent the agent away and then he and Hodge had spent the afternoon in Cloughie's office drinking whisky and sorting out a deal. I think he had some kind of exclusive deal with *The Sun* so he wouldn't talk to anyone else. I just said, "Come on, Brian, tell the people of Nottingham tonight what the people in London will read tomorrow" and he just went boof, and I went through these glass doors and landed on his Labrador. I thought that's a bit funny, I've just been punched by Brian Clough.

'I then went into the corridor and he said if I didn't leave he was calling the police. His assistant, Archie Gemmill, then took me outside and gave me an interview, no trouble. Then I walked back in to try and make friends with Cloughie and he was stuck in there with John Sadler from *The Sun* and some other smug tabloid types. I said, "See you next week, Brian" and held my hand out. He shook my hand and said, "Young man, you're the first reporter I've punched all season, but you won't be the last!"

'Later that season he did remember that he'd done something wrong. When they won the Littlewoods Cup I was in the tunnel trying to get a quote. He ignored everyone else, grabbed me, pulled me into the dressing-room and said, "Young man, let's work!" He was just wearing a towel and Stuart Pearce and Des Walker were naked drinking beer out of the Littlewoods Cup and he kept telling them, "Keep quiet, I'm working with this young man!"'

At least with Glenn Roeder, Jem will hopefully be safe from unexpected pugilism.

Nicholas refuses to play Tina Turner's 'Simply The Best' and Queen's 'We Are The Champions' at Upton Park (although unfortunately Queen's 'We Will Rock You' sneaked in as a Hammerettes' dance routine) and for that fact alone he deserves support. And like all lifelong Hammers fans he has a healthy sense of his side's failings. '"Simply The Best" is such a clichéd stadium record and as for "We Are The Champions", well, we're not really, are we?'

We leave the Central where the denizens are still singing 'Bubbles', and Nicholas departs for his car. Tomorrow he's attending a course for stand-up comedians. 'I've just split up with my girlfriend and I thought it would give me something to do on Sundays,' he explains. 'I did do a stand-up spot for a radio show once, which went OK, but I don't really want to become a comedian as yet.' Still, perhaps one day the stand-up clubs of London will be ready for such epic one-liners as: 'We go above Southampton! We go above Spurs! We're on the first half of page 324 on Ceefax!'

36. IAN PEARCE, SUPERSTAR

Tottenham 1 West Ham 1 – 13 April 2002

There could be a living in showing Americans the underbelly of footballing life in London. We're in the Victoria pub, just off Tottenham High Road, drinking pints of Whitbread Best Bitter from plastic glasses. The racing is on the telly, signs to Irish towns are on the wall and we're surrounded by a *Minder*-esque cross section of Spurs-supporting society, hunched over programmes, papers and pints.

'Gee, this is great,' says Reno, my American pal who attended the Southampton and Fulham games at Upton Park earlier this season, appreciating the most un-West End of ambiences. I'm explaining that in the away end he should get the full tribal atmosphere of English football, as opposed to the rather more sedate experience of sitting in the Upper East Stand at Upton Park. And that the Undertaker has come good and that if West Ham win today they'll be four points clear of Spurs in seventh place, making us the third best team in London. But if Spurs win they go above us.

We down two pints of watery bitter and head for the match, but only after Reno has decided to try the Chinese fish and chip shop next door. 'You won't believe it, but this is only the second time I've had fish and chips in England,' he announces. I'm a little apprehensive as Reno's wife Jackie has already told me to make sure he doesn't have any dodgy meat pies.

Reno soon wishes he'd stuck to just the one taste of fish and chips. He offers me some of his chips as we walk along Tottenham High Road and then peels a strip of batter from his fish. 'Look at the batter on this . . . I can't eat this, gee, there is just so much fat here!' he exclaims, dumping the said batter in a litter bin. Reno's inner Californian has just caught up with him.

There's an intimidating atmosphere on the High Road. A police helicopter drones overhead and six police vans and accompanying officers in luminous green bibs and black riot helmets are proceeding down the road escorting a

197

group of West Ham fans to the ground. A teenage Spurs fan in a replica top is giving lip to some of the police. He is roughly pushed back on the pavement by the police but comes back and bangs on the side of a van. Back on the pavement an officer in a Darth Vader helmet places his arm around him, telling him: 'Listen, you're just a little boy, you're out of your depth . . .'

'Hey, he'd never get away with that in the States,' says Reno, wondering how the kid has escaped the Rodney King treatment.

'This is all part of the authentic London derby experience, proper anti-social hooligan behaviour,' I explain.

Then we're queuing up outside the South Stand, where several stewards are waiting to search us. This presents a problem as Reno has brought a hip flask of bourbon with him and alcohol is banned from the ground. He conceals the flask inside a copy of the *Economist* and the stewards – perhaps dazzled by all that macro economic theory – fail to find it.

Then it's up to our seats where everyone is standing up and singing 'Bubbles'. Reno is instantly impressed, remarking that the home fans are not singing at all. Why, there's even some Dick Van Dyke to make Reno feel at home – 'Chim chiminy chim chiminy chim chim cheroo, we are those bastards in claret and blue!'

The game kicks off. 'GLENNROWERSCLARETANDBLUEARMY! GLENNROWERSCLARETANDBLUEARMY' chant the West Ham legions, desperately trying to make Glenn Roeder scan. Indeed, not since Billy Bonds have we had a manager with a name suited to mass chanting, which is perhaps a consideration the board should make in their next appointment.

Di Canio's injured knee will keep him out for the rest of the season, so Defoe is set for an extended run alongside 'King' Kanouté, as Jeremy Nicholas would call him. Joe Cole has pulled out with a thigh injury, so Roeder has reverted to a five-man defence, with big Ian Pearce coming in for Cole.

The five men at the back policy contains Spurs easily during the first half, with Rebrov anonymous and Sheringham slicing embarrassingly wide of the Hammers' goal. Dailly is again efficient in everything he does and there are chants of 'Super Tomas Repka!' after several typically robust clearances. Spurs best hope seems to be Simon Davies, who has the beating of Vladimir Labant, playing today instead of Winterburn. Earlier in the week Roeder announced that Winterburn will be released in the summer and hailed him as a role model for all young footballers. But with Labant still adjusting to the pace of English football, surely Winterburn should at least be kept on as a reliable deputy.

Even though most of us fans are probably from the home counties, or in my case North London, it's time to celebrate East London. Clearly some of the away crew have been performing some interesting gender research and have concluded that in East London there are – erm, women. 'Oh East London is wonderful! Full of tits, fanny and West Ham! Oh East London is wonderful!'

they holler. This is a traditional East End folk song, I explain to Reno. A bit like the Beach Boys' 'California Girls'.

Big Joe didn't fancy today's game because of the atmosphere of hatred that often surrounds these games and you can see his point with some of the anti-semitic songs being sung. I've explained to Reno about Tottenham being perceived as a Jewish club, and how the Spurs fans refer to themselves as 'Yiddoes'.

But with the Israeli army having defied international opinion and killed possibly hundreds of Palestinian refugees/terrorists at the Jenin refugee camp earlier in the week, a siege around the Church of the Nativity in Bethlehem and the BNP gaining ground in the forthcoming council elections, the anti-Jewish comments seem stronger than ever. There's a song that goes, 'We'll be running round Tottenham with our willies hanging out, singing I've got a foreskin haven't you!' which might just be interpreted as mere banter, only the chorus is now interspersed with a vitriolic, 'Fucking Jews!' It's sad, because last week Glenn Roeder used the Hammer programme to back a campaign against racism by the Association of Chief Police Officers, so there really is no excuse at all for the vociferous minority who continually chant, 'I never felt more like gassing the Jews, when West Ham win and Tottenham lose . . .' It's not ironic, it's not funny and it makes me ashamed to see it associated with West Ham.

The best chances are created by West Ham. Neat footwork by Defoe creates a shooting opportunity that Kasey Keller beats away, while another Defoe dribble results in his cross being knocked just wide by Fredi Kanouté.

At half-time I tell Reno that a point will be good enough as it still keeps us above Spurs. The important thing is not to lose. We then surreptitiously bend down and take some furtive sips of his contraband bourbon. For some reason a giant walkabout Sooty is paraded round the pitch only to be greeted with cries of 'Sooty takes it up the arse!', which is probably quite true when speaking of a glove puppet. Unless we've just had too much bourbon.

Early in the second half Fredi Kanouté shows just what a good player he can be by skipping away from two Spurs defenders and firing in a low hard shot that Keller again does well to beat away.

Then it all goes Chas and Dave-ish. Repka just fails to cut out Davies's through ball, Iversen shoots, James spills it and Sheringham slots home an easy goal. At last the Spurs fans come alive. By the high standards of potential World Cup keepers it's a shot that James should probably have held. There's an ominous sense of déja vu; last season West Ham dominated the first half only to lose 1–0 to a Sol Campbell goal.

Spurs have a good 20-minute spell, where James redeems himself by making two fine saves. Iversen shoots, he spills it again but recovers to make an excellent save from Sherwood. Then terrible marking allows Sherwood through again, but James saves with his legs.

However, the collective spirit among the West Ham side is much improved, for they keep going and come back into the game. Winterburn comes on for Labant and immediately crunches into Davies, grinning as he gets up from the ground. Carrick is, as ever, neat and economical, while Sinclair is working hard and starting to take players on. Schemmel is getting into crossing positions on the right and Lomas is working hard, although as Reno points out, 'That guy is not as skilful as the others.' But it amounts to little and the game is drifting towards the inevitable Spurs win. Free-kicks and corners are wasted, Defoe has a tame header wide and that's about it.

Only then, on 89 minutes Lomas skies a mishit cross into the area. Davies half clears it out to the edge of the area where Ian Pearce, yes Ian Pearce, emerges to hit an absolutely sumptuous volley that is still rising as it flies into the top corner.

Three thousand fans go barmy. Reno, who has just discovered that he is from the East End of San Francisco, is jumping up and down punching the air, people are kicking seats and hugging each other, my keys go flying from my pocket, as Pearcey runs to the fans with his fists clenched. It's the sort of goal Paolo Di Canio would have been proud to score, not Ian Pearce. After two years out with terrible injuries, it's a lovely moment for the man who after all was a striker as a kid at Chelsea when Glenn Hoddle was manager. 'He never hit one like that for me,' sighs Hoddle after the game.

There's still a minute or so for that will-they-concede-a-soft-winner-in-the-last-minute moment, as Poyet slices a half-chance wide and then the whistle blows. The players come over to the fans, and David James, as usual, gives away his gloves.

Reno finds himself chuckling hysterically at the verbal dexterity of the Irons fans still singing: 'Oh North London is full of shit, shit and more shit! Oh North London is full of shit!' As someone who lives in North London I find this sentiment a little unsettling, but you know what they mean. The River Lea is really quite scenic, you know.

'This is the best game I've ever been too . . .' says an enraptured Reno. 'There's nothing like this in America . . . They must have a repertoire of 100 songs . . . is this on television tonight . . . I like the fact they're blue collar regular working guy fans . . . Gee, they're passionate . . .'

37. KOREA OPPORTUNITIES

West Ham 3 Sunderland 0 – 20 April 2002

Poor Joey Cole. He produces a superb performance as a second-half substitute during England's 4–0 demolition of Paraguay in which he makes two goals while playing in the troublesome left midfield slot – only to be totally upstaged two days later by the revelation that England boss Sven-Goran Eriksson, who lives with girlfriend Nancy Dall'Olio, is having an affair with fellow Swede Ulrika Jonsson.

Forget all that intellectual, sophisticated continental coach stuff. Sven resembles the Swedish equivalent of Frank McAvennie with a penchant for blonde TV presenters. It's the sort of plot that would have been dismissed as being far too outlandish for the recent series of *Footballers' Wives*. At this rate it's tempting to look up the odds for Glenn Roeder being the father of Elizabeth Hurley's new child Damian. Still, at least Sven should treat Ulrika better than her ex-boyfriend Stan Collymore, who hit her in a bar in Paris. Collymore rightly earned the ire of the Bobby Moore Stand for that incident, who summed up the views of all those who oppose violence against women with their chant of 'You're shit and you slap your bird!' when West Ham played Aston Villa in 1997.

After the Paraguay game, Sven – who clearly knows more than we thought about tactical substitutions – had praised Cole's performance. 'I never said Joe Cole was too young and he made the right decisions tonight. He is a special player, full of fantasy and things few people have. He learnt from the mistake against Italy I know, because the whole country was talking about it.'

Cole had been unfairly criticised for losing possession against Italy. It was a mistake, but Montella's strike from the edge of the area was stunning. Most people subsequently forgot his tenacious contribution to making Fowler's earlier goal. After the Paraguay match Cole himself mentioned the Italy game, saying: 'I don't have anything to prove to anybody. I'm my own biggest critic, even the last game I took positives from. I feel good.' More and more fans are starting to feel that Cole can provide the element of surprise in 2002 that Gazza provided at the 1990 World Cup, and Sven too seems to be flirting with the idea of taking someone who is 'full of fantasy', unless that means Ulrika.

Before the Sunderland match there are fans at Upton Park tube handing out leaflets advertising a new initiative called the West Ham United Supporters Trust, part of the growing Trust movement in football. Membership is £20 and the Trust's laudable aim is to 'increase communication between the board and fans . . . and achieve supporter representation on the board at West Ham' – although sadly you suspect they'd get more members if the club was struggling rather than surging towards seventh place.

By the Dr Martens Stand a BBC camera crew is outside the main gates filming cockernee types shouting 'He's gotta go!' as the East End's contribution to the great Joe Cole debate. If only the Sunderland fans, still not safe from relegation worries, were so happy. A Sunderland fan, smelling more than a little of drink, accosts us in Tudor Road and reveals that Black Cats boss Peter Reid is now a hated figure. He says with some indignation that a fan was ejected from the Stadium of Light for criticising Reid, and in a conspiracy theory typical of football fans, that because Reid has shares in the club he won't buy any players. 'The police surrounded him because we were throwing shirts at him. I mean, what manager needs protection from fans throwing shirts at him?' adds the disgruntled Wearsider.

'A couple of years ago Reidy was God up there,' comments my pal Dave Kampfner, whose son Ben is a fan of the Mackems.

Fredi Kanouté has been hit by a late illness and so Trevor Sinclair, who has played on the left, right and centre of midfield this season, plays as a makeshift striker. Ian Pearce keeps his place at right-back with Seb Schemmel moving into right midfield.

West Ham's early football is as brilliant as the unseasonable April sunshine. After three minutes Joey appears to have scored his first league goal of the season, Sinclair crosses and Cole tucks home neatly. 'The time of the first goal was three minutes, scored by Joey "Always believe in your soul" Cole!' announces Jeremy Nicholas. Only our celebrations are aborted as a linesman's flag is spotted. 'Erm, I mean the time of the first goal kick . . .' ad libs Nicholas, salvaging the situation with some late humour. It must be those stand-up classes.

Cole is looking swift of foot and brain, and another raking ball reaches Schemmel who crosses for Lomas to volley just wide of the near post. Sunderland's Kevin Phillips chips a shot over but generally the side looks a class below West Ham.

Sinclair, who thanks to Glenn Roeder's influence is on the verge of signing a new contract, is looking a lively striker and on 28 minutes he opens the scoring. Repka crosses to Schemmel on the right wing, who nicely cushions a pass into the path of Tricky Trev, who fires a half volley past Sorenson for his fifth goal of the season. Sorenson makes three saves in succession to deny the Irons at the start of the second half, from Sinclair, Schemmel and Repka. By 52 minutes it's all over as West Ham score a superb team goal. Carrick works the ball to Cole, who plays a perfectly weighted ball into Sinclair. Trev crosses and Steve Lomas slots the ball home for his third goal in six games. Again we're all very relieved that the ginger-nutted midfield maestro remains fully clothed.

There's a carnival feeling among those West Ham fans not suffering from the bends. We're still seventh and huge roars of 'Bubbles' fill the air, followed by a chorus of 'Shit team from Scotland! You're just a shit team from Scotland!' directed at the impressively loyal Sunderland fans.

On 77 minutes Joey runs across the Sunderland defence from the left, plays the ball to Lomas on the right and old bog-brush head crosses for Sinclair to nod back and Defoe to head home from a yard out. Lomas has had a superb match, making several great tackles, scoring and making one, and displaying more skill than people credit him with. His role in West Ham's revival is probably just as important as the flashier skills of Cole, Carrick and Defoe.

For once we can relax during a home match and it's a sign of the side's progress that now we can win even without Kanouté and Di Canio. Nigel chants, 'We want Pottsy on the pitch!' wondering if Roeder will give the West Ham sub the chance of making his 400th West Ham appearance in front of his legions of adoring fans (or at least Nigel). 'I don't suppose anyone under 20 will remember seeing him play . . .' he then muses.

There's time for Richard Garcia to look lively and skilful in a cameo as sub, and Cole to miss a chance, proving that poor finishing remains his biggest failing.

Spurs have only drawn and we are now three points clear in seventh place, with three games left. Bizarrely, there's a small protest from a hundred or so fans in the Bobby Moore Stand after the game, chanting: 'Same old West Ham, taking the piss!' They seem to be part of the Independent Supporters Trust, but although many of us agree with at least some of their criticisms, West Ham's highest point of the season is not exactly a good time to ferment revolution in the stands.

Otherwise, even the Old Bill are happy. 'That was a lovely game, no trouble from anyone,' says the policeman marshalling the queues at Upton Park station. As we walk to Plaistow station, despairing of the huge queue at Upton Park, more friendly but depressed Sunderland fans moan about Peter Reid, telling us knowingly that he only uses one agent.

Meanwhile, the 20-year-old Joey Cole is talking with some maturity about his World Cup prospects. He recalls how he watched Gazza in the 1990 World Cup on 'the little TV upstairs' and would love to go to Japan and South Korea. He has showed mental strength to overcome his mistake for England against Italy and says: 'Every player loses the ball on occasions. This is

203

inevitable when you try to make things happen. So you have to have the right mental attitude. People talk about bravery in football but, to me, that's not about flying into tackles but always making yourself available to receive the ball, especially when the chips are down. If you've lost possession three or four times in a row it's easy to shirk your responsibilities and let someone else take the ball.'

He admits his frustration at not scoring more goals, emphasising: 'I'm looking for the perfect game, I made two goals today but I want to make two goals, score two goals, tackle everybody and clear a few off the line. I want to do everything.'

Eriksson will surely have been impressed. Even more so when he opened the following day's *News of the World* to read not only of his own sexploits with Ulrika, but that young Joe too apparently prefers blondes, although Cole is reported to be 'cooling' his relationship with former page three girl Ebony Gilbert (no, really, that is her name and she wasn't invented for an ITV drama) after her agent put her up for a part in the second series of *Footballers' Wives*. Ebony, who has a red bunny tattooed above her bottom, told the *NOTW*: 'Me and Joe were getting on really well, but I told him about how my agent was putting me up for *Footballers' Wives* and he didn't want me to do it. He just reckoned it would be weird because I'm a footballer's girlfriend in real life.'

Apparently Joe was worried people might not think he takes his football seriously. What dedication. Placing football above sex is a maxim Joe's England boss – who denies any relationship with Chardonnay whatsoever – might now wish he had followed.

38. KICK UP THE ARSENAL

Arsenal 2 West Ham 0 – 24 April 2002

Highbury is the one game of the season when I can be home in five minutes. Such close proximity to the home of the offside trap is really not my fault. When I moved in with Nicola back in 1994, shortly after meeting her, I had just been evicted from my short life gaff in Blackfriars Road. It was only upon entering her bedroom that I realised that you could glimpse the Arsenal ground through the window. It was tempting to run at this moment, but reluctant to turn down an evening with a woman who claimed to be the Ulrika Jonsson of Highbury, I decided to lie back and think of West Ham whenever I glanced at Arsenal's stands.

Then Nicola's flat suffered from subsidence, endless men in suits came to do verticality surveys, and after several years of meetings the flat is now surrounded by scaffolding, we are renting a place a couple of streets away and I'm still stuck with living next to the Gooners. Maybe it has been for the best, for I am now the sort of renaissance man who can appreciate the fine cuisine on offer both at Da Mario's deli and La Fromagerie on Highbury Barn and Ken's Café in E13.

Since my time as Hammer-in-residence in Highbury, I've seen Paolo Futre walk out in a strop because he wasn't given the number 10 shirt, Deadly Don Hutchison score the winner in his first incarnation, the late Les Sealey play up front as a late substitute, Ian Pearce score in a plucky 1–1 draw in the FA Cup, and the lads 4–0 down at half-time in a situation so bleak that there were cries from the West Ham fans of, 'We all agree, Dowie is better than Bergkamp!'.

A couple of seasons ago Di Canio gave an injury-hit West Ham the lead, young Bywater performed heroically in goal only for the ref not to spot Petit's handball before he fired home a deflected long shot in injury time. Sinclair was also sent off in the final minutes, but none of this stopped Paolo rushing over to the West Ham fans at the end, beating his shirt and uttering inspiring imprecations in the manner of a young Hadrian about to build a wall across Bethnal Green to keep away the northern hordes.

205

WEST HAM

In contrast, last season's dire 3–0 defeat was one of the worst West Ham performances I have ever seen and the memory of Davor Suker and Kaba Diawara strolling about up front as if perusing the delicatessens on Highbury Barn still brings me out in urticaria (yes, they were even worse than Newell and Jones as a front pairing). Dailly and Soma in midfield, Stuart Peace showing his age at the back, poor old Pottsy chasing Sylvain Wiltord . . . it could have been ten if Arsenal had bothered after the break. So any kind of performance tonight should be an improvement on that.

The Arsenal match has been moved to a Wednesday night with the Double-chasing Gunners top of the Premiership with a game in hand on Man United and Liverpool. Dan, Matt, Gavin and myself take our seats in the lower West Stand, while Nigel and Joe have used their influence with Arsenal fans to secure seats among the Gooner contingent.

The game begins with flashlights galore greeting the appearance of a contrite-looking Sven-Goran Eriksson sitting beside a beaming Nancy Dell'Olio, the dark lady's black locks contrasting fetchingly with a white trouser suit. It's 'Nancy 1 Ulrika 0' as the front page of the next morning's *Sun* puts it. Sven and Nancy – now wouldn't that be a good title for a movie?

The most shocking aspect of the whole affair was that Eriksson was prepared to date a Man United fan. There was Ulrika being photographed in the crowd at Chelsea versus Man United, brazenly cheering a Manchester United goal with her arms punching the air. Quite what link Ulrika has with Manchester United is unknown, although coming from Sweden she is probably a lot more local than most United fans.

Had Sven continued to whisper Swede nothings to Ulrika then there was a serious danger that Angus Deayton, Mick Hucknall, Gary Rhodes and Pete and Adam from *Cold Feet* would start coming round for smorgasbord and Sky. Sven would then become incredibly smug, start eating prawn sandwiches and demanding that the refs play at least ten minutes extra time for all England games . . .

At least West Ham have a solid family man in Glenn Roeder. Tonight, rather like Nancy, he's opted for containment. West Ham's formation has five at the back, with Roeder leaving Defoe on the bench and playing just Fredi Kanouté up front. As the teams emerge there's a sense of big-match expectancy among the Highbury hordes as, with four games left, they anticipate another step on their way to the Double.

After just 90 seconds Henry lays the ball off to Freddie Ljungberg, who fires in a low shot which James does well to tip past the post. The red-haired Swede is looking irresistible in midfield, cutting in from the left and appearing behind the Arsenal strikers. He then beats four West Ham defenders in a superb run from deep and is only stopped by a late combination of James and Ian Pearce. Despite myself, I reflect that Arsenal are really rather an attractive side to watch these days.

206

But the Hammers are defending with determination and slowly come into the game. Trevor Sinclair breaks down the left and crosses for Fredi Kanouté to head just wide. It's a good chance and, as Trevor Brooking might say, the lad really should have hit the target. Fredi, alone up front, is causing the ageing Keown and Adams problems with his languid strength. After a Cole dribble he places a half-chance just wide, then, picking up a long David James punt downfield, Fredi muscles aside Adams, controls the ball well but then chips the ball over the gaping goal when a more delicate touch is needed. He has created the chance brilliantly, but, typically with Fredi, his finishing has let him down. Our hopes might be hanging by a Fred, but you can't fault his perseverance and Kanouté is still looking for chances and doing a great job for the team as a lone striker occupying the Arsenal defence.

West Ham's cause is not helped after half an hour when Sebastien Schemmel limps off with a broken ankle, after a seemingly innocuous fall. It's tough on the Frenchman – many supporters' player of the year – who is replaced by Labant, with Ian Pearce switching to right-back.

Most West Ham fans cringe every time Repka clatters into tackles, fearing penalties and free-kicks, but tonight he's timing everything immaculately and alongside Dailly and Pearce is closing down Bergkamp and Henry superbly. Reformed journeyman Christian Dailly is having another unfussy game and, as I point out to Dan, he's hardly made a mistake all season since the Blackburn game.

At least Dailly's contribution to West Ham's position is now being recognised. Behind me his fan club – all two of them – chant 'Christian Dailly football genius!' to the rhythm of 'Glenn Roeder's Claret and Blue Army' and then 'Christian Dailly is fucking brilliant!'.

Then on 37 minutes comes the moment that will reverberate across the Premiership. Fredi skins Tony Adams, superbly dummies David Seaman, then rounds the prone pony-tailed keeper – still looking like a porn salesman from Soho as one Finnish paper memorably described him – and sidefoots the ball with his left foot towards the Arsenal goal in front of the North Bank. Fredi must score . . . Only, as we're cheering a goal, Ashley Cole appears to pop out of a trapdoor in the six-yard box and hack the ball from out of the net. The West Ham players are appealing that the ball was over. Even from our end it looks like a goal. But linesman Paul Canadine waves play on and referee Steve Dunn has no alternative but to let play continue.

As the TV replays will later confirm, the ball is not so much over the line as through the North Bank, halfway down St Thomas's Road and on its way to Finsbury Park. If it was much further past the line it would be designated as leading a reconnaissance mission for an expedition to the Arctic Circle. For a moment Fredi gives a quizzical shrug. He looks close to taking off his Walkman in protest. And let's be clear, if Fredi is near to uttering a word of complaint we know we are talking a major breach of international footballing rights.

WEST HAM

Just imagine if Paolo Di Canio had scored such a 'goal' and then been overruled by the referee and linesman. It would surely have made the Paul Alcock pushing incident look like a minor misdemeanour as Paolo faced up a lifetime ban for inappropriate usage of a linesman's flag.

As John McEnroe might have put it: 'Jesus Christ, man, that ball was over!'

'Alex Ferguson will go mental when he sees that,' I tell Dan, anticipating demands for a replay, allegations of anti-United conspiracies and the Fergie hairdryer turned up to 11. As Graham Taylor once memorably hollered, 'Linesman! Linesman! What sort of thing is happening here?'

The Arsenal crowd has turned decidedly edgy. 'It's quiet in the library! In the library it's quiet!' sing the buoyant West Ham fans to the tune of 'Go West'.

When we reach half-time the Gunners' scoreboard shows the first-half highlights, including Ljungberg's early chances and Kanouté's first three chances for West Ham. And then nothing. Perhaps the screen content is being coordinated by former contributors to *Pravda*. Fredi's 'goal' has apparently never happened. This is clearly an admission of guilt, M'lud. It has been eradicated from the tape by a combination of Arséne Wenger, The Cancer Man, the CIA and extraterrestrials from Roswell lest it damage the project.

There is a moment of disbelief and then a roar of, 'One-nil to the Cockney Boys!' and a chorus of, 'Show the fucking goal!' All around us people are receiving text messages on their mobiles saying that the ball was clearly over the line. At least with modern technology football democracy can now defeat these dark campaigns of disinformation. There is a rule that forbids clubs from showing controversial incidents which might inflame fans, but then again, by not showing them the sense of injustice is multiplied. Had Arsenal just shown the incident once, without any slow motion replays, it would at least have seemed fairer and a little less of an outrage. All together now: Oh lucky lucky lucky . . . lucky lucky lucky Arsenal.

Thankfully Gavin defuses the raging sense of injustice at half-time by producing a plastic bag containing eight packets of crisps, which he announces were a bargain at his company canteen. We suggest that he sets up a stall.

At the start of the second half David Seaman takes his place in front of the Clock End goal to chants from the West Ham fans: 'England's England's number two!' For David James is having one of those heroic games like he did at Old Trafford, towering over the Arsenal forwards, almost nonchalantly cushioning a loose ball on his chest, tipping away crosses one-handed and generally looking unbeatable.

Joey Cole beats Adams for speed with pleasing ease, but then Arsenal step up the pressure. 'We can't hold out forever,' remarks Matt, as Arsenal force another corner, and Vieira, looking world class, goes on another storming run through the middle. However, it's a testament to the new-found professionalism that Roeder has instilled in the side that we really do look like holding the future champions to a draw. Ian Pearce, rediscovering his form of two seasons ago, makes a superb headed clearance under pressure.

Only the reason Arsenal are top is because they have the mental strength to keep probing, even after 77 minutes of fruitless battering at the Hammers defence. Bergkamp plays a typical through ball and Ljungberg pops up in the area again to dissect the West Ham defence and sweetly redirect the ball into the corner of James's goal. Highbury erupts.

'You fucking glory-hunting cunts!' hollers a fan behind me as the Arsenal fans burst into a chorus of, 'Freddie! Freddie!' followed by 'We Shall Not Be Moved!'. 'You'd better note that one down, "glory-hunting cunts",' chuckles Gavin, impressed by such erudition.

West Ham are forced to go forward now. Three minutes later Trevor Sinclair is dispossessed on the left and Ljungberg goes down the wing to ping over a high cross which substitute Kanu mishits into the ground, the ball then luckily bouncing over James and into the net. Now people will think it was easy for Arsenal.

With Keown and Adams at the back you know that Arsenal are never going to lose a two-goal lead. Highbury is awash with noise as the Gunners' fans celebrate another huge step towards the Premiership title. It's a big big night for Arsenal, and at least we're part of football history, I suppose. The Double is surely theirs. But who knows what might have been if West Ham had gone in at half-time a goal up?

At the end of the game the Arsenal fans chant Nigel Winterburn's name as he leaves the pitch after what may be his final appearance at Highbury. 'Would they be doing that if they'd lost, though?' asks Matt.

At least Arsene Wenger gives West Ham credit in the post-match interviews, saying that 'West Ham were brilliant, and we needed a great team to beat them.'

Glenn Roeder sounds almost angry enough to loosen his tie, declaring, 'Championships are won and lost on things like that. It was a goal. I've seen the video and it crossed the line.' He adds that the goal that never was changed the game: 'If we'd have come in at half-time 1–0 up they would have become edgy and nervous.' GR then reclaims his nicest man in football reputation by saying that it was 'an honest mistake' by the linesman and that he is not in favour of video replays. 'I should be saying I am, as it cost us, but you have to have that bit of excitement, mystery, romance. I'm not a lover of what you see in American sports, stopping every few seconds to see if you've got it right.'

It's also hard to disagree with Wenger's verdict that 'we were a machine in the second half'. This Arsenal side will surely prove to be worthy champions.

The post-match Cockney knees-up at my house doesn't materialise. Matt and Dan plead the earlier closure of Arsenal tube as mitigating circumstances, while Gavin discovers that he has left his car keys in the office, with his car parked at Greenwich, and will have to return to Canary Wharf before travelling home.

At least the Arsenal fans walking down Stavordale Road are muttering things like: 'West Ham made it really hard for us . . . there was no space at all out there' in the animated throng of departing fans afterwards.

After sitting with his Arsenal-supporting mates Nigel has turned up at my place and offers some consoling words over a cup of Earl Grey: 'At least we've progressed, if you compare that to watching Suker and Diawara up front last year . . .'

Nor is the evening entirely wasted, for Nigel discovers the joys of the West Ham site on page 520 of Teletext, before we search vainly for footage of the disallowed goal. Bizarrely, the ITV News just shows the Arsenal goals and not Fredi's crucial 'goal'.

It's not until the next morning's news that I see Fredi's effort, and it is indeed several thousand billion miles over the line. My daughter Lola asks who won as we walk to her Highbury nursery and I tell her it was Arsenal.

As we arrive at nursery, Lola's favourite teacher Tracy Jones, who is perhaps Arsenal's number one fan, admits, 'I saw it and the ball was over the line . . . We might even do it at Old Trafford now . . . West Ham played well though.'

'I wanted West Ham to win!' cries Lola, with admirable loyalty to her father's strange dementia.

'If only it was that easy. But West Ham scored a goal only the silly referee didn't see it,' I explain.

How will I ever explain to poor Lola what it feels like to be kicked in the Arsene Wengers? Enjoy the innocence of childhood, my dear daughter, for life is but a series of perfectly legitimate goals ruined by the vagaries of dodgy linesmen.

TOP TEN DIABOLICAL DECISIONS AGAINST WEST HAM

Fredi Kanouté's goal that was clearly over the line being disallowed at Arsenal.

Tony Gale being unjustly sent off in the 1991 FA Cup semi-final.

The Football League ruling that we had to replay a 1999 Worthington Cup tie against Aston Villa, just because Manny Omoynimni failed to remember that he'd already played in the competition for another club.

Finishing fifth in 1998–99 and still not automatically qualifying for the UEFA Cup.

Bobby Moore being fitted up for nicking a bracelet in Bogota in 1970.

The TV companies deciding to go on strike the season West Ham nearly win the League in 1985–86.

The ref playing so much injury time that Oldham score a late winner, depriving us of the second division championship in 1991.

West Ham finishing third in 1986 but failing to qualify for Europe because English clubs were still banned after the Heysel Stadium disaster.

Oldham being allowed to play the Hammers on a plastic pitch in the first leg of a Littlewood's Cup semi-final and beating West Ham 6–0 in 1990.

Every other bad decision against West Ham, ever.

39. THE HIGHEST SEATS IN TOON

Newcastle 3 West Ham 1 – 27 April 2002

West Ham's penultimate game is away to Newcastle, who have just qualified for the European Champions League after drawing at Blackburn and securing fourth place. It's a marvellous achievement for their 69-year-old gaffer Bobby Robson, and the talk around St James's Park is that Geordie-born Bobby should be knighted immediately, having taken the club from the bottom of the league in just three seasons.

Having interviewed Robson after England reached the 1990 World Cup semi-final, it's good to confirm that he is a thoroughly decent man in an increasingly ruthless game. That impression is confirmed in the programme notes, where Robson takes time to praise ex-Newcastle player Glenn Roeder: 'Here was a young manager going to a club with big players, and they got off to a bad start. But Glenn handled it well, stood no nonsense, stood his ground, and guided West Ham up the table to the point that they are now a very strong side indeed. At the time when a lot of people are talking about the likely Manager of the Year, I think Glenn Roeder is very close to it.'

We have combined the trip to Newcastle with staying with our friends, Richard and Fleur, in North Yorkshire. I'm taking Fleur and her two eldest sons, Thomas and George, aged nine and eight, to the game, all three being football virgins. Although it's interesting to note that the boys' first reaction is: 'Somebody in *Harry Potter* supports West Ham.' If West Ham can just exploit the Potter link then the next generation of kids is ours. After driving past the Angel of the North – heavily plugged in photoshoots for tomorrow's revival of *Auf Wiedersehen, Pet* – we find a parking spot with surprising ease in the centre of Toon and enjoy a relaxed lunch in China Town.

An hour before the kick-off we give the boys a circular tour of the ground, viewing the numerous beer guts billowing under black and white replica shirts and stopping to stroke a police horse as an old Geordie geezer says something indecipherable to the kids, and we all smile where it seems appropriate. Fleur shows me a superb Georgian terrace – a similar one was knocked down to build the new stand, something she says would never have been allowed in London, but here the Toon is religion. We show the boys a footballer's wife in white trouser suit at the reception of the Milburn Stand and then enter the turnstiles of the Sir John Hall North West Corner Upper Tier.

We climb up one set of featureless concrete steps, then two, then three, then four . . . 'This is like the gods at the theatre,' suggests Fleur. After several more sets of stairs you start to wonder if it will count as bagging a Munro, as we are almost in Scotland. More than 200 climbers have died attempting to scale Mount Everest, but you sense even more might have shuffled off to the great Toon above attempting to scale the Sir John Hall North West Corner Upper Tier. Even its unfeasibly long name is enough to give you vertigo.

Finally we emerge blinking into the spring light. It feels a little like we're standing on top of the spaceship in *Close Encounters of the Third Kind*. The West Ham supporters are perched in a small eyrie in the top corner of the vast stand that now sweeps around two sides of St James's Park. There's an architecturally pleasing glass roof which covers the place in light and gives vast sweeping views of the city. 'Look, there's Gateshead over there, and that's the rest of Newcastle stretching down there by the Tyne,' says Fleur. This is the highest I have ever been at a football match, no drugs reference intended. Normally you only get such a view after taking a cable car up the Ben Nevis range. That's probably the Post Office Tower to the south.

The main problem, though, is seeing what happens on the pitch and really you need opera glasses to see the action. We are dimly aware of some pre-match entertainment way below us.

Bizarrely, a giant walkabout cigarette is being chased by a man who has given up smoking and is being beaten with pillows. The PA plays something that might be Ant and Dec's underwhelming World Cup single but we're so high up that all sound waves are being sent in the approximate direction of Gateshead. The thought occurs to me that if Bob and Terry from *Whatever Happened to the Likely Lads* wanted to avoid the score of the match now they could achieve it by the simple feat of sitting in the Sir John Hall North West Corner Upper Tier.

Incredibly, West Ham dominate the first half – that is if it is West Ham way below us, as no names or numbers on shirts are visible. After a few minutes your eyes do adjust a little to the distance and it's possible to recognise West Ham players by their gait and, in the case of David James, dayglo hairstyles (that barnet had to be useful for something). Alan Shearer is recognisable but the rest of the Newcastle players are more or less unidentifiable.

The action is distant but encouragingly Fredi Kanouté is causing big problems for the Newcastle defence. First he feeds Defoe who has a reflex shot brilliantly stopped by Shay Given. Then from Sinclair's cross Kanouté places a relatively easy header wide of the post. After qualifying for the Champions League Newcastle look complacent and sluggish.

'Look, he's really enjoying it,' says Fleur – who is incidentally possibly the only person called Fleur ever to sit in the away end with West Ham fans – observing her son Thomas looking with fascination at the West Ham fans singing 'Bubbles'. George looks pretty impressed too at the public use of rude words as a chorus of 'Stick your blue flag up your arse!' breaks out.

In front of us a possibly very drunk West Ham fan with a Dagenham cleavage is standing up and hollering: 'Glenn Roeder's claret and blue army!' periodically turning round and urging us fellow fans to accompany him in a slightly intimidatory manner.

As the mother of four boys Fleur is used to dealing with such things. 'It's all right,' she tells her boys. 'He's just full of aggression and testosterone.'

Kanouté flicks the ball on with his head, and way way below us Jermain Defoe delivers a crisp half-volley into the corner of the Newcastle net. Jermain whips off his shirt to reveal a white vest. Everyone is up cheering and the boys have seen their first Premiership goal.

'Chim chiminy chim chim cheroo, we are those bastards in claret and blue!' sing our small contingent, as the boys grin some more and George from North Yorkshire shouts, 'Come on you Irons!'

Steve Lomas should double the lead when played in cleverly by Kanouté but screws the ball wide. Cole and Carrick are dominating midfield and West Ham should be three–nil up. St James's Park, full with 51,127 fans, is silenced so the West Ham fans chant 'Shall we sing a song for you?'.

Then on 41 minutes Newcastle score with their first chance. West Ham's offside trap goes horribly awry and from Robert's through ball Shearer calmly slots home the kind of chance he's been dispatching with ease for years, to score his 202nd goal for Newcastle. Suddenly our singing is as nothing compared to the Toon roar.

'We should have scored more. Sadly I don't think Newcastle can play as badly again in the second half,' I announce to the boys, with the natural air of pessimism that comes from watching West Ham away from home for three decades.

Newcastle replace O'Brien with Distin and proceed to play like Bobby Robson has given them a thorough bashing with his pension book. Robert and Solano start taking on their men on the flanks and suddenly it's hold-on-to-a-draw time. Only on 53 minutes David James, unsure if he is in or out of his area, heads away Repka's back header rather than picking it up, the ball spins to Robert who cuts inside and fires in a shot. James makes a great save, but the ball falls kindly to the alert Lua Lua, who scores his third goal for Newcastle and celebrates with a mere one somersault.

'Sing when you're winning, you only sing when you're winning!' chant the Hammers fans. There is some serious baiting of the Toon fans to our left now.

Rival fans spend most of the half just looking at each other, and making wanker gestures.

Then comes the killer goal. On 66 minutes Solano's pass with the outside of his right foot supplies Robert, who flicks the ball over the onrushing James and onto the post. It holds up around the line for the winger to tap into an empty net.

'Blaydon Races' echoes down the impossibly steep inclines of the Sir John Hall stand. The vociferous geezer in front of us starts waving a £20 note and chanting 'Two bob a week!' at the Toon fans. 'He really does think he's better than them, doesn't he?' observes Fleur with some fascination.

Taking a middle-class anthropologist to a match can be instructive. Fleur also has a degree in history and today her husband Richard has gone to Cambridge to attend a lecture on the English Civil War. When I ask her how this compares with the other civil war as she observes the taunting of the rival claret and blue and black and white factions and remarks: 'You can see why young men between 16 and 25 are used as cannon fodder in wars. Look at all that testosterone. You can really imagine some of them holding pikes . . .'

A couple of West Ham fans are pulled out by the Geordie police for threatening behaviour, which at least gives the boys some extra entertainment as they listen to people boasting about nearly getting arrested. Careers in the ICF may beckon. Fleur concludes, with some shrewdness, that 'West Ham play too much to a formula, when Newcastle get the ball it's just bang and it's a goal'.

The despairing West Ham fans strike up a chorus of 'Ten men went to war, went to war at Millwall!' as West Ham, to their credit, create a half chance for Cole and at least win some free-kicks and corners at our end. 'We're gonna win 4–3!' chant the West Ham fans, celebrating imaginary goals every time the Geordie fans sing.

At the end there's an outpouring of Geordie pride as Robson and his men take to the pitch for a lap of honour.

The boys tell their mum that they would have enjoyed it a little more if the man in front of us had been arrested, but were very pleased by the naughty words and seeing grown men behave so badly.

'It would have been better if West Ham had won,' announces eight-year-old George. I try to explain that we never expected to win up here anyway. Tickets I can fix, but not results. 'And at most grounds you can actually see the players,' I add.

'But really most people go to taunt the other side's fans, so it doesn't matter,' counters Fleur.

In the post-match inquest Bobby Robson speaks of Newcastle's 'poetic' football in the second half, while Roeder bemoans West Ham's terrible finishing. 'I counted six clear chances on top of our goal in the first half. That's not bad luck, that's bad finishing.'

The next morning over breakfast at their farmhouse, the boys tell their father of their football induction and it's not been quite as poetic as Bobby Robson thought. They announce, 'Dad, we learnt lots of swear words like "wanker" and "arse"!' West Ham might have lost but at least another generation has been won over to the people's game.

40. SEVENTH HEAVEN

West Ham 2 Bolton 1 - 11 May 2002

The Queen has been down the 'Ammers. The West Ham programme has devoted the front page and four pages of photos to her opening of the Dr Martens Stand. As the chant goes: 'Royal supporter!' This causes some reflection in Ken's Café, where Dan, myself, Part-time Mike and his son Scott, are sitting with our final teas and chips of the season before West Ham entertain Bolton.

'It was the Queen Mum's dying wish that Liz should get down to her beloved West Ham and open the Dr Martens Stand,' claims Mike.

'Look at her signature, all she's written is "Elizabeth R",' comments Dan. 'She could have put something like "Why not try 5–4–1 next season?".'

Most of the players were at training, but Joe Cole was presented to Her Royal Highness. You can imagine Liz asking young Joe: 'And what do you do, are you one of the ball boys?' While the name of the new stand might have been a little puzzling – 'Ah, Dr Martens, he must be the club physician . . .'

There are numerous pictures of Terry Brown guiding the Queen and the Duke of Edinburgh (cue his legendary bad jokes such as 'Are you Cockney chappies still wearing pearly king suits and having knees-ups round the old Joanna?') round his manor.

It's reported that the Queen stayed for 'luncheon', which can only mean that she was taken to Ken's Café for a luncheon of sausage, bubble and beans, but only after taking her numbered meal ticket like everyone else. Then she was offered a reconditioned fridge from Upton Park Domestic Appliances and some new mops from Derrick A Cross's ironmongers store.

'Well, it beats King Olaf of Norway,' I tell Mike, referring to West Ham's other celebrity royal fan, once featured on the cover of *Fortune's Always Hiding*. Mike then reveals that his son Scott has just discovered a video of the legendary 1991 West Ham side and played it that morning. 'We were terrible,

219

it's just Trevor Morley missing chance after chance!' We agree that at least we're making progress.

My trip to Upton Park has been painful, for smug flag-waving Gooners are everywhere around Highbury and Islington station celebrating the Double before Arsenal's game against Everton. It's been eight months since September 11 and Osama Bin Laden has still not been found, but the thought occurs that as a Gunners fan he'll surely be somewhere around Upper Street attending his first game of the season, waving a 'champions' flag and singing 'We won the league in Manchester!'.

West Ham can finish seventh today and with our expectations sadly reduced over the years then perhaps that's our equivalent to doing the Double – at least until George Lucas (flogging another *Star Wars* movie this week) decides to become our wealthy benefactor. It's better than anyone anticipated and with a good young side and a promising manager we might even be able to aim for top six and the UEFA Cup next season. Glenn Roeder says he can only afford 'quality Bosmans' in the summer, although maybe we secretly have millions, for in *Over Land and Sea* fanzine Roeder confesses: 'My dad was a shopkeeper and he always taught me you never told anyone what you have got in the till.' West Ham – we're open all hours.

Further good news is that two Hammers are going to Japan and South Korea. On Thursday Joe Cole and David James were named in Sven-Goran Eriksson's World Cup squad, although it's tough on Trevor Sinclair, whose ability to play anywhere in midfield or attack would have made him a valuable utility player.

But even as the season ends there are the obligatory rumours of the giant clubs sniffing around our young stars. Now it's claimed that if Liverpool fail to sign the on-loan Nicolas Anelka they will try to get the £12 million-rated Fredi Kanouté, presumably by luring him with a top-quality portable mini-disc player. This might just be a way of forcing Anelka's camp to reduce their demands, although Fredi himself is quoted as saying that, although he is contracted to West Ham for two more years, 'There may be much to think about over the summer. I have always said I wanted to stay at West Ham, but I cannot close my eyes to other horizons.'

There's a festive feeling around Upton Park, with Bolton fans celebrating their survival by arriving dressed as Elvis Presley, giant green dragons and convicts. Before the kick-off Sebastien Schemmel is given his Hammer of the Year trophy – he received my vote and it's a sign that West Ham fans will always appreciate unremitting, Billy Bonds-style commitment to the club. Sadly, though, it seems Seb is ruling himself out of any BBC costume dramas like *Henry the Eighth*, as, following a bet with Trevor Sinclair on the result, he has agreed to have his flowing hair trimmed.

For the first 15 minutes Glenn Roeder remains seated – the only time he's sat down all season – and this lack of agitation on his part seems to get to the players. It's a stroll in the sun for both sides, enlivened by Gav ending the season as he started it, and taking his seat six minutes late. Row F stands in his honour as Nigel chants 'Legend!' at his fellow Uriah Heep fan.

We discuss Fredi's possible move to Liverpool ('He can't go to Liverpool, he'd get his Walkman nicked up there') and who will take penalties in the absence of Di Canio. Nigel thinks it should be Steve Potts, who's on the bench today and stuck on 399 appearances. And, of course, whenever Pottsy scores West Ham win 7–1. Joe Cole is another penalty possibility. 'Only Joe would miss because you can't dribble it in,' reflects Matt.

After the first 15 minutes Roeder stands up again and the Hammers start peppering the Bolton goal. Winterburn is still racing into the opposition box and we agree that he should be given another season at least by Roeder, who is apparently releasing him this summer. (Thankfully, he does later agree to stay another year.) Trevor Sinclair is playing with admirable skill and industry after his World Cup disappointment and Cole is still in great form. Even Roeder himself looks pretty good when he juggles the ball as it goes out of play by his technical area. Roeder is now less like an undertaker and more like a proper Premiership boss. He's almost become a showman.

But, as ever, Fredi misses a couple of good chances and with West Ham overelaborating it takes a humble ginger yeoman to finally beat Jaaskelainen. Sinclair makes a penetrating run into the Bolton half, and plays it on to Carrick who finds Defoe. The young striker shoots from the edge of box, Jaaskelainen parries and Steve Lomas appears to half-volley into the net. Clearly defenders have been scared to come anywhere near Lomey since he scored against Man United and revealed a torso that John Cooper Clarke might have termed 'flesh the colour of cold potatoes'.

Lomas has scored four more league goals than Japan-bound Joe Cole. If only he wasn't from Northern Ireland he'd be a certainty for Sven's World Cup squad I tell the lads at half-time . . . only they don't sound convinced. There's yet more West Ham pressure in the second half as Joey Cole attempts again to score his first league goal of the season. He brilliantly accelerates past a statuesque Simon Charlton only to crash his shot onto the post. Fredi hits the keeper, puts the rebound onto the bar and then heads it over an empty net. A few minutes later he completely miscues another chance and is having one of those games where his transfer value looks to be 12 Walkman batteries rather than £12 million.

Then suddenly, Bolton equalise. World Cup winner Yuri Djorkaeff hits a free-kick that is slightly deflected off Steve Lomas in the West Ham wall beyond David James, who beats the turf in frustration. It's our own fault for, as ever, missing so many chances. However, news has filtered through that Spurs are now losing at Leicester and it looks like we'll have to scrape a draw

WEST HAM

to reach seventh spot. The Bobby Moore stand consoles itself with a rousing chorus of 'If you 'ate Tottenham stand up!'.

Full time nears and West Ham win a corner. One of our number – who will not be named and shamed for humanitarian reasons – has even left his seat. Now we've only scored one goal from a corner all season – Don Hutchison's header against Sunderland – and it's not likely to change now. Only the doomsday scenario happens. Carrick floats over the ball and Ian Pearce, unmarked, meets the ball with a thumping header into the roof of the net, runs over the corner flag and, in seventh heaven, makes strange hand gestures as if he were the older, more embarrassing brother of Spandau Ballet's Tony Hadley.

There's still time for Roeder to bring on Garcia and Moncur and to unsentimentally ignore Nigel's cries of, 'We want Pottsy on the pitch!' The whistle sounds on the season and Glenn Roeder allows himself a quick punch of the air before crossing his arms again.

Enter Jeremy 'The Hit Man' Nicholas. The match-day announcer is on the pitch now, microphone in hand, a kaleidoscope of Ceefax pages turning over inside his head. 'It's only a latest score, not a result, but the latest score we have from Filbert Street is Leicester 2 Tottenham 1! he announces to huge cheers. I have a terrible sense of déja vu about the Notts County game of 1991, when the latest score from Oldham was announced as being 2–2, thousands of fans invaded the pitch to celebrate winning the second division championship, only Oldham won 3–2 in injury time and we finished as runners-up. But for once pessimism is unfounded. Nicholas announces that Spurs have lost: 'That means most importantly that we go above Spurs! We're seventh!' he hollers hoarsely. Huge cheers reverberate around the stadium, for we are now the third best team in London.

Typically, Roeder has a word with Joe Cole at this point, later revealing: 'I took him aside on the pitch and told him to focus on learning and enjoying this experience. And that I was envious of him.'

Nicholas then introduces each player individually: 'They're off to the World Cup, Joe Cole and David James . . . The Hammer of the Year Sebastien "Archie" Schemmel . . . The only man who's played in all 42 games, Mr Christian Dailly . . . and put your hands together for Mr Glenn Roeder!'

The players lap the pitch, as 'Celebration' plays over the PA, including the injured Don Hutchison with kid in arms, and even Pottsy gets a namecheck. The only person who isn't mentioned is Paolo Di Canio, recovering from his injury in Italy, which seems a strange oversight. Even if some of the magic of two years ago has diminished, as the Opta stats reveal, he has still been one of West Ham's most effective performers in his 26 games.

Sadly Michael Carrick has to pull out of the England Under-21 tour after the Bolton match, although after injuries to Kieron Dyer and Steven Gerrard Trevor Sinclair is placed on stand-by for the England squad, and with Danny Murphy dropping out, West Ham end up with three players in the squad –

222

just like Moore, Hurst and Peters – which will result in England inevitably winning the World Cup. Perhaps.

For the fourth time in five years West Ham have finished in the top half of the table. It's certainly an improvement on last season where the club was not safe from relegation until the penultimate game and finished with just 42 points, compared to this season's total of 53 points. If you'd said ten months ago that West Ham would lose 7–1 to Blackburn, Hayden Foxe would be caught pointing Percy at the bar in Sugar Reef, Paolo Di Canio would turn down a move to Manchester United to spend more time with his piranhas, Glenn Roeder would keep his job, West Ham United would have the joint best home defensive record in the Premiership, we'd triumph at Old Trafford, win a couple of games without Paolo, Steve Lomas would turn into a deadly goalscoring machine, Christian Dailly would be hailed as an ever-present football genius, Sven-Goran Eriksson would cop off with Ulrika Jonsson, the Queen would turn up at Upton Park and West Ham would end up finishing seventh, you'd have got some healthy odds.

More than anything the season has been the story of Glenn Roeder, initially derided as a 'yes man' and 'cheap option' by even his own fans. Yet he has performed a quiet but remarkable transformation, turning a set of underperforming high-class individuals into a team. Harry Redknapp deserves immense credit for bringing the likes of Defoe, Carrick, Cole, Sinclair, Kanouté and Di Canio to the club, but under Roeder the club seems to have adopted a more professional approach and the side has a better shape. Roeder's stemmed a player exodus, signed an England goalkeeper, found the bargain of the season in Schemmel, taught Joe Cole how to be a team player and succeeded in most things bar getting David James a decent haircut.

A year ago a disgruntled fan greeted Roeder's appointment by e-mailing the club website with the message: 'If you think small in the Premiership you are small.' Were the board just lucky in their appointment or could they, for once, have been thinking long term and shown great prescience? A season on, with a bright young coach, a superb collection of youngsters and a ground capacity that has increased by nearly 10,000, the club might just be on the Roeder somewhere and some of us might see West Ham win another trophy within our lifetimes. Or we might be relegated – with West Ham you never know.

Final proof that the world is against the Hammers comes with the news that Ipswich – yes, relegated Ipswich – have qualified for the UEFA Cup through a fair-play lucky draw. Maybe West Ham should have gone for the drop rather than finishing seventh.

As ever, the season has produced numerous memories, good and bad. Sinclair's wondrous scissor-kick against Derby, Ian Pearce's rocket into the top corner against Spurs, Jermain Defoe's winner at Old Trafford, crafted by the peerless Di Canio, a shirtless Steve Lomas terrifying the fans after scoring against Man United at Upton Park. Plus Shaka keeping it down to seven at Blackburn, Hayden Foxe turning himself into a one-man sprinkler unit, and Paolo's piranhas keeping him away from the Reds. It's certainly never been boring. And that, perhaps, is why so many of us still have Irons in the soul.